GRANTA

12 Addison Avenue, London W11 4QR
email editorial@granta.com
To subscribe go to www.granta.com or call 845-267-3031 (toll-free 866-438-6150)

ISSUE 104

EDITOR	Alex Clark
SENIOR EDITOR	Rosalind Porter
ONLINE EDITOR	Roy Robins
ASSOCIATE EDITORS	Adelaide Docx, Helen Gordon, Liz Jobey
EDITORIAL ASSISTANT AND DEPUTY ONLINE EDITOR	Simon Willis
CONTRIBUTING WRITERS	Andrew Hussey, Robert Macfarlane, Xan Rice
DESIGN	Carolyn Roberts
FINANCE	Geoffrey Gordon, Morgan Graver
MARKETING AND SUBSCRIPTIONS	Anne Gowan, Joanna Metcalfe
SALES DIRECTOR	Brigid Macleod
PUBLICITY	Pru Rowlandson
VICE PRESIDENT, US OPERATIONS	Greg Lane
MARKETING AND ADVERTISING, US	Greg Lane, glane@granta.com
IT MANAGER	Mark Williams
PRODUCTION ASSOCIATE	Sarah Wasley
PROOFS	Lesley Levene
MANAGING DIRECTOR	David Graham
PUBLISHER	Sigrid Rausing

Granta USPS 000-508 is published four times per year. *Granta* 12 Addison Avenue, London W11 4QR, United Kingdom at the annual subscription rate of $45.99
Airfreight and mailing in the USA by Agent named Air Business, C/O Worldnet Shipping USA Inc., 149-35 177th Street, Jamaica, New York, NY11434. Periodicals postage paid at Jamaica NY 11431.
US POSTMASTER: Send address changes to *Granta*, PO Box 359 Congers, NY 10920-0359.

Granta is printed and bound in Italy by Legoprint. This magazine is printed on paper that fulfils the criteria for 'Paper for permanent document' according to ISO 9706 and the American Library Standard ANSI/NIZO Z39.48-1992.
This magazine has been printed on paper that has been certified by the Forest Stewardship Council (FSC).
Granta is indexed in the American Humanities Index.

Cover Design: Graphic Thought Facility
ISBN 978-1-929001-34-7

CONTENTS

Audubon: Early Drawings

Introduction by Richard Rhodes
Scientific Commentary by
Scott V. Edwards
Foreword by Leslie A. Morris

"Prior to the publication of *Birds of America*, John James Audubon spent decades honing his talents. *Audubon: Early Drawings* sheds insight into Audubon's trajectory as an artist and naturalist, offering 116 bird and mammal images from the fledgling stages of his career...[A] reminder of Audubon's timeless relevance."
—Julie Leibach, *Audubon*

116 color illustrations / 288 pages
Belknap Press / new in cloth

Egg & Nest

Rosamond Purcell, Linnea
S. Hall, and René Corado
Introduction by Bernd Heinrich

"What kind of genius is Rosamond Purcell? Is she an artist? A scholar? A documentarian? A living cabinet of wonders? Her originality defies category, as does her newest triumph, *Egg & Nest*. Crack its shell."
—Jonathan Safran Foer

183 color illustrations / 232 pages
Belknap Press / new in cloth

HARVARD
UNIVERSITY
PRESS
www.hup.harvard.edu

The men who made us

B ringing together these pieces about fathers and fatherhood for my first issue as *Granta*'s editor has been both exhilarating and very instructive. Apart from the deep satisfaction of seeing writers develop and refine their ideas and settle on the most fruitful way of expressing them, sometimes ending up in a quite different place from where they started, there has been another imperative in play. When the issue at hand involves asking people to address a subject as personal and as necessarily complex as their earliest and often most intimate relationships, to recreate and dissect the experiences that helped to form them, there is a delicate balance to be struck between maintaining the impartiality of the outside reader and intervening in private and inner lives. As the truism has it, we can all say what we like about our own families, but woe betide anyone who presumes to characterize our parents, our siblings or our children for us.

The immense rise in the popularity of memoir in recent years has made observing such delicacies far more problematic. Those who voluntarily strip bare the details of family life must, surely, be extending to the reader the right to form their own opinion; to take against, if they choose, the individuals concerned, to make judgements about their behaviour, to come to the conclusion that, after all, someone else's family romance is simply not as interesting to us as our own.

Our criteria for selecting the pieces in 'Fathers' were based on the hope not that each piece of writing would extend to the universal – that seemed far too grandiose, unlikely and even

Part personal journey, part manifesto, this book is a snapshot of England at a precarious moment in its history

undesirable an aim – but that they would be suggestive and beckoning in their specificity. I have never, for instance, played basketball, but the feelings that Benjamin Markovits describes in his meditation on the sporting coaches who steered him through high school flooded me with memories of the ambivalence that an adolescent harbours towards an authority figure; the strange mixture of embarrassment, affection, curiosity, aggression and what he perceptively calls 'all the varieties of wrong-feeling'. One of childhood's most furtively treasured games is to imagine how life would be if other circumstances had prevailed, and it is perhaps misguided to think that that stops when one grows up. Here, meeting fathers who were doctors, vicars, hairdressers, comedians, men who married in secret or more than once, fathers who have been faced with serious illness or bereavement, who laughed or smacked or left or made everything better or, in the end, died, feels as though it affords a fleeting understanding of why I am different from you.

Several of the fathers in this book have, indeed, died; but their children's relationships with them have not ended. Writing about our family provides fairly incontrovertible evidence that our business with the dead, and the conversations that we have with them, not only continues after that initial separation but changes and mutates almost ceaselessly. 'That's what happens if you don't do your paperwork,' David Goldblatt writes in his frequently painful account of his father's violent death. 'Time comes round and takes your stories.' He's right: in our effort to preserve our parents and, in the process, to preserve both the particularities of our personal history and our more inchoate and communal sense of the past, we are also engaged in a battle with time. Time works on us, and it works on our memories of those closest to us: how best to confront the temptation, often unconscious, to supply definition to imperfect recollection, to exonerate or to lay blame, to commemorate or to settle scores, to downplay or to dramatize? But behind that world of difficulty is the thought of what might happen if the attempt is not made at all.

It is *Granta*'s job, and my ambition for it as its editor, to provide a place where all kinds of attempts can be made, whether they are provisional and preparatory or highly polished and as near definitive as might be possible. It is a particular pleasure to be able to introduce in this issue a number of new writers whose work is not yet widely known – Daniyal Mueenuddin, Francesca Segal and Justin Torres among them – alongside far more familiar names and, indeed, to witness those more well-known writers strike unfamiliar poses. At a time when the latitude granted to emerging voices to locate and connect with their readership seems increasingly under threat, and when new writing must make itself, more than ever before, easier to define, to package and to market, we hope to say as simply as possible – here is the space. Now tell us the story. ∎

Cyan

I'm one of those model men
in barbershop or unisex
salon windows. I've held my breath
here, like this, for decades.

O distant youth, O brilliantine,
I saw myself the other day
across the street in running time:
gabardined, red-faced, gone grey.

The cow's-lick and the kiss curl.
I'm holding out. I'm blue in the face.
Telstar still orbits the Earth.
We don't like what you've done to the place.

The fount of all smoky wisdom

I hardly know where to begin when it comes to describing a single object in my writing room. We're talking the literary equivalent of Francis Bacon's studio here, for the room is a dusty, mildewed slew of stuff, a terminal moraine of yellowing paper, and a slurry of tat. The walls are covered with a myriad Post-it notes upon which are inscribed ideas, gags, aperçus, images and tropes; the floor is piled with books and typescripts; the shelves have more books, pill pots, Band-Aid boxes, disposable toothbrushes (I like these a lot and collect them assiduously whenever I fly long haul), shoelaces – and so forth.

The desk, which runs around two sides of the room, has been purpose-built to be slightly scaled up (I'm six feet five), and while there are favoured objects studding the papers on it – an Olivetti Lettera 22 typewriter, a bust of Schumann with a speech bubble stuck to his forehead reading TAKE ME TO THE BRIDGE, a Neolithic handaxe, a giant ball bearing, etc. – there is no single thing that typifies that whole, no synecdoche, or exemplar.

Now I am not a collector per se. To collect seems to me an acknowledgement of defeat; the substitution of a set for its setting. Rather, I think of my relationship with these things as akin to that of a shaman with his symbol set: they may be arranged and rearranged to produce remote and magical effects, such as texts. However, the tobacco pipes that are ranged along the mantelpiece are of a different order: these are transactional objects, at one time invested with enormous power and significance, but now merely briar monuments, a Woodhenge around which I once danced, heavily intoxicated.

We're talking drugs here. I gave up smoking for a year from 2002 to 2003. I could cope without nicotine – I could even write. I just couldn't bear people. I wrote my novel *Dorian* during this period, in which the character Henry Wotton says, '*Au fond*, I think I will always be smoking.' Prophetic words, but part of the reason I'd given up cigarettes was that I was beginning to think 'pipe', and even look at them lovingly in the windows of tobacconists. When I relapsed and resumed sucking the miasma I tried a pipe and discovered – gulp! – that it was an infinitely more effective nicotine delivery system than cigarettes, or even cigars.

As with every other kind of drug-taking I've ever indulged in, once bitten, for a long time smitten (there's even a phenomenon known to pipe smokers as 'tongue bite', when you puff so heavily that it feels like just that). My first pipe purchases were modest enough – a churchwarden, a London-style 'bent' – all costing around thirty-five pounds, but soon enough I learnt about the mechanics of pipe construction, how the straightness of the briar grain imparts a certain coolness and balance to the smoke, how the bigger the bowl, the looser the fill.

I toyed with meerschaum – I flirted with clay. I haunted specialist tobacconists, spending quite obscene quantities of money on pipes: a natty Savinelli straight set me back £150 (predictably, while the Italians make beautiful pipes, their tobacco blends suck). I awoke in the night dreaming of pipes, and I got up to surf the Internet looking for them. Marc Quinn, the artist, told me about a 'car pipe' he'd seen in Milan, the magnetized bowl of which you could stick to the roof of your vehicle – I longed for it.

But most of all I longed for the big black pipe in the window of Jayems, the tobacconist on Victoria Street. It was in all respects a pretty standard pipe – not notably different to the iconic pipe of which the painter says '*Ceci n'est pas une pipe*', but writ large. Very large. That's what I liked about it – it seemed to me as near as possible to being the ur-pipe, the fount of all smoky wisdom. Being very black and very large and very straight-grained, it must've required a huge chunk of briar root to make it (briar, being the only kind that carbonizes without burning, is the sole wood that pipes can be made from). I goggled at that pipe, I went inside and hefted it, I checked out its 'grip', which is for the pipe smoker as key as a saxophonist's embouchure. It was inevitable that despite the insane price tag – £500 – sooner or later I was going to buy the thing.

And there it sits in the rack on the mantelpiece: a parenthesis of an implement that brackets nothing, for soon after its acquisition I more or less gave up pipe-smoking. The hit was great – but the effects, my dear! A tongue like a carpet and an exponential increase in bronchitis I couldn't be doing with. Instead, to explain what I now feel for the pipe I must paraphrase the writer Robert Stone's remarks on hard drugs: I admire it from afar.

Well, perhaps not that afar – only a few feet in fact – but such is the queer jumble of this room, it might as well be miles. ∎

The summer I turned twenty-five, I met my parents for a vacation in northern Spain. On our first night together, we went for a stroll by the sea. Along the stretch of a deserted coastline, we happened to glimpse a cafe by the water, suspended in a perfect evening, cool and blue, its wicker tables flickering with candles. 'Let's go have a glass of wine,' my father said. But we were tired – my parents had just flown from Russia, I from America. It was only our first evening here, my mother and I said. Let's not rush things; we'll come back. 'We'll never come back,' my father replied. 'Things that aren't done right away are never done.' We laughed, but he was right: we stayed there for two weeks, and every evening something happened to prevent us from returning.

A year ago my father passed away and this was what I found myself remembering – not the things that were, but the things that were not: the places not visited, the words not said, the stories not shared. And this, like so much else, I inherited from him: he marked his whole life not by his accomplishments and the books he published – brilliant works of philosophy and sociology, studies of mass consciousness, of public opinion – but by the vast territories he still wanted to cover, knowing always that he was bound to run out of time. His unwritten works occupied cabinets, thoughts, years, in sheaves of manuscript pages, in elaborate colour-coded charts thumb-tacked to his walls, meticulously mapping out the future landscape of his life.

He was in his seventies when he embarked on a monumental endeavour summarizing his scientific discoveries, a multi-volume *Four Lives of Russia* that was to encompass the country's evolution through its past fifty years. Yet he believed that gargantuan labour to be but a precursor to the true work of his life – the memoirs that would use as fuel the thousands of pages of diaries he had kept since the age of twenty, photographs stored in neatly marked boxes, poems composed in whimsical moments, his magnificent drawings of Prague (his favourite city), his study of Czech beer folklore, his unparalleled knowledge of classical music (entire operas learned by heart), his love of art and cinema, and more, and more, so much more – the story of

Boris Grushin, Moscow, 1989

twentieth-century Russia through the prism of one man's life. He talked about it, he wrote outlines, he sorted his archives without cease, even when his Parkinson's disease had progressed so far that he could not read his own handwriting without a magnifying glass.

He died while working on Russia's 'Third Life' and for months the empty spaces, the bitterness of things that had not happened, haunted me like the cafe by the Spanish seaside where we never drank wine. Yet now, a year later, I find myself moving on, slowly, step by step, walking past the candlelit terrace that never became a memory towards other moments that did – diving for crabs off a rocky Bulgarian coast; reading poetry to each other while making redcurrant jam at our dacha; giving my father a draft of my first novel, waiting to see his face as he turned the last page – an album thick with three and a half decades of shared memories, through which I am learning to leaf with gratitude rather than pain. ∎

Photo booth: Bobby and Ivor, Toronto, c. 1963; right-hand side, top to bottom, Ivor and Bobby's wedding, Kenton, 1964; David and Ivor, Ruislip, Yom Kippur, 1970; David and Ivor, Ruislip, c. 1968

DOING THE PAPERWORK

Life in the aftermath of a violent death

David Goldblatt

I t just wasn't his strong suit. He hardly did it. He barely kept it, and as he got older he cared even less about the consequences of not doing his paperwork. It wasn't a form of learnt absent-mindedness or elderly decline. It wasn't a kind of shallow front or brittle bravado but a cussed indifference to authority, a refusal to live with fear of any kind. The old man really didn't give a fuck what happened. It became more pronounced as my mother, Bobby, was dying and the tedious bureaucracy of car ownership that had been her domain went untouched. The summonses and the fines began to mount up, but still no tax, MOT or insurance. In fact, a year after Bobby's death he had taken to sporting a beer mat in his tax disc holder. Why? He didn't need to. For years Ivor had had access to backdated tax discs, MOT certificates and insurance papers. Anyone unfortunate enough to be stopped by the police and asked to produce their documentation, anyone who had through no fault of their own overlooked their renewal, could remedy the situation for a small fee. Notices of fines from magistrates' courts across the south-east of

England kept rolling in for another three or four years. The total value of those fines – the interest on unpaid fines and the fines for not paying fines – peaked at around three grand. Then it stopped. Maybe he paid up, maybe they gave in? They probably did a deal where he agreed to pay twenty-five pence a week until the end of time and then he put the paperwork in the bin.

Although Ivor spent the last years of his life as a reasonably legal motorist, this did not mark a sea change in his personal administration. He made a will, but that was as far as it went. Among the many elements of his estate that I dealt with after his death were over four thousand pounds' worth of unpaid parking tickets, a wide variety of pending utility bills and a number of unresolved court cases involving motoring accidents and insurance claims. More impressively, he hadn't paid any council tax or made any mortgage payments for eight years and, despite running a considerable small business, he had not passed on a jot to the Inland Revenue or the VAT. He had, however, had a small but useful injection of cash from social security on the grounds of disability. In truth, for the first year after Bobby's death he was good for nothing. The other seven are harder to account for.

Sometimes, the bailiffs arrived, but his response was always the same. They would knock on the door and introduce themselves. He would then greet them, step out of the house, close the door behind him and walk out on to the neat green in front of his flat, ringed by six other mock-Tudor blocks, and shout at the top of his voice, 'This man is a bailiff. He wants to take my possessions away to pay for unpaid bills and unjust fines, but he will not be getting anything.' They never did.

For the most part my paperwork is in better shape than his. My car is legal and my tax records are so clean that, after a random going-over, the Inland Revenue decided they owed me money. I'm not neat, organized or obsessive about paperwork – I do the easy stuff first and then I procrastinate – but I do eventually get round to it. The boxes, however, remain unsorted. They contain what's left of his paperwork; the stuff that I took from his flat when we cleared it out

and sold it, minus the choicest items, which were taken by the police
and the lawyers. The boxes have been through various incarnations:
thick plastic bags, taped-up grocery cartons, old book boxes. I think
that they have, at last, taken their final form. In their current state, there
are four. There used to be more, but over the seven years that I have
carted them from one cupboard, shelf or attic to another, their contents
appear to have contracted. Although I have unpacked and repacked
the boxes, stopping along the way to dwell on the odd paper, I haven't
really opened them. I'm always squinting, half shielding my eyes.

The paperwork first arrived in black plastic sacks and putting it
into in some kind of order had helped. It felt like an act of salvage. That
was the easy bit; then it stopped helping. My partner Sarah said to me,
'Are you sure you want to open the boxes? You know what happens
when you open the boxes... I'm not saying don't open them, but you
know what happens... and... I just wonder if it's helping any more.'

I knew what happened when I opened the boxes. I started crying.
Not moist eye crying, or dabbing with tissues crying, or tears down
the cheeks crying. I mean raging, head banging, animal noise crying.
Crying that made my skull tighten and my head throb, crying that
wouldn't stop. After she spoke I was angry that she was on to me.
Angry that she couldn't bear another night of standing by helpless as
I wailed. Angry that I had so much bile to swallow. Angry because
she was right. I'd done enough anger to know how addictive and self-
satisfying the acid burn of rage can be and how it corrodes what's left
of your love. When my brother broke the news to me, I said, 'I don't
know what we are going to do, but we are not going to get angry.'

I made a choice. I chose not to be angry. I put the boxes away and
I left my paperwork undone. If I was more like the old man, that
would have been that. The boxes would have mouldered in the loft
until my kids got their hands on them. Their contents would,
I imagine, be all but incomprehensible to them. I worry that they are
becoming incomprehensible to me. That's what happens if you
don't do your paperwork: time comes round and takes your
stories, characters flatten out into the two-dimensional shapes of

comfortable family legend. But I'm not like the old man. I can't let it ride, I can't front the bailiffs, I can't put the paperwork in the bin.

W hen anyone is murdered the police want to take a look at their home. When they're murdered in that home, the police want to take a good long look. In Ivor's case they examined his flat for almost a month. They looked at him for just as long – time enough for three autopsies, one for the prosecution and one for each of the two defence cases. We got to see him for ten minutes in the Uxbridge morgue, a low brick building of studied anonymity. Unadorned, it is surrounded by stark beds of cracked earth and leggy municipal roses strewn with a thousand cigarette butts. Inside, it's suffused with seedy, thin yellow light, furnished like a cheapskate undertakers. We couldn't touch him or even be in the same room at the same time; he remained a piece of evidence. They let my brother and me into a viewing room with a gridded glass window through which you could see the broken corpse ruddy with smashed capillary beds, his battered jowls drooping heavily down his face, his eyes tiny black crosses sunk in his skull, his thick dark pelt still lush on his greying skin.

When the police had finished inspecting his flat, there remained the matter of his blood; lots of it and all over his new pink carpet. We agreed it would be a good thing if the carpet was removed and if someone washed the woodwork. When I asked the police, for no reason in particular, who would be doing it, they replied, 'Rentokil.'

Early April, a blank white sky, and we're driving down the Westway, heading out of London towards Ruislip. In the car we are tight-lipped, wondering whether they really have taken out the carpet, whether they really did clean the woodwork, wondering what we'll do if we have to clean the flat before we clear it. I didn't think I would dare play it, but I slide in the cassette, a battered copy of AC/DC's Highway to Hell. *It's already wound to track eight: 'If You Want Blood (You've Got It)'. We pull off at the Polish War Memorial. I see his smile, not his wounds. I hear his laughter and swallow my horror.*

I see myself enter the house through the back door. The air in the flat is hard and still and cold. At the edge of my vision I can see strange but familiar landmarks: his collection of tannin-stained mugs, the deep-fat fryer and its crust of oil sludge and dust, the stacks of duty-free Rothmans cartons. But the coin jars have gone and so has most of the linoleum. It's been cut away and removed. He must have bled all over it as he lay slumped in the hallway. I look through into the hall. The carpet is gone. They've taken the lot, leaving dirty boards, copies of the local freebie, the sharp tips of the exposed runners, but no blood. I feel relieved and suddenly emboldened.

Walking into his bedroom, it feels even staler: the curtains are drawn, dust hangs in the air. My parents' private space – their drawers, their papers, their clothes, their bed. I head straight for the top drawer on his side of the dresser. I am looking for a letter. I paw through lighters, hip flasks, old casino chips, scraps of paper with scribbled addresses, rotting Polaroids, cufflinks – and the letter. He wrote it twenty years ago, the first time they left James and me at home while they flew off on holiday somewhere. 'Only to be opened in the event of our demise,' he had said, theatrically but in earnest. We never opened it. It sat for a long weekend on the coffee table. They didn't die, they came back. I always supposed the letter would be in the drawer. It is handwritten, with an air of mock seriousness. He tells us that he and Bobby love us and are proud of us. We are to go and see the solicitors, Cathcart and Co., which, of course, we've already done. He tells us, 'David look after James. James help David.'

Now I'm crushed. I'm heady with my find. I am lost. I can hear a distant rasp that is my sister-in-law vomiting: Rentokil scrubbed his blood up, but they overlooked the steak he was going to cook that evening defrosting on the draining board. She found it in a pool of stinking brown blood. We are grabbing papers and folders and anything official: letters, postcards, photos, paperwork. I'm opening Bobby's bedside cupboard. Sarah's talking to me, close to my ear: 'We don't have to do it all today; we can and will come back.' He hasn't touched it. He hasn't touched it for eight years. It's exactly as she left it; the old exercise books, lip balms, her last handbag. I rub the dust from the zip and open it. Inside there's an appointment card from Northwick Park Hospital, bearing a date for two weeks after she died. There is a small orange pill pot, with a single tiny capsule of diazepam left.

After that day, I put Bobby's handbag and her diazepam in the boxes. I kept her letters and her books of poetry. I sorted the birth, death and marriage certificates for three generations, immigration papers and passports. I collected the cards that celebrated my birth and my brother's, our bar mitzvahs, Bobby's twenty-first birthday and the cards that consoled us when she died. I sifted what was left of her schoolwork, and mine and James's, kids' artwork, holiday mementos: this was treasure. But the old man's paperwork remained unsorted and unexamined, still toxic to the touch. I shovelled it all in – bulging folders and files, bundles of bills and summonses and judgements, photos and fan mail, correspondence with lawyers, bank and business papers wrapped in rubber bands – and put it away.

The boxes move slowly from loft to landing to study. I circle around them, delaying. I read the letter. I hold the pill pot up to the light. Finally, I begin to sort his paperwork, but I am not being thorough; I'm jumping ahead of myself. Like the letter in his drawer, there are things that I know are here and I am looking for them, and there are things I want to overlook. I don't want to do our fights. I don't want to do how he sent my brother all the wrong messages and fucked his head up. I don't want to do all the shit he put Bobby through. I want to start with the legend.

I've got his certificate from the Morris School of Hairdressing in Piccadilly, which recalls his adventures as an apprentice hairdresser, working for Raymond 'Mr Teasy Weasy' Bessone in his Knightsbridge salon. Ivor at work with a faux French hairdresser, the sought-after stylist to the debutantes and blue-bloods of west London and the star turn on a BBC variety show: a hint of camp, a swirl of cigarette smoke, a pencil-thin moustache. Ivor escaping from his suburban prison into the penumbra of the London set, louche cocktail parties and weekends in the country. I've got his discharge card from the RAF and the tale of how he reported sick for three months and got an honourable discharge three months later, how he never did drill or fired a gun or received a uniform that fitted him. I've got the transcript of a police interview with him in the embezzlement case he managed to escape scot-free, but for the cannabis plant they found in his office. I've got the betting slips and casino cheques and his days of low-rolling and high-rolling, card marking and cheating, betting coups and scams in private rooms at the back of west London gambling dens. This is the easy stuff. I know these stories and they're good ones. The stories of his first lives and selves: secure, fixed and funny. Shall I break the habit of a lifetime and do the difficult paperwork first? The stuff that's not settled? That's not funny? I pick up his notebook – I've only ever glanced through it before – and I start to read and I start to write.

I vor is sitting on the sofa with the notebook. It's 1994, he is fifty-five and this is a low. Bobby has been dead for nine months: breast cancer that came and went and came back again and ate her liver and shrank her body to a husk before it snuffed her out. She was fifty-one. There had been plenty of cancer in the family and there's the luck of the draw, but the thought nags at me; he didn't do their paperwork. If the pressure of their life didn't kill her it made the fight too hard.

Seven years earlier, Ivor and Bobby were running Robertero, a women's clothing shop in Ruislip Manor. It was a shoestring operation, but run with great charm and acumen. No one earned a fortune, but all the bills were paid without pain and that definitely constituted an advance. Of course, one of the reasons it went so well was that Ivor had learned a few lessons from previous brushes with commercial law and bookkeeping. Instead of not keeping any books, he kept two sets of books. In 1987 Customs and Excise showed up on the not entirely unreasonable grounds that the business had paid barely any VAT for the previous five years. The Inland Revenue were a bit perplexed by the numbers too. The ensuing bankruptcy proceedings would last six years. Bobby would get breast cancer and, although they did eventually clear all the debts, she was dead before the case was closed. The old man never did finalize the paperwork.

For the first time in my life I saw him helpless. James and I arranged Bobby's funeral. She had to be buried at Bushy cemetery, where everyone else in the family has ended up, but they had blown out the synagogue and the burial plans a decade ago, so that was £1,500 now and another £4,500 later. I gave the United Synagogue Burial Society the bounciest cheque you've ever seen and we put her in the ground and cancelled it.

A few days later, we told him and he was delighted; he rose from the sofa, put on a jacket and headed up to town, where he told the burial authorities that we weren't going to pay, we didn't want a headstone and they could make their own arrangements. He and Bobby's father had the row they'd been waiting to have for forty years and met only once again before they both died. The thin web of family networks and friends sustained by Bobby was either left to gather dust or sharply and deliberately broken. Ivor's gambling crew were personae non gratae; everyone was persona non grata. For maybe six months he sat on the sofa in impenetrable despair.

He has reduced the sagging golden sofa to a pulp of wood, springs and stuffing. He's been lying on this sofa a lot, but today he's sitting, probably cross-legged, slightly hunched over a pad of lined paper that lies on an old marble coffee table. Around him is a sea of ashtrays, mostly full, Rothmans packets, lighters, mobile phones, pens, toothpicks, business cards, Post-its, playing cards, torches and nail care equipment, glasses, spare glasses, a magnifying glass. There is at least one, but most likely more than one, very strong cup of tea stewing. The TV is on, a cable sports channel, probably with no sound and definitely with no subscription. He's smoking and carefully,methodically, he writes, making his points, then reading and rereading his notes.

I have the notebook in front of me. Flipping through it I find his usual hieroglyphics and doodles, lists of things to do and bills to pay, names, numbers and addresses including my own, but they are all to come. On the opening pages, in capitalized script, is a list of complaints. It's odd to read through this moment of self-reflection. I never saw the old man on the wrong end of a power inequality before. I never heard him admit that slights had hurt or that he had ever tasted humiliation. I'd seen him grieve, but this was a part of his psyche that never went on public display. He blows out a long slow stream of acrid smoke and taps each point on the page with his biro.

> Believing rumours and not checking with me (and not apologizing when proved wrong)
> Making decisions without consulting me
> Milking club funds for personal use or worse to help other groups
> Making the newsletter a personal voice
> Not helping me to clear my name
> Not paying me the money I am owed

He stubs out his cigarette, drains the tea and turns the page.

> Hitting Heidi in the face at Framfield
> Watching experienced girls and ignoring novices
> Telling members to strip girls off without consulting the girl
> Interfering with members scenarios
> Always jumping in at party's and in so doing preventing paying members getting their fair share of the action

Since Bobby died he hasn't picked up a playing card. He doesn't drink and the last time he smoked weed he got the whites. He's not interested in anything stronger that might dull the pain. Cigarettes and tea are his drugs of choice. They serve to mark the time, structuring his loneliness, helping pass the agonizing tedium of every day. It wasn't working. We have conversations on the phone where no one knows what to say and no one can tell who is trying to help whom. Ivor has crawled out of the wreckage of past lives and shed his skin a dozen times, but this time I really wonder if he has run out of conjuring tricks.

But he hasn't. In the depths of his grief, he has turned to his remaining obsession: spanking, in fact the full range of corporal punishment. It's a long-held peccadillo but now he thinks he's found a way not only to have fun but to make a living. He is in with Keith and Abi at the Posterity Club (like the hairdressing fraternity, fetish clubs are fond of a cheesy pun). They are operating out of deepest Berkshire, putting on afternoon spanking parties in detached houses for paying guests. Keith is the main man, he's been running the club for two years, but I can see Ivor is not happy. Not because he's not the boss – he knows he's still learning this game – but because he's not being respected, the girls are not being respected, the punters are not being respected. What should be a mutually satisfying and above all profitable affair is being run as an ego trip and at a loss.

I turn the pages: there's a bespoke scenario laid out for Mr Freddie Romero involving the silent treatment in a limousine followed by a trip to the dungeon; a party in Surbiton to be arranged, guests and girls to be paired; fragments of scripts for movies and routines for a cabaret club. And then there is the Red Stripe Club. He has two or three goes at writing his opening pitch and then he finds his voice:

> Thank you for writing to Red Stripe. We are the only hands-on spanking club in Great Britain and these are the reasons why. Red Stripe is run by people who are as enthusiastic about the spanking scene as you are. Because the girls who attend Red Stripe parties are truly submissive and really enjoy the spanking scene, and because we listen to the opinions of our members. So if you enjoy putting a cheeky schoolgirl over your knee, pulling down her knickers and giving her a thorough and well-deserved spanking then you will definitely enjoy a Red Stripe party.
>
> We haven't forgotten all the submissive gentlemen either. Our dominant ladies are just as enthusiastic as our submissive ladies and really understand what is required.
>
> If you would like to join Red Stripe, meet the girls and other like-minded men please send a cheque for £25. This is to cover the cost of post and the printing of our newsletter which will keep you informed of the monthly upcoming events for you to choose from.

A month later he splits from Keith and Abi. He puts a few ads in the back pages of the *Sunday Sport* and the specialist press and the cheques come rolling in. List after list of party guests and girls fill the final pages of the pad. For a time after this he went very quiet on the details of his life. His phone was suddenly always engaged, but who was he talking to? No, he couldn't come over because he had to go to Manchester. Manchester? This man wouldn't go to Uxbridge normally. The real giveaway, though, was the nine video machines in his sitting room, all wired up together and each showing a paused picture of a woman being caned. I made him tell me about it. It didn't come as much of a surprise: my brother and I had discovered his stash of spanking porn a long time ago and thought little more about it. Sure it was kind of weird, but he was kind of weird. Whatever it was all about, it wasn't turning us on. We had enough of our own stuff to sort out without trying to fathom the old man's fetishes. When we talked it over and he tried to explain what the turn-on was, we never got very far. In the end he didn't care, he just knew that he liked it. Self-reflection was no substitute for having fun.

Ivor never looked back. Seven years on the Red Stripe Club had 2,000 members, held four or five parties a month and made ten movies a year. The girls loved him because he was an old-fashioned gentleman. He made them feel safe and never failed to pay them on the day, generously. Some, as his pitch claimed, were enthusiasts, others less so; but he couldn't abide faking, believing it bad for both business and the soul. There was a queue round the block to audition. He set very clear rules of behaviour and enforced them assiduously; at the parties, encounters were carefully policed, with code words that girls could use at any time to terminate a session. There was as little nudity as was possible given the nature of the fetish, and there was absolutely no sex. The punters loved it because it was safe, suburban and regulated, and what turned Ivor on is what turned them on. The whole circus was conducted with an air of endless and effortless bonhomie.

Money, love, fame and fun were flooding into Ruislip Court. On a business trip to New York, Ivor was recognized in a fetish club as 'the Headmaster' – his alter ego, who appeared in the fabulously successful Red Stripe College Classic series of movies. He recalled with relish a high-pitched New Yorker in a leather cat suit and furry ears who exclaimed, 'It's the Headmaster! It's the Headmaster!' A buzz ran through the club and proceedings were halted to allow the Headmaster and his escort to take to the podium and give an impromptu masterclass in the finer points of using the cane and the paddle. I stopped worrying that he might top himself and started worrying that the tax man would come calling again.

In the mass of unopened post in his flat was a letter from Uxbridge Police. It read:

> Dear Mr Goldblatt,
> We are sorry to hear that you have been a victim of crime.

In a world where Rentokil is hired to clean up homicide sites, this was surely a grotesque but routine response from the police to the recently murdered. It had, in fact, arrived two days before his death and he had been the victim of a crime a few weeks before that. The two were not unconnected. That's what I like about the letter: not its irony, but its prescience. When I read it I think about the question everyone asks – 'Why? Why him?' – and it reminds me of the only answer that makes sense. 'Why not?' Do the paperwork. Shuffle the files and stack the cards for long enough and you can make the inconceivable feel inevitable.

He'd lived with the sofa and the swirling orange carpet it had arrived with for thirty years and now they were all used up, threadbare and finished. Even he had had his money's worth, and just maybe it was time to start moving on from Bobby and that life. Suddenly a pair of white leather sofas and a pale pink deep-pile carpet filled his living room and hallway. Pale pink? What was he thinking? There had been method in the swirly orange carpet madness and a month later there were tea stains on the sofas and cigarette burns in the new carpet.

Ivor calls for a running repair and two men show up to fix the carpet. The small pale one is actually the carpet fitter. The big bearded one doesn't seem to do that much and mooches about. The old man barely notices as he waves them into the sitting room, the phone clamped to his head and Nigel from Loughborough or Gareth from Nuneaton bending his ear about some minor breach of party protocol at the switch do in Leicester last week. Or maybe it's Ken calling to say that he's finished recording the big video order; or he's counselling one of the girls on some issue in her life, money problems, boyfriend problems, housing problems; and all the time he's making very strong tea, smoking Rothmans and laughing.

The carpet fitters must be taking a good look round. There would have been no effort to disguise what was going on. The Red Stripe show would certainly have been diverting, but much more interesting, I suspect, was Ivor's wallet and the five grand in cash that he invariably carried with him, secured by a very large, old-fashioned paper clip. They palm that as they finish the job and, as they go through the kitchen, the change bottles must have caught their eye. Three-litre plastic soft-drinks bottles with the tops cut off; ten to fifteen of them crammed on to the kitchen work surfaces between the toaster and the cooker, stacked around the bread bin and sitting on the open shelves, all overflowing with pound coins and fifty-pence pieces. Five hundred coins a bottle, ten bottles, another five grand at least. And where there's that much coinage and that much cash in a wallet, there's bound to be more.

He reported the theft to the police; he knew who had done it. He even had them round to investigate the crime. He cleared up a bit, but he wouldn't let them into the sitting room, where the carpet had been fixed and the crime committed. So what's anyone going to do? The police left it and wrote him a nice letter. He left it and never got the letter. At another time he might well have taken matters into his own hands, or pulled in a few favours from the wide range of heavies and knuckle merchants that he knew. But he didn't. He didn't really need the money back, he didn't need revenge, he didn't need the aggravation. The *News of the Screws*, with whom he had advertised in the past, had infiltrated the Red Stripe Christmas party. He was appalled at the photograph of him that they had used but he was unshakeable in his insouciance: 'It's the life I chose... Might even end up bringing in a few new punters.' Only once did he hint that his casualness might mask fear. He had told me just a few weeks earlier that he couldn't quite march on like he used to. Yes, he had felt something move across his heart.

A month later, March 1, 2001, the carpet fitters are in the pub in Hayes. It's lunchtime. They're drinking their second or third lager of the day and then they retreat to the toilets to do the last line of a very large bag of cocaine. The five grand is spent, the cupboard is bare and the party is coming to an end. Except it doesn't have to. Everyone around the table knows this; they know exactly where to go to refresh their funds. A friend drives them the twenty minutes from Hayes to Ruislip Court and, some time around two o'clock, they knock on the door. Ivor, alone, knows exactly who they are and what they want, but you can't play the kinds of games he played with the bailiffs with this lot. He's pushed back down the narrow hall and the door closes. After that the precise details are a matter of conjecture but we know this much.

Ivor is stabbed twenty-six times with one of his own kitchen knives. His lungs are punctured and there are deep wounds in his shoulders and his flanks. He receives a variety of other blows to his head, neck and arms. At 2.08 the emergency services receive a call from him. The carpet fitters are grabbing whatever they can and leaving. The conversation was recorded and it was played in court.

I faced almost everything. I watched them argue over the diagram of his knife wounds, I looked the carpet fitters in the eye, but I couldn't listen to the tape. What do you want: some justice or no justice, some truths or no truths, enough of the story or all the story? I reach the limit of my paperwork. I am told the tape is gentle and dignified. I'm told he didn't panic, but just explained the situation and waited for the ambulance to arrive. It came twelve minutes later.

He was dead in a pool of his own blood, which was ebbing away into the deep pile of his new pink carpet.

I sifted the contents of his house for another five months. After the trial I finally felt strong enough to empty it: the furniture, his clothes, my mother's clothes, the nine video machines, the box of butt plugs, the bamboo canes and the leather paddles, the vaulting horse and the blackboard. Then I started stripping and cleaning. I told myself that it would help sell the flat. How could anyone think of buying it? But I also imagined that if I cleaned long enough and hard enough, the dull patina of dried blood that seemed to cling to every surface would finally go. I hoped that if I emptied the flat of its objects, and pared back its contents to nothing, I would uncover the place that I grew up in, before Ivor was the old man, before he was a legend. I couldn't find that place and I didn't think I would find it in the boxes and among the papers either.

I make a final trip. I know I'm going to say goodbye, but it feels like a hollow journey. There's nothing left to take, no scraps of memory remaining. I'm standing in the bathroom in front of the sink, looking at the light bending and breaking through the textured windows. The sink is still leaking. A patch of the rough, greasy brown carpet is wet. I look up at the waste water pipe and see that an old rag is wrapped around the leaking joint; an old grey fraying rag. Along its edge, woven into the fabric, are two lines of small navy rectangles. I bite on my own breath. The navy rectangles edge a huge white soft towel. My father is standing over the bath holding it up for me. I'm four. My brother has just been born and tonight, for the first night that I can remember, my father and I are alone and he is bathing me. He's bathing me and lifting me out of the bath in the rectangle-edged towel. I unwind the rag from the pipe and spread it out in my palms and I'm crying. The towel is huge and soft and enveloping. He dries me. There's the sweet smell of baby powder in the air. He brushes my short, tightly curled hair and dresses me in my finery: my orange cords, my smart pink shirt, my orange braces. I'm holding the rag and I'm crying, but not because I can't stand the bloodstains and the gash in the linoleum. We eat, side by side, at the marble coffee table. He bathes and dresses and sings to me. I gather up biscuits for my new brother, knowing full well that I will eat them. He holds a gigantic, ostentatious bunch of roses for Bobby. I'm holding the rag and I'm crying, but not because the grime and the dust have obscured every moment of the everyday life I lived here. I'm crying because he's taking my hand and he's leading me out and we're walking down the hall and we're going to the hospital and I feel safe and warm and loved and tingling with anticipation. ■

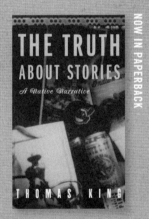

My father left school at thirteen; his family needed the money. When I asked him what he'd like me to say in this piece, he said, 'Tell them I was in the Navy from 1942 to 1947, in four different invasions, in North Africa, France, Italy and I forget the other one. Tell them I'm eighty-four and a half. Tell them I'm a good salmon fisherman and so's my daughter, who caught the third biggest fish of the year last month at Delphi in Ireland.' No I didn't, I said. It was the gillie. I just held the rod a bit. He laughed. 'Aye, but don't tell them that.'

My father put all five of us, my brothers and sisters and me, through university with a passion and foresight it took me decades to appreciate.

My father is English. Whenever people in the Highlands, where he's lived since he married my mother in 1949 (she died in 1990), comment on his Lincolnshire accent, he says, 'I came up to work on the Hydro dams and never had the train fare back again.' He was the main electrical contractor in Inverness and the Highlands in the Sixties and Seventies, until the coming of Thatcher, Dixons, Currys. 'Tell them I'm still Conservative after all these years,' he said. There's no way I'm telling them that, I said.

My father, one afternoon, sat at the dinette table, unscrewed my talking bear whose cord had broken, and screwed it back together. It worked. 'When people are dead, graves aren't where to find them. They're in the wind, the grass.' That's the kind of thing he said. When I asked him what you do if you see something in the dark that frightens you, he said, 'What you do is, you go up to it, and touch it.' When things went wrong in the neighbourhood, people would come to my father for help. When we went to visit an old neighbour last autumn, in her eighties too, she called him Mr Smith. 'Call me Donald, now, Chrissie,' he said. She shook her head. 'You'll have another biscuit with your tea, Mr Smith,' she said.

My father, as a boy, was a champion footballer, boxer, ping-pong player. His handsomeness, as a young man, is legendary. Every time I left for university, he tucked twenty pounds and a folded sheet of stamps into my pocket. 'Write to your mother,' he said. ∎

Ali and Donald Smith, 1971

CATERPILLARS

James Lasdun

ILLUSTRATION BY AUDE VAN RYN

A t first they thought the white things in the trees were plastic bags. You saw that back in Brooklyn all the time: scraps of sheeny litter caught in the branches of sidewalk ginkgos and sycamores. But out here in the middle of the French countryside it was a shock.

'Human beings,' Craig said calmly, 'are disgusting.'

But as they came closer they saw that what they were looking at were in fact cocoons, with shadows of caterpillars moving inside them.

The trees were pines and the cocoons had been anchored to the bendy twigs of different branches, using them for tension like the guy ropes of marquees. Clusters of needles had been trapped and flattened under the skeins of milky webbing.

Craig peered in at them.

'I guess it's some kind of tent caterpillar.'

Caitlin smiled cautiously.

'Oh well. At least it's not people...'

He shrugged; it wasn't his style to recant.

Luke, his son, poked at one of the cocoons with a stick. The branches moved, but the dense, opaque fibres stayed intact. He poked again, harder.

'Don't do that,' Craig told him.

They walked on, passing through vineyards and a long orchard of almond trees. On the far side of this they came to another stand of pines with the cocoons in them. There were more of them this time and the trees looked more blighted than the others, the branches around the webby fabric drooping downward, with dead needles dangling from their twigs. The three hurried on past.

At lunchtime they picnicked under a stone watchtower on a hill. The trees up there were oaks and birches and there were no cocoons in them. But when they moved on, turning on to the trail that led back to the hotel, they passed again through pine woods and there were white cocoons lodged in the green branches wherever they looked. Around each one, large volumes of needles had desiccated and turned brown. Inside, among the moving shapes of caterpillars, were strangled clusters of brown needles showing milkily through. Dead branches hung crookedly from the trunks. On some of the trees there were ten or twelve cocoons in different places.

Caitlin turned to Luke.

'They look sort of like invalids, don't they, the trees? Covered in bandages?'

The boy gave her the unnerving sidelong look that had so far greeted most of her attempts to befriend him.

Back at the hotel the owner told them the cocoons were made by processionary caterpillars: '*chenilles processionnaires*'. They were called that, he explained, because they travelled in long lines joined head-to-toe. Most years the winter killed enough of them that they weren't a problem, but the past few winters had been warm, so now there was an infestation. He smiled as he said this, as if it were something to be proud of.

Craig asked if they were everywhere in this area.

The man nodded enthusiastically.

'*Ici, oui, partout.*'

Wagging a finger, he added, '*Faux pas les toucher...*'

You shouldn't touch them, or you could get a painful rash.

They had been planning to do another walk from the village the next day, to a cave with an underground lake. But after this conversation Craig said it would be too depressing to spend another day surrounded by half-dead trees and that they should leave early in the morning instead.

'Let's head on up to the mountains.'

'What about the cave?' Luke asked.

'There'll be other things to see.'

So the next morning they drove to the mountains. Their ears popped as they climbed. The air grew cooler. Vineyards gave way to stony lavender fields and sheep pastures bounded by low stone walls. Above these a vast pine forest began.

The three fell silent, staring out through the windows. The trees looked healthy enough; tall and straight, their branches spreading a pelt of deep, dark green over the bony ridges and slopes of the mountains. On the steepest slopes the trees grew more sparsely and you could see the grey mountainside rubble between them, but even in these places they seemed to be flourishing; their massive, upward-curving branches bearing thick swathes of unblemished black-green needles.

Only as the forest became interspersed with pasture again did Caitlin see a cocoon; just the one, glistening like a tuft of cotton candy high in the branches of a tree above the road. She didn't say anything; the others seemed not to have noticed.

The road turned to gravel, following a shallow river until it arrived at the stone buildings of the farm where they were staying. After they had checked in and eaten lunch, Craig spread out the hiking map. There was a pair of *bergeries* in the area that he wanted to see: old drystone sheepcotes that had been designated historic sites. According to the guidebook you could only get to them on foot, which was a part of their attraction as far as Craig was concerned. They were set below a high ridge, and the woman who ran the farm pointed out a ring walk they could do that would bring them past each *bergerie* before circling back to the farm in time for dinner.

The first part of the trail led over a saddle of grassland with sheep grazing on it. There were no pylons or cellphone towers to upset Craig, and for this Caitlin was grateful. Not that she liked these things any more than he did, but his diatribes had an unsettling effect on her. Since being with Craig she had found that it was necessary to guard, rather carefully, what remained of her affection for her own species.

Over the saddle the trail fell through a valley to a stream where it entered a dark wood of deciduous trees. The stream was deep in places, with pools of green water under ledges of moss-covered rock. Along its banks were patches of buttery yellow that turned out to be primroses. There were also purple flowers that Craig said were *Hepatica*.

'It's nice here,' Caitlin ventured.

'Not bad,' Craig agreed.

As they came out of the wood and began climbing again they saw something on the path ahead of them that appeared to be a long, dark snake, moving very slowly forward over the red dust.

Luke ran towards it.

'It's the caterpillars!' he shouted.

They walked up and stood over the creatures. They were an inch and a half long; grey, with an orange stripe along the top, and covered with pale spikes of fur. Each shiny black head was attached to the tail of the caterpillar in front. Their progress along the path was slow, but the quilted, rubbery pouches of their bodies moved in vigorous undulations.

Craig squatted down. After inspecting them closely for some time, he called to his son.

'Come here, Luke.'

The boy squatted beside him.

'We don't kill animals, do we?'

'No. Mom does. She kills mice.'

'Okay, but I don't and you don't and Caitlin doesn't. But these animals, I'm thinking – they aren't part of nature, exactly. They're here because the winters haven't been cold enough to kill them, and you know why that is, right?'

The boy thought for a moment.

'Oh,' he said in a dull voice. 'Global warming.'

'Right. Which makes them partly a human phenomenon. Now, look at those pine trees.' Craig pointed to the wooded ridge ahead of them. 'These guys can probably smell them from here. I imagine it's a good smell to them. They're going to go up there and start making their cocoons which means pretty soon that whole forest is going to be infested like the one we saw yesterday.'

The boy blinked, then gave a grin.

'Are we going to kill them, Dad?'

'Yes we are. But I want to make sure you understand why. Do you?'

'Yes, yes. How are we going to do it?'

'Like this.'

Craig stood up and stamped on the first caterpillar in the column, bursting it under the thick sole of his hiking boot. The line started breaking apart immediately, each individual uncoupling itself and striking out in its puff of fur with an appearance of panicky disorientation. The boy jumped on a group of them, crushing them to a dark pulp in the dust. Then he and Craig proceeded to obliterate the entire column.

'That takes care of that,' Craig said.

But a little further along the trail they came upon another procession, crawling slowly up towards the ridge. This time father and son set about destroying them without any discussion, Luke yelling gleefully as he jumped about, Craig preserving a neutral air, as if he regarded himself as the instrument of some purely impersonal force of necessity.

They didn't see any more caterpillars after that. The path climbed through an area of the sweet-smelling scrub of juniper and wild rosemary that they had learned to call 'garrigue'. Luke and Craig were chatting, at ease with each other for the first time in days. Caitlin walked behind them, conscious of the need to give them their space.

As their trail turned for the final, steepest part of the ascent, they saw something shiny rising towards them over the brow of the ridge, a couple of hundred yards ahead. It was a car, a silver SUV – the small kind they had here in France – and it was driving down the footpath. A moment later another one, identical, appeared behind it, then another, and then another. Very slowly the four vehicles came down the near vertical-looking top section of the trail, before turning on to the horizontal path that branched off along the ridge toward the *bergeries*. There, in tight convoy, dust puffing up from their tyres, they rolled slowly onward, disappearing into the trees.

'What the fuck was that?' Craig said.

He unfolded his map.

'They're on a footpath,' he said. 'There's no road there, and there's no road on the other side where they came from either.' He folded the map back up, quickening his pace towards the ridge as if he thought he might be able to catch up with the cars. They were out of sight, of course, by the time the three of them reached the intersection. But the smell of their exhaust hung in the air, and you could still hear the sound of their engines over the tinkle of sheep bells down in the valley.

'They're driving on a goddam footpath!' Craig said.

They took the same turning as the cars had taken. Once they entered the woods they saw that there were in fact cocoons all over the pine trees. Caitlin glanced at Craig, but he didn't seem interested in pursuing the implications of this. His jaw was set tight, his grey eyes glaring ahead along the trail. His bearing, as always, was calm, but she could tell he was furious. He would have liked to crush the cars, she sensed, just as he had crushed the caterpillars. Suddenly he stepped off the path into the woods. He stooped down for something, then came out backwards, dragging the bleached trunk of a fallen tree.

'Luke, give me a hand!'

The boy helped his father drag the tree across the footpath.

'What are we doing?'

'We're giving those people something to think about when they come back from their expedition. A little roadblock.'

'Oh. Cool.'

'In fact maybe a series of roadblocks,' Craig said, scanning the woods again. 'Make sure they get the point. It'll be like those Stations of the Cross they had outside that first village. Some little opportunities for reflection. There's another tree…'

He and Luke dragged out several other trees as they walked along, setting them across the path every fifty yards or so. Caitlin looked on, unsure this was a good idea, but not wanting to get into an argument. With Craig you had to be utterly convinced of your position if you wanted to disagree with him, and she suspected her misgivings might be nothing more than cowardice. Besides, she didn't want to interfere when he and Luke were getting along like this.

At one point they found some large rocks.

'We'll use these too,' Craig said.

He and Luke braced themselves against the rocks, manoeuvring them into the middle of the path.

A little further along they saw a tractor tyre lying by a gate at the entrance to a field. They heaved it up on its edge. It was enormous: almost as wide in diameter as Luke was tall. Together they rolled it into the path where they tipped it over, water splatting from a gash in its side as it fell.

'Okay,' Craig said. 'That should do the trick.'

They walked on along the flat, stony path. After a while Luke began lagging behind.

'Wait for me!' he shouted.

'Keep up,' Craig called back. 'We have a ways to go.'

It was another half-hour before they arrived at the first *bergerie*.

The four cars were parked in a line at the top of the steeply sloping meadow, in the middle of which stood the small domed and arched sheepcote and shepherd's hut. A group of people stood outside, gathered around a large woman in an outfit of mauve tweed.

'I'll wait here for Luke, shall I?' Caitlin said at the entrance to the meadow. The boy had fallen back again. Craig shrugged, then walked on down.

She watched him approach the buildings. Several faces from the group turned towards him with smiles of greeting, and she saw his tall, straight figure stride past them into one of the buildings without so much as a glance in their direction. She couldn't see his face, but she knew the severe expression it would be wearing. A familiar, half-fearful, half-admiring feeling came over her as she pictured it. She found it so difficult, herself, to judge other people's behaviour, even when she could see it was wrong. But Craig regarded it as an obligation. He had told her once that if he'd been born in a time when it was possible to believe in a god, he would have felt compelled to become a preacher. He had gone into furniture-making instead, but even this he had turned into his own kind of crusade, with his recycled materials, his all-natural stains and varnishes, his rejection of all elements of ornamentation and superfluous comfort from his designs. 'It's what Jesus would have done if he'd stuck to carpentry,' he liked to joke. Or not joke exactly; just say with a glint in his eye that you felt you were permitted to take as humorous. She'd never been with a man quite like him before. She didn't love him exactly; not in the usual way of wanting to be always kissing and fooling around together. She didn't even like him, she sometimes thought, observing his cold manner with people he disapproved of, which was most of the human race. But he had engulfed her somehow; taken up residence in her imagination like some large, dense, intractable problem that had been given to her to solve.

By the time Luke caught up, the group had begun walking back up towards their cars. The woman in the mauve outfit was talking to them in English, with a French accent.

'What you will see at the next *bergerie* will be a completely different technique of construction. Instead of the vaulted ceilings we have here, you will see that it will be built in the tunnel style…'

The people were mostly middle-aged, some of the men wearing ties and sports coats under green waterproof jackets, the women in wool and tweed outfits like their guide, though in more subdued colours. They looked like professors, Caitlin thought. They smiled at her and she smiled uncomfortably back, wishing that she wasn't having to encounter them like this, in person.

The guide gave her a polite nod as she passed. Her eye lingered a moment on Luke. Caitlin looked back and saw that the boy had lifted his T-shirt over his large belly, which he was scratching vigorously. It was a bit embarrassing, but she didn't feel it was her place to tell him to stop. Up beyond him the people were climbing back into their cars.

Craig emerged from the dark interior of the sheepcote. He stood in the entrance, watching the cars as they set off in a line along the footpath, heading for the second *bergerie*.

'I was thinking,' he said, 'if they were in wheelchairs or something, that might be an excuse, but really I don't even believe that. It's not like if I was old or disabled I'd feel entitled to be driven places off the road that I couldn't walk to. Anyway those people are perfectly capable of walking. They're just lazy, and selfish.'

They wandered through the buildings. Craig explained how the arches and domed roofs were built without any tools or cement, just with the careful piling and balancing of all the flattest stones the shepherds could find in the area. There was a rare note of approval in his voice and Caitlin brightened, as she always did at such moments. He loved this kind of patient, anonymous craftsmanship and his enthusiasm when he spoke about it made her want to cheer him on even though she didn't find it that exciting herself.

After they had finished looking, they went back to the path and started walking to the second *bergerie*. The boy was scratching himself again.

'What are you doing?' Craig asked.

'It itches.'

'Leave it alone. What is it, a mosquito bite?'

He peered at his son's stomach.

'I don't see anything. Except too much of this.' He grabbed the roll of fat on Luke's belly. 'Come on, let's burn some off.'

He set off at a brisk march. The boy soon started lagging behind again.

'Wait!'

Craig turned. 'Keep up, kiddo. And stop the scratching.'

The boy was panting when he caught up. His face was mottled pink.

'I can't walk this fast,' he said. He was scratching his forearms now; clawing them with his plump, nail-bitten fingers.

'What is going on?' Craig said.

'I don't know.'

'Well stop scratching. And try to keep up.' He tousled the boy's hair. 'You want a nature quiz?'

'No.'

They walked in silence along the path. The sun had dropped below the other side of the ridge and they were in shadow now. Here and there pale cocoons hung in the pines above them; stretched and bulging in a way that made Caitlin think of something hawked up from a lung. She tried not to look. Before long the boy had fallen behind again.

'Wait for me!' he wailed.

This time when he caught up, his face was an angry red and there were yellowish welts standing out on his arms.

'My God,' Caitlin said, 'are you okay?'

He ignored her, as usual. Craig examined his arms.

'It looks like hives. He gets allergies sometimes. You didn't touch one of those caterpillars did you? With your skin?'

'No.'

'Well, listen, we're not halfway yet. We have another couple hours walking. Think you can make it okay?'

'I don't feel good.'

'I know. We'll get you some antihistamine when we get back. But you're okay to go on, right?'

'I'm tired.'

'I could take him back the way we came,' Caitlin heard herself say, 'I mean if you want to go on…'

'No!' the boy said, clinging to his father.

Craig opened the map. He didn't say anything for a while.

'How much shorter would it be?' Caitlin asked.

'To go back?'

'Mm.'

He looked at her; a faint sardonic light in his eye, as if in acknowledgement of some small but unexpected challenge.

'A bit. Yeah, I guess it would be quite a bit shorter.'

He looked again at Luke. The boy seemed dazed. The soft flesh around his eyes had begun to swell up, and the eyes themselves were bloodshot.

'All right,' Craig said, folding the map away. 'We'll go back. We'll go back the way we came.'

And so they turned around and started walking along the trail the way they had come. This time they moved at Luke's pace: it took them a good twenty minutes to reach the *bergerie* again; twice as long as it had coming.

'Can we have a rest?' the boy said as they passed above the buildings. He was panting heavily.

'No. We should keep going now.'

'But I'm tired. My eyes hurt.'

'Come on.'

The boy stood still on the path.

'I can't!' His lip trembled. 'I'm not walking any more!'

Craig stared down at him.

'Okay,' he said gently. 'Get on my shoulders.'

He stooped down and the boy climbed on his shoulders. Slowly, with a slight backward lurch, Craig stood up, his thin frame looking perilously top-heavy under its burden.

'Christ,' he muttered.

They walked on along the path, their progress even slower than before. Luke huddled over his father, resting a swollen cheek on his head. The air was cool but after a while beads of sweat began to slide down over Craig's face. A vein stood out on his forehead. He looked at Caitlin.

'I'm not going to be able to carry him all the way.'

She nodded, saying nothing. There was nothing she could think of to say.

A few minutes after this she heard the cars returning along the trail behind them. She had been listening for them, but even so a feeling of dread came over her. It seemed to sink through her, twisting slowly as it fell, like some heavy object drifting down through oil. As they drew near, Luke raised his head and turned back groggily to look. His eyes were thin red slits in the cushions of flesh around them. Craig moved to the side of the path but went on walking steadily forward, acknowledging nothing.

It occurred to Caitlin that he wasn't going to be able to ask the people for a ride. She could feel, as if she were him for a moment, the impossibility of it. He couldn't carry the boy all the way but he would break his back trying rather than ask these people for help. At the same time he must have been able to see that that would solve nothing. Dimly, it seemed to her that somewhere in the stubborn grid of his thoughts there must be a calculation that she would do the asking; that if she did, it would be possible to accept. A part of her rebelled at being counted on like this. For a moment she was tempted not to play along, just to see what he would do. But even as she tried to assume the necessary attitude of indifference, she knew that his calculation was correct: that she didn't have the heart for it. She turned to face the cars, smiling helplessly and putting out her hand to stop them. As it happened they were stopping anyway, and the driver's window of the front car was sliding down.

'*Il est malade, le petit?*' came the voice of the guide.

'Excuse me?'

'Your child is sick?'

'Yes, yes he's sick!' Caitlin shouted. 'Can you help us? Craig! Stop!'

Craig swung slowly around, his face streaming sweat now.

The guide got out of the car, looking up at Luke.

'What happened to him?'

Caitlin answered. 'We don't know. We think some kind of allergy...'

'I thought this when I saw him before. Did he go near to some of the caterpillars who make these nests?' She pointed up into the trees.

'He was near them, but he didn't touch them.'

'You don't need to touch. Even if you just go near to them and breathe the air it can be dangerous. Especially for the eyes.' She came close to where Craig stood with the boy on his shoulders. 'Ah! But you must bring him to the hospital immediately! Come with us. We'll drive you.'

Craig said nothing, but he lifted Luke from his shoulders. The guide took charge, installing the three of them in the back seat. A grey-haired couple moved over to make room for them. In the passenger seat in front was a man with a shrewd, pointed face. He and the couple made sympathetic noises to Luke as the woman led the convoy off again. The boy buried his head in his father's shoulder.

'Where are you staying?' the guide asked. She was driving fast; much faster than she had before.

Caitlin named the farm.

'Ah. This side of the mountain. The hospital is on the other side. You'll have to take a taxi after you—'

She slammed on the brakes:

'*Mais c'est quoi...?*'

They had come to the tractor tyre.

'I'll move it,' Craig said, opening his door.

Passengers got out of the cars behind. Caitlin thought she should stay in the car with Luke, even though the boy wriggled free when she tried to hold him. She watched the people help Craig move the enormous tyre; laughter and puzzlement on their faces as they returned to their cars. She heard someone say a farmer must have dropped it. Craig climbed back into his seat and stared fixedly out through the window. Caitlin's heart was beating fast, almost fluttering in her chest as the car started up and they sped off once more.

'Are you all professors?' she asked. 'Is that why you're—'

'Heavens no!' The man in front chuckled.

The woman of the couple spoke.

'We're members of a rural preservation group from Suffolk. We go on a jaunt somewhere abroad every year.'

Again the guide slammed on the brakes.

'*Mais...!*'

They had come to the rocks.

Craig was out of the car almost before it had stopped. Others got out to help him once again. This time there was less laughter. The man in the front seat looked at Caitlin in the mirror. She turned away, blushing. He said something very fast in French to the guide as they set off again. The woman looked disbelieving, but at the first of the fallen trees she stopped more gradually, as if half-expecting it.

Craig jumped out and this time only a couple of people from the cars behind came to help him. At the next tree nobody did. The four cars stood with their engines idling while he dragged the heavy, skeletal trunk back into the woods. Then they rolled slowly forward to the next, where he got out again. He was armouring himself, it appeared, in a kind of stoical detachment. But for Caitlin the situation was unfolding with excruciating vividness. An almost physical sensation of pain filled her as she sat among her fellow passengers, watching him get out and move the remaining obstacles, one after another. Alone on the path he seemed to her a strange, parched, remote, beleaguered figure. His face was expressionless, but the straining muscles at his neck and the sweat on his face as he dragged the dead trunks across the dust and stones gave him an agonized look. She felt a desire to comfort him, even though she knew he would have repudiated any hint of pity. Climbing back into his seat after the final tree, he took out a handkerchief and mopped his face. The guide looked at him in the mirror.

'That's the last one?' she asked.

He stared back at her a moment. Then he nodded, and she drove on.

Nobody spoke after that. Caitlin felt the silence bearing down on her. What made it worse was that there was nowhere to look that gave any relief: Craig, Luke, the guide, the other passengers, the trees outside hung with their cocoons; everything seemed to add its own oppressive weight to the moment.

At the intersection they turned right, crossing over to the far side of the ridge. The valley below them was much larger than the one they had crossed on the way from the farm, and it was built up. Houses began halfway down the slope opposite; scattered thinly at first, but growing more dense towards the bottom, their lights hanging pale against the grey-green hillside. Caitlin glanced at Craig, then flinched away. She told herself that the hospital was down there; that these people helping them had also come from down there somewhere. But it was impossible not to think of the cocoons. She closed her eyes, but even then she could see them: pale shapes in the darkness behind her own eyelids, with the shadows of the caterpillars crawling around inside them. ■

 **Wrought**

BY ALISON BECHDEL

I RECENTLY WROTE AND DREW A GRAPHIC MEMOIR ABOUT MY FATHER WHICH OPENS WITH THIS DRAWN VERSION OF A SNAPSHOT.

CHAPTER 1

OLD FATHER, OLD ARTIFICER

THE MOMENT IT DEPICTS IS NOT PART OF THE STORY. I SELECTED IT FROM A LARGE STORE OF FAMILY PHOTOS FOR THE WAY IT SEEMED TO SUM UP MY FATHER AT A GLANCE.

SEDUCTIVE, IMPERIOUS.

WE CALLED IT HIS MICK JAGGER SHOT.

I WAS ABSORBED FOR SOME TIME WITH THE TECHNICAL CHALLENGE OF RENDERING THE TONALITY AND BLURRY MOTION USING ONLY LINE.

BUT MY DRAWING IS AS CRUDE A SCHEMA OF THE COLOR PHOTO AS PERHAPS THE PHOTO IS OF THE RAW, UNSPOOLING LIFE IT PURPORTS TO CAPTURE.

I KNOW I TOOK THIS PICTURE. BUT WHEN? I HAVE A VAGUE IDEA IT MIGHT HAVE BEEN THE SAME DAY DAD TOOK SOME PICTURES OF ME THAT I REMEMBER FROM A FAMILY ALBUM.

I LOOK THESE UP.

INDEED, THE SIZE, COLOR, AND TEXTURE OF THE PRINTS MATCH. AS DOES THE QUALITY OF LIGHT— THE LENGTHENING SHADOWS AND MELLOW AIR OF AN ETERNAL, JAMESIAN TEATIME.

FROM THE PRESENT TO THE PAST TO THE FUTURE IN THE PAST.

I'M 14. I DIDN'T KNOW THAT FIVE SUMMERS LATER, DAD WOULD BE DEAD.

COME SIT ON THE WROUGHT IRON BENCH.

I WAS USED TO BEING DAD'S PROP.

BUT NOW I REALIZE THAT HE WAS TAKING A PICTURE NOT SO MUCH OF A BENCH AS OF A MOMENT. A GIRL ON A BENCH IN A GARDEN...

HOW CURIOUSLY WE SHIFT TENSES WHEN DISCUSSING A PHOTOGRAPH.

... IN "THE PERFECT MIDDLE OF A SPLENDID SUMMER AFTERNOON."

NEXT, WE WALKED AROUND THE HOUSE.

HENRY JAMES DIDN'T THINK MUCH OF FIRST-PERSON NARRATIVE. THOUGH IT CONFERS ON THE HERO THE "DOUBLE PRIVILEGE OF SUBJECT AND OBJECT," HE FELT THIS WAS NOT WORTH THE LOSS OF OMNISCIENCE.

IT WAS MISCHIEVOUS OF ME TO SNAP THE UNPOSED SHOT. FILM WAS EXPENSIVE.

DAD, LOOK!

SNICK!

IT'S IMPOSSIBLE TO CAPTURE A MUTUAL GAZE FROM A FIRST-PERSON PERSPECTIVE, BUT PERHAPS ONE CAN BE INTERPOLATED.

MY FATHER LOOKS AT ME.

I LOOK AT HIM.

FOR A MOMENT, WE SEE EACH OTHER.

MY FATHER MYSELF

Siri Hustvedt

Determined thereto, perhaps by his father's ghost,
Permitting nothing to the evening's edge.
The father does not come to adorn the chant.
One father proclaims another, the patriarchs
Of truth...

Wallace Stevens, 'The Role of the Idea in Poetry'

There is a distance to fatherhood that isn't part of motherhood. In our earliest days, fathers are necessarily a step away. We don't have an inter-uterine life with our fathers, aren't expelled from their bodies in birth, don't nurse at their breasts. Even though our infancies are forgotten, the stamp of those days remains in us, the first exchanges between mother and baby, the back and forth, the rocking, soothing, the holding and looking. Fathers, on the other hand, enter the stage from elsewhere. More exciting than pacifying, they often bring with them rousing games and rough and tumble play. I vividly recall my own baby's joyous face as she straddled her father's jumping knee. He regularly turned her into 'Sophie Cowgirl', and the two took wild rides together as my husband provided the shoot-'em-up sound effects.

I cannot remember bouncing on my father's knee, but I can recall the noise of the door opening, his footsteps in the hall, and the supreme happiness that accompanied his homecoming. Every day for years, my three sisters and I greeted our father as if he were a returning hero, running to the door, shrieking, 'Daddy's home!' We were only daughters in my family. The boy never arrived, and I have often thought that in the end, his absence served us all, including my father, whose relationship with a son would have been coloured by an intense identification he didn't have with his daughters. I think that was oddly liberating. My sisters and I were born into a culture that didn't expect great ambition from girls. The irony is that because we didn't have to share our father with a brother, our interests were able to bloom. A boy would inevitably have felt more pressure from both his parents to *become* someone, but I feel sure we would have envied that pressure, nevertheless.

God the father, land of our fathers, forefathers, founding fathers all refer to an origin or source, to what generated us, to an *authority*. We fall into the paternal line. Patronymic as identity. I have my father's name, not my mother's. I didn't take my husband's name when I married, but the symbolic mark of paternity is inscribed into the signs for me: Siri Hustvedt. We were called 'the Hustvedt girls' or 'the Hustvedt sisters' when we were growing up, four apples from the same tree. The father's name is the stamp of genealogy, legitimacy and coherence. Although we know when a woman gives birth that she is the child's mother, the father's identity can't be *seen*. It's hidden from us in the mysteries of the bedroom, where potentially clandestine unions with *other* men might have taken place. In Judaism, this difficulty is circumvented by establishing Jewish identity through the mother, the known origin. Doubt or confusion about paternal identity and the scourge of illegitimacy have been the stuff of literature in the West since the Greeks.

In the Oedipus story, the hero commits patricide and incest *accidentally*, but once the crimes are known, the world's foundations shake. The Virgin birth in Christianity is the ultimate evocation of paternal mystery, for here the progenitor is God himself, the Holy Spirit, who by means beyond human understanding has impregnated a mortal woman. Edmund in *King Lear* bemoans his fate as illegitimate son, 'Why brand they us / With base? With baseness? bastardy?' But Edmund's treachery is part and parcel of his position as an outsider, a child born from the right father but the wrong mother – a crooked line. Charles Dickens populated his books with illegitimate children and articulated and rearticulated the drama of fatherlessness as a nullity to the self and to others. The illegitimate Arthur Clennam in *Little Dorrit* is repeatedly referred to as 'Nobody'. In another pointed passage in the same novel, when asked about the mysterious Miss Wade, Mr Pancks answers, 'I know as much about her as she knows about herself. She is somebody's child – anybody's – nobody's.' Without an identifiable past, the route to self-knowledge has been closed. The father's power to name fixes and defines us in a relation that allows us to become somebody, not nobody. This is the source of Jacques Lacan's famous pun on the dual symbolic role of the father. He names and he sanctions: *le nom du père* and *le non du père*.

When I was a child, *Father Knows Best* was on television. This benign series evoked an orderly family, which is to say everyone in it knew his or her place in the hierarchy. Every week, the structure was rattled by a minor storm, which then passed over. I am sure that the mythical dads of that post-war era mingled with my internal fantasies about my own father. They weren't despots, but they were in charge, and they had the last word, those ideal fathers of a period determined to re-establish a familial order that had been dismantled during the war when the fathers of many American children were overseas.

My father wasn't a disciplinarian, but he had an unchallenged, unspoken authority. Even a hint of anger or irritation from him was enough to mortify me. Those occasions were rare, but the power of paternal sanction ran deep. I wanted so much to please him. I wanted to be good.

It has been said, and is true –

And this is real pain,
Moreover. It is terrible to see the children,
The righteous little girls;
So good, they expect to be so good...

That is how George Oppen ends his poem 'Street' and for me, the last two lines have always had the force of a blow. I was a righteous little girl. They are so delicate, these attachments of ours, these first great passions for our parents, and I have often wondered what would have become of me had my father used his power differently. In the hospital where I teach a weekly writing class to psychiatric patients, I have listened to many stories about fathers – violent fathers, runaway fathers, seductive fathers, negligent fathers, cruel fathers, fathers who are in prison or dead of drink or drugs or suicide. Shameful fathers. These are the paternal characters who fuel the stark narratives of 'abuse' that people in our culture gulp down so eagerly. It is simple then to create cause and effect, to eliminate all ambiguity, to ignore the particulars of each case, to march down the road of moral outrage. There are brutal stories. We have all heard them, but there are also subtler forms of paternal power that create misshapen lives.

I think of a man like Henry James's father in *Washington Square*, Dr Sloper. He intervenes when he understands that the young man courting his daughter, Catherine, is a fortune hunter. His assessment is by no means wrong, and his desire to protect his child is eminently reasonable, but beneath his acumen lurks not only coldness to his offspring, but an ironic distance that borders on sadism. In a remarkable exchange between Sloper and his sister, they discuss Catherine's decision not to marry her beau immediately, but to wait in the hope that her intractable father will change his mind.

> 'I don't see why it should be such a joke that your daughter adores you.'
> 'It is the point where the adoration stops that I find it interesting to fix.'
> 'It stops where the other sentiment begins.'
> 'Not at all – that would be simple enough. The two things are

extremely mixed up, and the mixture is extremely odd. It will produce some third element, and that's what I'm waiting to see. I wait with suspense – with positive excitement; and that is a sort of emotion that I didn't suppose Catherine would ever provide for me. I am really very much obliged to her.'

Sloper's comment that Catherine's emotions for him and her lover are 'extremely mixed up' is irrefutable as an insight, and it carries far beyond the boundaries of James's novel. Our deepest adult attachments are all coloured by our first loves. They are extremely mixed up. But it is Catherine's love for and fear of her father that give him power. Her desire to please him holds her captive to his will.

In James's story, however, there is a further irony, the third element, which is that the struggle over the bounder Morris Townsend uncovers what might have remained hidden: the father's contempt for his daughter. The revelation gives Catherine an iron will, and when Sloper insists she promise that after his death she will not marry Townsend, she refuses, not because she has any intention to wed, but because it is her only avenue of resistance.

My father was gentle, not severe, kind, deeply interested in whatever we did and proud of our accomplishments. The man basked in his young daughters' love. I have understood this only in hindsight. During my childhood, I wasn't able to put myself in his position, to imagine what that adulation must have felt like. He was a magical being then, enchanted, I think, by excitement, by the glamour of his otherness. He seemed to know the answer to every question. He was tall and strong, a carpenter, woodchopper and builder of fires, friend to all mammals and insects, a storyteller, a smoke-ring-blower and, of course, a man who went to work, where he taught college students and engaged in various other cerebral activities, the nature of which was a little dim to me. It is natural for children to idealize their father. It is also natural for children to grow up and recognize that same father's humanity, including his weaknesses and blind spots. The transition from ideal to real isn't always so easy, however, not for the children or for the father.

Identities, identifications and desires cannot be untangled from one another. We become ourselves through others, and the self is a porous thing, not a sealed container. If it begins as a genetic map, it is one that is expressed over time and only in *relation* to the world. Americans cling desperately to their myths of self-creation, to rugged individualism, now more free-market than pioneer, and to self-help, that strange twist on do-it-yourself, which turns a human being into an object that can be repaired with a toolbox and some instructions. We do not author ourselves, which is not to say that we have no agency or responsibility, but rather that becoming doesn't escape relation. 'You do not stop hungering for your father's love,' my husband, Paul Auster, wrote, in the first part of *The Invention of Solitude*, 'even after you are grown up.' The second part is told in the third person. The 'I' becomes 'he':

> When the father dies, he writes, the son becomes his own father and his own son. He looks at his own son and sees himself in the face of the boy. He imagines what the boy sees when he looks at him and finds himself becoming his own father. Inexplicably, he is moved by this. It is not just the sight of the boy that moves him, nor even the thought of standing inside his father, but what he sees in the boy of his own vanished past. It is a nostalgia for his own life that he feels, perhaps, a memory of his own boyhood as a son to his father. Inexplicably, he finds himself shaking at that moment between both happiness and sorrow, if this is possible, as if he were going both forward and backward, into the future and into the past. And there are times, often there are times, when these feelings are so strong that his life no longer seems to dwell in the present.

Here the identifications are seamless. Three generations mingle and time collapses in *likeness*. I am you. I have become you. But we cannot write, *When the father dies, the daughter becomes her own father and then her own son.* The daughter never becomes a father. The sex threshold is a thick seam, not easily crossed. It complicates identification and desire.

Paul didn't have a daughter when he wrote those words, our daughter. She came later. Once, when she was very small, she asked us if she would grow a penis when she got older. No, we told her, that would never come to be. It wasn't the moment to introduce the subject of sex-change operations, but one may wonder in all seriousness about Freud's much maligned comment that 'anatomy is destiny'. To what degree are we prisoners of our sex?

I, too, have felt the continuities among generations of women in my family, the maternal as an unbroken chain of feeling. I loved my maternal grandmother, whom I knew well, my *mormor*, mother's mother in Norwegian. She adored my own mother, her youngest child, and she adored me. I remember her hand on my face when I said goodbye after a visit, the affection in her eyes, her mildness. My own mother's face, her hands, her touch and voice have resonated in me all my life and have became part of a legacy I carried with me to my own daughter, an inheritance which is like music in my body, a wordless knowledge given and received over time. In this, I was lucky. There is little dissonance in that tune that was passed from one woman to the next.

Mother love is everyone's beginning, and its potency is overwhelming. I remember once finding myself with a group of women – it may have been at a baby shower – when one of them proposed a ghoulish choice: if your husband and child were drowning, which would you save? Every woman, one after another, said the child, and as the confessions accumulated, there were also several jokes (told by more than one woman) that fell into the *no contest* category, which were greeted by peals of laughter. I remember this because it spoke to the ferocity of the love most women have for their children, but also to an undisguised hostility, at least among those particular women, towards the men whom they had left to die in an imaginary deep, a feeling I honestly didn't share.

It is impossible, then, to talk about fathers without talking about mothers. For both boys and girls, the mother begins as a towering figure, source of life, food and feeling. The sentimentality that has lain thickly over motherhood in Western culture, at least since the nineteenth century, strikes me as a means of taming a two-way passion that has a threatening quality, if only by dint of its strength. Children must escape their mothers, and mothers must let them go, and separation can be a long tug of war. Every culture seeks to organize the mysteries of maternity – menstruation, pregnancy, birth and the initiation into adulthood. Taboos, rituals and stories create the frames for understanding human experience by distinguishing one thing from another and creating a comprehensible order.

The anthropologist Mary Douglas contrasts two kinds of power in her book *Purity and Danger*: one that exercises a legitimate articulated authority inside a known social structure and one which is implicit, unarticulated and unknown. She points out that the witch is a perfect example of a threatening counter-power, one that is not part of a culture's explicit architecture. 'Witches,' she writes, 'are social equivalents of beetles and spiders who live in the cracks of walls and wainscoting.' But there is a third kind of power, as well, one Douglas calls 'the legitimate intruder', an ambiguous figure who may occupy, at least for a time, a position of sanctioned authority. Joan of Arc was such a person: 'a peasant at court, a woman in armour, an outsider in the councils of war'. And, of course, in the end she was branded a witch.

In classical psychoanalysis, the conscious articulate power is the father, who comes between mother and son as a kind of saviour from the unarticulated and unstructured; maternal engulfment. But he also thwarts the son's desire for his mother and inspires rivalry; the Oedipal drama. Once it is resolved, the father's law is internalized, and the boy can go on to occupy the father's place. Using Douglas's model, the mother in psychoanalysis comes very close to being a witch. Moreover, where all this leaves little girls in relation to their fathers has been something of a muddle in the field. Turning the story around doesn't work because little girls also want to leave their mothers. In 'The Dissolution of the Oedipus Complex', Freud continues his observation on anatomy as destiny and argues that when a little girl is faced with a boy's penis, she suffers feelings of inferiority, and while she may hope that in time she will acquire more impressive genitalia, her wish is, of course, doomed to failure. It isn't strange that feminists have found the idea of penis envy uncompelling.

Girls can certainly identify with their fathers. Many do. In fact, it is far more usual for a girl to admit to *being like* her father than for a boy to say, *I'm just like my mother*, which would impinge on his masculinity by summoning his dependency on her. What the girl cannot do is take her father's place, which remains the articulated position of power and authority in the culture. The Oedipal conflict has been criticized inside psychoanalysis for some time, and it's widely recognized that Freud's focus on the father underestimated the mother and her vital role in a child's early life. The importance of mothers, however, doesn't change the fact that it is still harder for girls to find a place in the sexual divide, to embrace an articulated position of power. The witch is always hiding in the background.

Of course, life never corresponds exactly to any myth. The sharp divisions erected to explain sexual *difference* elude the ambiguities of what it means to be a person growing up in the world with real parents. I was not a tomboy. As a small child, I liked girls' games, and I liked dolls, and I can't remember a time when I didn't have love feelings for boys. I cried easily. I was extremely alert to my parents' expectations, rather passive and empathetic to a fault. My animistic tendencies lasted longer than most people's. I remember personifying just about everything. My greatest happinesses were drawing, reading and daydreaming. Most of the action in my life took place internally. This is still true. In my neck of the woods, the expression for such a person was 'femmy' or 'wimpy'.

Virginia Woolf's 'Angel in the House', the person she had to defeat to write, exemplifies the wimpy feminine ideal of the Victorian era:

> She was intensely sympathetic. She was immensely charming. She was utterly unselfish. She excelled in the difficult arts of family life.

She sacrificed herself daily. If there was a chicken, she took the leg;
if there was a draught, she sat on it – in short she was so constituted
that she never had a mind or a wish of her own, but preferred to
sympathize always with the minds and wishes of others.

The Angel is a mirror held up to the desires of others. Arguably,
she no longer exists as a paragon of womanhood, but there is
something about her that isn't easily dismissed, because her
'sympathy with the minds and wishes of others' is part of maternal
reality. What the paediatrician and psychoanalyst Donald Winnicott
called 'good-enough mothering' is the maternal ability to feel an
infant's needs, to answer, mirror and calm. A mother's harmony with
her baby is physiological, essential not only for what we think of as a
child's emotional growth, but for its developing brain. Woolf's Angel
is like a mother during her baby's first year of life, when her child's
vulnerability and needs are intense and draining. The Victorian trap
for women was multiple. It idealized maternal qualities, isolated them
as *the* distinctive, rigid features of womanliness, entirely separate
from the qualities of the paternal, and linked feminine traits to
childish ones, which infantilized women. The good-enough mother
is not the perfect mother. The good-enough mother is a person with
interests, thoughts, needs and desires beyond her child. Nevertheless
the lure of other people's needs can be strong, not just for women,
for men, too, but it may be that for many reasons – psychic,
biological, social – most women have found the pressure of 'the
minds and wishes of others' more difficult to resist than men. The
continual suppression of the self for another will inevitably produce
resentment, if not rage.

Accommodation, squeezing oneself into the expectations of
others, however, is part of every childhood. Children of both sexes
are dwarfed by their parents in every way. Small and powerless, they
are easily crushed by parental authority. Obedience to mother's and
father's wishes is hardly enslavement, but all children are in thrall to
the people they've been born to, and the desire to please can easily
become a form of internal tyranny. In a letter he wrote to his father,

which never reached its destined reader, Franz Kafka presented a stark picture of childhood puniness:

> I was, after all, weighed down by your mere physical presence. I remember, for instance, how we often undressed in the same bathing hut. There was I, skinny, weakly, slight; you, strong, tall, broad. Even inside the hut I felt a miserable specimen, and what's more, not only in your eyes but in the eyes of the whole world, for you were for me the measure of all things. But then when we stepped out of the bathing hut before the people, you holding my hand, a little skeleton, unsteady, barefoot on the boards, frightened of the water, incapable of copying your swimming strokes, which you, with the best of intentions, but actually to my profound humiliation, always kept on showing me, then I was frantic with desperation and at such moments all my bad experiences in all spheres fitted magnificently together.

Here the father's body is huge and before it the child becomes a shrinking 'little skeleton'. It is a boy's experience because a woman's body would not be 'the measure of all things' for a male child. I distinctly remember the feeling of awe and alienation I felt when I saw naked adult bodies as a child, but here Kafka's experience of his naked father is terrifying, an impossible standard which humiliates him and very quickly becomes bound to all his 'bad experiences'. Desire, fear, shame are extremely mixed up. The letter as a whole is one of only intermittently suppressed rage, an overt bid for dialogue that is in reality a statement of grievance. Why is it so hard to *talk* to fathers?

Montaigne argues in his essay 'Of Friendship' that there cannot be friendship between children and fathers:

> From children toward fathers, it is rather respect. Friendship feeds on communication, which cannot exist between them because of their too great inequality, and might therefore interfere with the duties of nature. For neither can all the secret thoughts of fathers be

> communicated to children lest this beget an unbecoming intimacy,
> nor could the admonitions and corrections, which are one of the
> chief duties of friendship, be administered by children to fathers.

Montaigne is right. Inequality engenders necessary silences. Young children don't really want friendship from a father, but a heroic figure to look up to. Is there something in fatherhood as we know it that by its very nature blocks communication?

My father liked instructing us, liked working in the garden with us, liked to explain just about anything to us, and he listened to us, but there were distances in him that were difficult to breach and, unlike my mother, he found it hard to speak directly to his daughters about anything personal, especially as we got older and sexually mature. Sometimes he would communicate his worries about his children through his wife, which generally meant that his comments had been screened or edited by her judgements about the situation, so exactly what had alarmed him had become rather foggy once it reached us. The older I became, the more hidden I felt he was, and there were moments when he seemed unavailable to a degree that startled me. It could be difficult for him to *say*, so sometimes he would *do*.

My father drove me home after I had been fitted with braces for my teeth, painful and gruelling hours made worse by the fact that the orthodontist was a truly unpleasant man who gruffly told me to stop moving my feet when I squirmed in discomfort, to open my mouth wider and to stop flinching when he hit a tender spot. I left the ordeal with tears in my eyes. My father didn't say much, but then he stopped at a gas station, left the car and returned with a box, which he handed to me. I looked down: chocolate-covered cherries. My father's favourite. I was eleven years old and, even then, I felt poignancy mingle with comedy. I didn't like chocolate-covered cherries and was in no shape to eat them had I liked them, but the mute gesture has stayed with me as one of infinite, if somewhat wrong-headed kindness, and as a token of his love.

By all accounts, my father was a good boy. He was the oldest of four, as I am, upright, sensitive, intelligent, with a perfectionist streak that showed up strongly in me. My aunt once told me that some of the boys who attended their one-room schoolhouse in rural Minnesota teased my father for reading too much. Apparently, it was a pursuit that lacked manliness. In my father's childhood, masculine and feminine roles were strictly defined by the kinds of labour done on the farm. My grandfather and grandmother both worked hard, but at different jobs. In his memoir, my father wrote, 'Adolescence, as it is now understood, did not exist. A boy became a man when he could do a man's work.' He confessed to hot competition with his fellows when it came to rites of passage: 'At what age had so and so been entrusted with a team of horses, a tractor, the family automobile, and how many cows did one milk.' But, then again, by his own admission, it was his sister who was the athlete: 'She could run faster than her brothers, do cartwheels, walk on her hands, and wielded a mean bat at the softball plate.' He was proud of his sister's physical prowess, and when two of his daughters, his oldest not among them, turned into champion horsewomen, no one was more pleased with their trophies than my father.

Despite his beginnings on the farm, my father became an intellectual and worked as a professor. Reading too much took him elsewhere. But like all of us, he was shaped by his early experiences. He watched his parents' farm fail during the Depression and suffered the indignities and humiliations of extreme poverty. His boyhood helplessness in the face of these terrible events became the catalyst for a life lived to repair what had been broken. The winds of chance and devastation were not going to blow down *his* family if he could help it. He would work himself to death if he had to. This is an old story of the good boy who becomes the duty-bound father. What he could never say was that his parents' marriage was one of conflict and alienation. He, too, idealized and identified with his father, a tender-hearted and rather meek man who by the time I met him seemed resigned to his fate. My grandmother, on the other hand, was indomitable and outspoken, admirable traits that sometimes veered towards the screeching and irrational. For a temperamentally sensitive boy like my father, his mother's invective must have cut him to the quick. But these were wounds he hid.

About three years after my father's death, I had a conversation with my mother that made such an impression on me I can reproduce it almost word for word.

'He wanted his girls to marry farmers.'

'He wanted us to marry farmers?' I said. 'You can't mean that seriously.'

'Well, farmboys like him, who went on to other things.'

'Farmboys who became professors?' I said incredulously.

My mother nodded.

'But, Mamma,' I said, 'how many farmboys-turned-college professors are there? It's tantamount to saying that we shouldn't marry or that we should have married *him*!'

My mother and I laughed, but this strange notion of my father's reinforced the fact that it was difficult for him to let go of his daughters, to tolerate our growing up. He wanted to continue to find himself reflected in our childish eyes and see the ideal father shining back at him. It took me a long time to understand this, in part because I never stopped hungering for his love and approval, and he remained a measure for me, if not of all things, of many. But I suspect now that there was a part of him that thought he had lost me, to my husband, to my work, and because real dialogue was often difficult for us and unequal to some degree – I remained a respectful daughter – there were unspoken misunderstandings between us.

I don't remember when I began to realize that I wanted to be *like* my father, but it wasn't in my earliest days. I think I became ambitious around eleven, which was just about the time I was suddenly able to read 'small print' books, when I first read William Blake and Emily Dickinson. Poems and stories became an avenue for my psychic cross-dressing or, rather, discovering my masculinity. I was twelve when I first heard the story of Joan of Arc, that legitimate intruder branded as a witch. The man who told it to me was my seventh-grade English teacher at a Rudolf Steiner School in Bergen,

Norway: Arne Krohn Nilsen, a tall rangy man with long whiskery eyebrows that made him look as if he were permanently surprised. He was an intense teacher, and he told *Jeanne d'Arc*'s tale of glory and woe with a fervour I have never forgotten. He told it to the whole class, but listening to it, I felt like the recipient of a secret gift. I could not have said that the girl warrior appealed to me because, for a while anyway, she was allowed to play a role normally prohibited to women, but I am certain that I felt it. As my teacher spoke, as his voice rose and fell, and his sweeping gestures emphasized the drama, I was Joan of Arc. In a blank book, he drew me a picture of the historical heroine in armour with a sword on a white steed. I still have it. I relate this because not only did Joan collapse the hard lines of sexual difference, but she came to me through a man who genuinely believed in my abilities, a father figure.

PORTRAIT OF THE ARTIST AS A YOUNG WOMAN: 'Identity and memory are crucial for anyone writing poetry,' says Susan Howe in her book *My Emily Dickinson*. 'For women the field is still dauntingly empty. How do I, choosing messages from the code of others in order to participate in the universal theme of Language, pull SHE from all the myriad symbols and sightings of HE.' Emily Dickinson constantly asked this question in her poems:

> In lands I never saw – they say
> Immortal Alps look down–
> Whose Bonnets touch the firmament
> Whose Sandals touch the town–
>
> Meek at whose everlasting feet
> A Myriad Daisy play–
> Which, Sir, are you and which am I
> Upon an August Day?

Dickinson stayed at home to read and write. There she inhabited the immensity of her own inner life. Her mentors lived on the page.

Hundreds of fathers. But Howe takes her title from a letter Dickinson wrote to her cousin after reading in the newspaper that George Eliot had died. 'The look of the words as they lay in the print I shall never forget. Not their face in the casket could have had the eternity to me. Now, *my* George Eliot.' And *mine*. Translator, scholar, intellectual, brilliant novelist, Mary Ann hid behind the mask of George. How well I understand that pseudonym – the need to evade the fixity that comes with the brand 'woman writer'. If reading was for me the route to legitimate power under the sign of my professor father, it was nevertheless my mother who fed me books, one after another, to stave off a mounting hunger which at times veered towards the compulsive. She had read widely, and so the *idea* of literature belonged to both my father and my mother, and my literature, the English books I read at eleven, twelve and thirteen, were my mother's choices for me. I read under the auspices of two pole stars, one paternal and more remote, the other maternal and closer.

What did I want? *More*. Reading is internal action. It is the intimate ground where, as my husband says, 'two consciousnesses touch'. I would add two unconsciousnesses as well. Reading has become so attenuated in our culture that all reading is now considered 'good'. Children are admonished to read in general, as if all books are equal, but a brain bloated with truisms and clichés, with formulaic stories and simple answers to badly asked questions, is hardly what we should aspire to. For the strange thing is that even books we can no longer actively recall are part of us, and, like a lost melody, they may return suddenly. Not long ago, I reread Djuna Barnes's *Nightwood* and discovered how deeply one of her characters had affected my own work, but I hadn't been aware of the influence at all. As a young person, I read the canon, as I perceived it. Great books signified achievement and mastery, but also apprenticeship. I wanted to know everything, to enlarge myself, to get a fat mind, and that mind, as it has turned out, is mostly made of men.

'The process of literary influence,' Harold Bloom wrote in *The Anxiety of Influence*, 'is a battle between strong equals, father and son as mighty opposites.' Freud's *Civilization and its Discontents*, with its rapacious sons murdering the tyrannical father, isn't far away from Bloom's blanket declaration that literature is the domain of men duking it out – *strong equals*. There are no daughters in this narrative. And there's the rub. It is too easy to say that the canon is patriarchal, that casting out John Milton for George Sand is a solution to the problem, but that is to ignore quality in the name of parity.

What of women who write? We, too, have literary fathers and mothers. For most of my life, I have felt that reading and writing are precisely the two places in life where I am liberated from the constraints of my sex, where the dance of being the other takes place unhindered, and the free play of identifications allows entrance into a multitude of human experiences. When I am working I feel this extraordinary freedom, my plurality. But I have discovered that out there in the world 'woman writer' is still a brand on a writer's forehead, not easily erased; that being George remains preferable to being Mary Ann.

I am not arguing that Bloom is entirely wrong. I think he is right that many male writers struggle to overcome influence. I have seen it up close in some men I know who have had to tangle with a beloved author before they can write themselves. A classic example from literature is Beckett's overwhelming admiration for Joyce, an influence he had to purge before becoming the writer he became. The question is not whether women writers are influenced; every writer takes from the past. It is how it happens. I was a sponge for books, but I have never had a bellicose relation to writers I love, men or women, even those who have influenced me the most strongly. My love for Henry James doesn't make me want to fight it out and get *over* him. Is this because, as a woman, I have a different relation to the paternal and the maternal? Are writers like Emily Dickinson, Jane Austen, Emily and Charlotte Brontë, George Eliot, Gertrude Stein, and Virginia Woolf not part of the pantheon of English letters? I don't believe that their sex is what one thinks of first when one thinks of their books, is it? But didn't they make themselves in a different way from men who write? Didn't they have to? Is the question of equality with men so fraught for women that their battle is a different one? Are we part of a crooked line outside the patrimony? 'Which, Sir, are you, and which am I?' Immortal Alps or Daisy? Note that Dickinson's alps wear bonnets. Howe quotes Dickinson's second letter to the mysterious 'Master', in which she writes:

> If you saw a bullet hit a bird – and he told you he wasn't shot – You might weep at his courtesy, but you would certainly doubt his word. One more drop from the gash that stains your Daisy's bosom – then would you believe?

Is she not both alps and daisy? Wounded here. Whole elsewhere. Is she not myriad? Howe directs her reader to *David Copperfield*, to David, Master Davy, but also to Daisy, Steerforth's affectionate and feminizing name for his younger friend. Literary mingling. Sexual mingling. Language isn't owned by anyone. It is inside and outside; it belongs to men and to women. Does it matter that women are mostly latecomers to the table of literature? Perhaps. Perhaps not.

There have been moments in my life when I felt like the legitimate intruder – at the defence of my doctoral dissertation in English literature, for example. I sat at a table with six men, my judges. They were not unsympathetic. Most of them were admiring. The single exception was an ageing pedant who had painstakingly checked my footnotes for accuracy and, finding no errors, resorted to the comment, 'I did find some of the editions you used egregious, however.' As I waited in the hall for their verdict, I didn't expect them to suggest any changes. I knew what I had written was good, but for me that seven-year adventure of getting a degree was an ongoing encounter with paternity, not because most of my professors were men, but because the institution itself offered a fatherly stamp of approval, as Dickens would say, 'three dry letters': PhD. The fact that my father had also undergone those rigours no doubt haunted the entire enterprise.

I have since discovered that it is much harder for young women to resist the lure of a higher degree than it is for young men. A poet who had been languishing in a PhD programme for years confessed to me that although she had no intention of becoming a professor, giving up the hope for a degree felt like a painful loss of stature. I understand. For women letters after their names can be a form of armour. This is probably even more true in the sciences where there are fewer women than in the humanities. It is in these worlds that one feels the problem of femininity most deeply, because it is here that it shouldn't *show*. A physicist friend of mine revealed that women in his field generally disguise their bodies in manly attire to fit in with the powers that be, but he had also noticed a trend: when a woman has reached a position of respect and acclaim, when she has secured her reputation as brilliant, her sartorial discipline begins to unravel. Colours formerly unseen, high heels, make-up and jewellery appear in rapid succession on her body, as if these accoutrements of womanliness are the tokens of a long-restrained sexual energy, as if the poor thing has suddenly been allowed to burst into bloom.

The awareness of sex acts as a disturbance to the collegial pursuits of the mind – those unnameable openings in the structure begin to emanate dangerous powers, and the maternal witch is back. For all its strides in the right direction, the Enlightenment elevated Reason to an impossible stature, and because women were lumped with its opposite, with the irrational forces in human life, no longer inexplicable or mystical, just situated on the wrong side of the fence, women languished there until they could claim Reason and the Rights of Man as their own. But climbing into the patriarchy entails some distortion. I learned to lower my voice when I spoke at seminars in graduate school, to try to sound dispassionate, even when I was quaking with feeling. I called on masculine forms to ensure I was taken seriously, to hide the girl. Over time, those forms became me, too. We are not static beings. We age and change.

In my novels, I have written as a woman and as a man. I have written as a father. I have written as a son. In my last novel, I became my own imaginary brother, the boy who was never born to my family. A young woman dresses as a man. She puts on her armour and wanders the streets. A man paints his self-portrait as a woman. A man dresses as a woman and comes into his own. We are myriad, all of us. Daisies. Witches. Alps. Masters. And skeletal little children looking up at the enormity of Dad. Contrary to Montaigne's statement about fathers and children, late in his life, not so long before he died, my father and I became friends. Although he was proud of me and carefully pasted my good reviews into a scrapbook, he had never said much to me about my work. I had become accustomed to brief cryptic comments that could be construed in many ways. My father was very ill when I finished my third novel and sent my parents the manuscript, but he was still living at home. That book was the first I wrote in the voice of a man. One afternoon, the phone rang, and to my surprise it was my father. He rarely called. I usually spoke to my mother, and she would put my father on for a chat. Without warning, he launched into a discourse on the book, heaping praise on my literary efforts. And I began to sob. He talked, and I sobbed. He talked more, and I sobbed more. Years of tears. I would never have predicted so violent a reaction. But then, you see, he *knew*. He knew how much I wanted his sanction, his approval, his admiration, and his knowing what I had mistakenly assumed he had always taken for granted became the road to each other. We were changed then, my father and I. The distance between us fell away, and when we sat together in the months before his death, we talked as friends, as strong equals, as two real, not ideal people who had found each other again. ■

In 1958, when he was nineteen, my father, Kevin O'Neill, got a job with Chicago Bridge & Iron, an American corporation active worldwide in the construction of industrial plants, at Whitegate refinery in Cork, which is my father's hometown.[1] His subsequent career, mainly in hard-hat managerial positions, yields this chronology:

1959: Dinslaken, Germany (building a BP refinery).

1960: Mersin, Turkey (Atas refinery).

1962: Skælskør, Denmark (refinery for Gulf Oil).[2]

1963: Ingolstadt, Germany (refinery for Esso).[3]

1964: Rotterdam, the Netherlands (refinery for Gulf).[4]

1965: Neuchâtel, Switzerland (refinery for Shell).[5] Teheran, Iran (setting up an office for a CB&I fabrication plant). Limassol, Cyprus (mechanical issues at a cement factory).

1966: Ras Sel'ata, Lebanon (small job for Esso).[6]

1966: Umbogumtwini, South Africa (spheres and aluminium distilled water tanks for African Explosives and Chemical Industries).[7]

1967: Matola, Mozambique (chemical plant for a client now forgotten).

1968: Ras Lanuf, Libya (oil terminal for Mobil).

---

1 'My boss was the great Fred Lane, from Panama City, Florida.'

2 My mother: 'We lived very close to Korsør, where Louis-Ferdinand Céline, *le poète maudit*, had lived.' *Voyage au bout de la nuit* is one of only two books my mother has read in one nocturnal sitting. The other? *The Catcher in the Rye.*

3 Here, my parents once strolled across the frozen Danube.

4 Remembered for the ball lightning that whirled around the living room of our house at Brielle.

5 Where my father, by now a field supervisor, briefly quit Chicago Bridge after accusing Fred Lane of having a 'paper ass'.

6 'There's a poem in Arabic about a naughty girl from Ras Sel'ata.'

7 'We lived in Amanzimtoti – "the water is sweet".' By now my father was a resident manager (camp boss).

Kevin O'Neill, left, working in the desert during the 1960s

1969: Kermanshah, Iran (refinery for National Iranian Oil Company).[8]

1970: Rotterdam, the Netherlands (multiple projects, including a huge oil terminal at Maasvlakte, a BP refinery at Europoort, tanks for Esso).

1973: Asab, Abu Dhabi (gas plant for Abu Dhabi Petroleum Company).

1975: Porsgrunn, Norway (ammonia storage facility for Norsk Hydro).[9]

1979: Aughinish Island, Ireland (alumina extraction plant for Alcan).[10]

---

8 My father went to dinner with Farah Pahlavi, Empress of Iran (and a couple of hundred others). He and my mother spotted Ms Pahlavi forty years later at a Ralph Lauren store in New York.

9 He lived at Skien, source of Henrik Ibsen and the verb *to ski*.

10 Nicknamed Anguish Island and then, when the job started to go well, Treasure Island. My father, now a project manager, got to meet 'H. B. Horton, the legendary designer of Horton spheres.'

After Aughinish, my father left Chicago Bridge & Iron.[11] He joined the Bechtel Corporation and in 1982 went as project manager to Balikpapan, Borneo, to build a refinery in the coastal jungle.[12] In 1984, Bechtel sent him as a field superintendent to Pembroke, Wales, on a refinery job for Texaco.

In 1985, my father joined Wimpey Engineering. His first job was at Sullom Voe, in the Shetland Islands, managing the shutdown of a gigantic refinery. From 1986 to 1990, he was resident manager at Fawley oil refinery. Then he joined John Brown Engineering and worked on the Cellobond phenolics project at Barry, south Wales; and in Al-Jubayl, Saudi Arabia, on the Ibn Zahr polypropylene project and an industrial alcohol plant for SAMAD. In 1995, Kevin O'Neill went to Uppsala, Sweden, as project manager on a secondary pharmaceutical plant for Pharmacia & Upjohn. In 1997, he helped build the biggest silicon plant in the world, in Barry, south Wales (client: Dow Corning). In 2000, Kvaerner John Brown sent him to Dublin, Ireland, to build a Bristol-Myers Squibb primary pharmaceutical plant.

In 2004, my father joined Tepe Insaat and was the project manager for building pump stations on the Baku-Tbilisi-Ceyhan pipeline (Turkish section). My father, who is sixty-nine, still works for Tepe.[13] He has four children and eleven grandchildren (ten boys, one girl). He and my mother live in Turkey, which by chance is where they met, forty-seven years ago, when she was a secretary employed by Foster Wheeler. Their marriage still works. ∎

---

11 There was litigation. My father was advised by an able barrister named Cherie Booth.

12 Vijay Singh not long afterwards became the pro at the local golf club (VS: 'the lowest point in my life'). It was in Indonesia that my father met George P. Shultz.

13 'All my companies were good to me.'

PROVIDE, PROVIDE

Daniyal Mueenuddin

S eated at a dinner in Lahore one winter in the late 1970s, for the third time in a week Mr K. K. Harouni was forced to endure a conversation about a Rolls Royce coupé recently imported by one of the Waraiches, a family whom no one had heard of just five years before. The car had been specially modified in London and cost an absurd amount of money, and the mention of it inevitably led to a discussion of the new Pakistani industrialists, who at that time were blazing into view. Like other members of the feudal landowning class, Harouni greeted the emergence of these people with condescension overlaying his envy. He had capital, as he observed expansively. Why shouldn't he play along a bit, how difficult could it be?

Toying with the idea in the following weeks, then deciding, Harouni resolved not to do things by halves. He began selling tracts of urban land and pouring more and more cash into factories, buying machinery from Germany, hiring engineers, holding meetings with bankers. Caught up in these projects, he spent increasingly less time at his family estate in the southern Punjab, relying instead upon his

manager, the formidable Chaudrey Nabi Baksh Jaglani. Tall and stooped, wearing heavy square-rimmed glasses, his face marked with deep lines of self-control and resolution, Chaudrey Sahib grew paramount in Dunyapur, the place along the Indus where the Harouni farms lay.

Thus, Chaudrey Jaglani's moment struck. The more money that Harouni sank into the factories the more they seemed to decline in a bewildering confusion of debts and deficits, until finally his bankers advised him to fold. A few months after this catastrophic event, Harouni summoned Nabi Baksh Jaglani to his house in Lahore. When the manager went into the landlord's study, a dark place with a famous ceiling painted by the great surrealist Sadequain, and incongruously adorned with Indian miniatures and temple bronzes of dancing girls and Hindu gods, he found the old man sitting with his steno. Jaglani remained standing.

'Come on, Chaudrey Sahib,' said his master. 'After all these years you can sit down.'

They enacted this scene every time Jaglani came to Lahore. He complied, not quite sitting at the edge of his seat, as the steno Shah Sahib did, but keeping himself rigid.

'How are things on the farm?' asked the landlord.

'The crops are good but the prices are bad.'

'How are land prices?'

Jaglani had been expecting this and saw in a flash where it would take them. 'Low – buyers get nothing from the lands, so they don't pay much for them. The Khoslas sold four squares at sixteen hundred an acre.' He failed to mention that this land stood far from the river, at the tail of an unreliable canal.

'In any case we need to sell. Have them prepare powers of attorney so that you can arrange the transfers.'

They spoke for a few minutes about a murder recently committed by one of the tenants, a matter of a girl. Jaglani knew to do this, in order to paper over the embarrassment his master must feel at having to sell land held by his family for three generations.

Walking out under the cool white veranda of Gulfishan, the name by which Lahore knew the great house, Jaglani reflected, *Well there's plenty of it. He can sell for thirty years and he'll still have a farm.*

The chauffeur, Mustafa, stood by the car. Seeing Jaglani coming he discreetly threw away his cigarette and went around to open the door. A short man with a chipped tooth, a small, careful moustache and wavy hair, Mustafa had earned Jaglani's confidence by his discretion and by his excellent qualities as a courtier. Although they spoke frankly and easily on the long drives to Lahore, Mustafa became mute in the presence of others, stone-faced as a chauffeur should be.

Getting into the car, Jaglani said, 'Well, now the game heats up.'

'Good news?' asked Mustafa.

'Not bad, not too bad.'

Accustomed to having almost unlimited amounts of money, K. K. Harouni began selling blocs of land, sold it with the sugar cane still standing, the hundred-year-old rosewood trees on the borders of each field thrown in for nothing. Jaglani would receive a brief telegram – NEED FIFTY THOUSAND IMMEDIATELY – and he would sell the land at half-price, the choice pieces to himself, putting it in the names of his servants and relatives. He sold to the other managers, to his friends, to political allies. Everyone got a piece of the quick dispersion. He took a commission on each sale. He became ever more powerful and rich.

Harouni's children, seeing their inheritance bleeding away, said to their father, 'Jaglani's fleecing you. He's a thief. You should cut down your expenses. If you must sell, for God's sake sell at a proper price.'

'If I believed that Jaglani had cheated me,' said the father, 'I wouldn't believe in anything anymore.'

The old man sentimentally thought that the people of Dunyapur, the village in the heart of the Harouni lands, revered his family, whose roots had been in that soil for a mere hundred years.

*

Though he had become crooked on a large scale, Jaglani did not believe himself to have broken his feudal allegiance to K. K. Harouni, but instead felt himself appropriately to be taking advantage of the master's incapacity and lack of oversight, not seceding but simply expressing a more independent stance. He continued to run the farm extremely well and profitably, and continued sending money to Lahore, a larger share of the net in fact than he used to send, because he himself had developed other sources of income. As his political ambitions grew, he moved his family and household from the village to a large but plain house in the small city of Firoza, the sub-district headquarters, in order to be closer to the courts and to the government administration. He kept his house in Dunyapur, and often spent nights there. An old sweepress cleaned the house, and he ate the food prepared in the *dera*, the administrative centre, where many visitors, buyers and sellers, came and were fed and housed.

One spring day, while driving Jaglani from Firoza to Dunyapur, among the rising green sugar cane fields, with partridge and the migratory quail calling, Mustafa the driver, sensing his master's good mood, begged to speak.

'That's fine, go on,' said Jaglani, who knew that the driver had chosen this moment to make some request. Mustafa rarely asked for anything on his own behalf, but often acted for other people who needed something from his master. He advanced carefully, speaking only at the correct moment, when he knew Jaglani would accede; and Jaglani, who often sounded out his ideas on Mustafa, did not mind this slight bit of manipulation. His own career had been built on calculations of give and take. Mustafa took care to make requests that reflected Jaglani's interests, or at least that would not harm them.

'My sister,' said Mustafa, 'just fled back from Rawalpindi, leaving her husband there. He works in 'Pindi as a peon in a bank. You were good enough to get him that post. She couldn't stand the city, the dirtiness, the bad food, the lack of friends or family. Her husband doesn't send any money, because he wants to starve her out and force her back to his home. You often have said that the food they prepare for visitors doesn't suit you. Viro, who cleans your house, is getting old. Let my sister cook for you and keep the house. Let her try for a week or two. If she doesn't do well then please let her go. I beg pardon for troubling you with this.'

Mustafa always managed to ask favours in a way that made Jaglani glow, choosing moments when his master felt satisfied, with work or with politics, the moment when the day seemed sweetest.

'That's fine,' said Jaglani tersely, not wanting to show his pleasure at obliging his driver in this almost personal matter. 'Tell the accountants to put her on salary, and put the old woman wherever they will.'

The next evening Jaglani returned to Dunyapur at dusk, after a day spent on the farms, the jeep's twin lights poking into the night. Peasants bringing their buffaloes back from watering at the canal stood aside and saluted, the heavy bells hanging from the animals' necks making a mournful hollow gonging. Some had old shoes tied around their necks, as amulets against the evil eye. Only Jaglani's house had electricity, and as they drove along the dusty main street of the village, lanterns glowed in the unshuttered windows and cook fires threw orange light on the mud walls. The village smelled of dung and dust and smoke and of the mango blossoms in the surrounding orchard.

Entering his house through a side door Jaglani saw a woman crouched over the hearth in the courtyard lit by a single bare bulb, cooking parathas in clarified butter. She looked back at him and then covered her head, turning her face away.

'Salaam, Chaudrey Sahib,' she said.

'Salaam, Bibi.'

He went into the whitewashed brick house, the rooms overcrowded with ugly carved wood furniture. In his bedroom he took off the revolver that he always wore under his kurta and hung it on a hook, then washed his hands and face at a sink in the bedroom and said his prayers.

Returning to the courtyard he sat down on a charpoy, a bed strung with rope, and put his feet up. She had already lit his hookah, and he began to smoke.

'How long have you been back in Dunyapur?' he asked.

'Two months.'

'Are you staying with Mustafa?'

'Yes, he took me in.'

'What's your name?'

'Zainab.'

When she brought the food, four or five small dishes of curry on a steel tray, with the parathas in a woven reed basket covered with a napkin, he looked up at her suddenly, wanting to find out what kind of woman she might be.

Slowly looking down, she avoided his eyes. She had a hard pale face, angular, with high cheekbones, almost beautiful, but too forceful, reminding him of a woman who had been caught years ago on the banks of the Indus, a cattle thief. No woman had ever before been known to lift cattle, and people came from miles around to see her, sitting defiantly on a charpoy in the *dera*, waiting to be turned over to the police.

As Jaglani finished eating Zainab slipped away. The food could not have been better. Smoking the hookah and listening to the village going to sleep, the last few voices, the animals bedded down, he decided he would keep her on.

In late March the wheat harvest began, and Jaglani moved to the village, as he did each year, in order to observe the weighing of the crop as it came in. That winter he had planted 700 acres of wheat, and now he hired the villagers to cut it by hand, moving across the yellow fields and setting up the cut bundles into shocks, women and men working together. Their babies swung in cloths strung in the shade between trees, and the tractors pulled steel wagons, which bumped over the field rows and gradually filled with the loose sheaves thrown up by the men. The threshing machines ran all day and night, powered by tractors which idled or roared as they ran light or had to bear a load, when the man on the wagon threw a big armful of wheat into the hopper. The chaff, blown out to one side, would grow into enormous golden piles, until finally the men would uncouple the tractor and move the thresher to another spot.

Jaglani sat much of the day in the *dera*, on a charpoy under a massive banyan tree, smoking a hookah and watching the trolleys come in. Two men would pull the burlap sacks down from the trolley along a wooden ramp, each holding one corner, dragging them over to the balance scales that hung from a far branch of the banyan. An accountant entered the weight of each sack into a ledger, and then the two men threw the wheat atop a growing pile, which they climbed, their bare feet digging into the hot grain, sinking to their knees, until they reached the top and upended the sack.

Once again neither hail nor winds had ruined the crop, and the fruits of Jaglani's management stood there beside him, growing, golden. This harvest mattered more to him than any other, more than the mangoes or the cane or the cotton. The men would be paid a portion of their wages throughout the year in wheat, which they preferred, saying that money might be spent, but as long as they had the monthly allowance of wheat their families would not starve. At noon each day Zainab sent out a tray of food to him, covered with a white cloth, and Jaglani ate under the breezy leaves of the banyan, while the men continued to work.

Late one evening, when he returned tired to his house, having spent the afternoon out along the river, dealing with a tractor that had foundered in a sandbank while returning to the farm with a load of grain, she brought him a glass of sherbet, as she now always did as soon as he walked in the door.

'Would you like me to press your feet?' she asked.

This too became part of the routine. He would lie in the shadowed courtyard of his house, smoking a hookah, leaning on one elbow, while she massaged his legs and feet, patiently, her hands red with henna. Her headscarf would slip down to her shoulders, and he admired her thick black hair, braided and oiled. She had strong hands.

Inevitably, one evening he reached for her and took her inside. Now often they would make love before she went home, if he was not too tired. She did this uncomplainingly, giving him whatever he wanted. He had little experience with women, other than the wife to whom he had been married by arrangement at the age of seventeen. Once or twice he had slept with the wives of peasants in the village, when the women threw themselves at him. He would give the husband a job, something that might as well go to one man as to another, but these women were unclean and crude, and once he entered his forties he stopped succumbing to them. He had two sons by his wife, and he continued to sleep with her when he needed release, though he didn't find her attractive, her slow mind and preoccupation with the household in Firoza, which smelled of cooking. Zainab, by contrast, knew how to please him. She wore no scent, but bathed always before he came home and wore attractive clothes.

When the harvest ended he still found some pretext to come every day or two to the farm. He would do his business and then go to the house, where Zainab would serve him the meal she had cooked earlier. He would bathe, she would massage him and feed him, and then they would make love. He said her name in a particular way, pronouncing the first syllable in his throat, and this became the emblem of their closeness, which otherwise they did not refer to. In the bedroom, with the lights off, she kissed him hard and soft and gradually persuaded him by her supple actions to lose his inhibitions. She had a way of falling on the bed, with her face buried in the pillow, on her knees. Driving around the farm, or in the city, the vision of her giving herself so trustingly would come to him.

One evening at bedtime they quarrelled. Next morning when she brought his tea, Jaglani reached around her waist and pulled her down beside him, wanting to be reconciled. 'You never ask for anything. Let me give you some money. You can buy clothes.'

'You buy me things and then later you'll think you bought me. I was never for sale,' she replied, standing up.

'Stop,' he called. He spoke in the voice he might have used with a servant.

She left, quietly closing the door behind her.

That evening they said nothing about this, but he left money on the table beside the bed. She did not take it that night, nor the next morning. He went to the city for a few days, and on the evening when he returned to the farm he found the money still where he had left it.

Each time he met her she approached him with the same reserve that she had displayed the first time he saw her. She spoke to him formally, called him Chaudrey Sahib. When he tried to kiss her, coming in at dusk, her lips would never be hungry. After they made love he would stroke her, run his hands over her slender body, tell her how much she meant to him. He never before had said these things to any woman. She did not caress him, and he felt that she herself was not touched in her core. After they made love she lay on her back, while he nuzzled her neck and threw one arm across her body. Although she massaged him, cooked for him, cleaned his house and made love to him, he found that after two months she still had not come any closer. She needed him, he knew that, but he had no idea whether she cared for him. Except when they made love, when she abandoned herself, a red patch of flushed skin brightening each cheek, he found no response in her eyes, except a willingness to serve him. He looked for contempt in her eyes, but did not find even that. He wanted more from her, for her to spend the entire night with him.

'Why do you care?' he asked. 'Are you afraid the other villagers will find out?'

She laughed humourlessly. 'The villagers! They knew the first night. They leave me alone because they're afraid of you. It's nice, it's a proof of just how much they do fear you. If you dropped me they would call me a whore out loud as I walked down the street.'

'Then why not spend the nights?'

'Then I *would* be your whore. At least now we still pretend. Leave it alone, I've already said more than I wanted. Please.'

In July the monsoon began, a strong monsoon, with rain and enormous clouds towering over the flat desert that fell right to the edge of the river. It had rained all day and all night, and Jaglani came to the farm in order to oversee the pumping of water from the cotton fields. Where the fields lay low the young cotton stood under four inches of water. Mechanics removed the turbines from the tube wells and powered them in the fields by shafts run from tractors. If the sun shone on the plants while they stood in the water the reflected heat would kill them.

That night, late, the watchman from the *dera* knocked on Jaglani's door. He rose quickly and took his revolver.

'Sir, may we use the jeep? Loharu's son just got bitten by a snake.'

Putting on his clothes, Jaglani sent for Mustafa and went to Loharu's house.

Lowering his head to walk under the lintel of the small door, stepping carefully in the slippery mud, he approached the family, an old woman and her husband Loharu, who had worked on the farm as a labourer since he became old enough to be useful. They were standing in the little single room by the light of a lantern, the woman quietly sobbing and dabbing at her eyes with her headscarf. A crowd of villagers stood around, some inside and some outside the hut. When Jaglani entered they murmured, 'Chaudrey Sahib.' Even in his grief the father fell into a posture of deference, taking Jaglani's hand and reaching to touch his knee.

The boy lay on a charpoy in one corner, very thin, just developing a moustache. Although still alive, his body had softened and lost all tension. A bit of white foam sat in each corner of his lips. Jaglani knew he would be dead soon, as did the villagers, who had seen this before. Only the parents refused to accept that their son would soon be gone. They heard the jeep coming along the muddy street of the village, splashing, whining in first gear. No one made a move to lift the boy, and after a few more minutes he died, curling now, his throat rattling, and then becoming limp.

The mother fell on to the body, quietly saying, 'No, no, no, no, no.'

Jaglani went outside. 'What happened?' he asked.

'A cobra came through the window, the water must have filled its hole. The boy's hand hung over the edge of the charpoy, and the snake brushed the hand.'

'Did they kill the snake?'

A man went inside and brought out the cobra, black, three feet long, dangling like a hose over the stick with which he carried it. It slid off into the mud, making a soft slapping sound.

Back in his house, Jaglani found that he couldn't sleep, that he wanted something, tea or some food. He hadn't known the boy, though he had seen him about. The father had worked on the farm for twenty years, since childhood. Now he was a heavy-featured man with a few days' muzzle of greying beard, his teeth almost gone, rather stupid, so that the other men made good-humoured jokes about him.

Jaglani pushed the bell button, which rang out where the watchman could hear it.

'I'm not feeling well,' he told the watchman. 'Call Zainab and tell her to make me some tea. I've got a fever.'

'Shall I send Mustafa for medicine?'

'No, in the morning I'll go back to Firoza. Just tea.'

Zainab came into the room, walking quietly as always. 'I'm sorry you're not well.'

'Come here,' said Jaglani. He took her by the wrist and pulled her down on to the bed. She didn't resist, but instead, with a practised motion removed her kurta, pulling it over her head. As she came on to the bed she kicked off her shoes.

Rolling on top of her, he searched her face.

'I need you to be here in the house whenever I'm here.' He looked directly into her eyes.

'I told you, I won't. I'll go away.'

'Where can you go?'

'My husband has written three times. He says he'll take me back. I'll go there.'

Jaglani lay on his back staring at the ceiling, his emotions tightened up almost unbearably.

'I'll marry you,' he said.

'What about my husband?'

'I'll arrange it.'

She turned and began kissing him, looking down on his face. He closed his eyes.

Jaglani knew that his wife, who was also his first cousin, would try to turn their common family against him if he took another wife. In the next few days he didn't mention his offer of marriage again, although it lay between them. Zainab became harder and more emotionally inflexible than before. She did what he asked. Again and always in bed, sexually, she opened and became almost vicious, pliable, biting him, on his cheeks, his neck; but after they finished she withdrew into herself. Only sometimes, when they lay in bed, she would cough or feel cold and he would offer to do something for her, to bring water or to find a blanket, and she would say, 'yes, please', in a girlish voice that wrung his heart. Finally he could not deny to himself that he had fallen in love, for the first time in his life. He even acknowledged her aloof coldness, the possibility that she would mar his life. And yet he felt that he had risen so far, had become invulnerable to the judgements of those around him, had become pre-eminent in this area by the River Indus, and now he deserved to make this mistake, for once not to make a calculated choice, but to surrender to his desire.

At the beginning of September, after the monsoon, the immense Punjabi heat began to subside. One morning when Zainab brought his breakfast he said to her, 'Your husband comes today.'

'Why?'

'I've called him. He needs to sign the divorce papers.'

'He won't do that.'

Jaglani looked up at her as she leaned forward, placing the tray of food on the table in front of him. 'You still don't know me, do you?'

In the late afternoon Zainab's husband, a peasant named Aslam born in Dunyapur, entered the *dera*, a small figure advancing through the whitewashed brick gates, having walked from the main road, where the intercity bus dropped him off.

Jaglani sat under the banyan tree, signing cash vouchers passed to him by an aged accountant wearing spectacles mended with wire.

Aslam approached, said his salaam, and touched Jaglani's knee.

'Hello Aslam,' said Jaglani. 'I'll call you, go sit.'

Seven or eight men sat in chairs under a veranda, all waiting to see Jaglani, with petitions of various kinds – a stolen ox, water issues, begging for jobs, needing letters to local government administrators.

Jaglani saw Aslam last of all, several hours later. The sky had darkened, and the *maulvi* in the plain but large marbled mosque built by the Harounis had finished the *maghreb* call for prayer, standing on a platform, his voice reedy.

'Aslam, you can't seem to control your wife,' began Jaglani, without any preamble.

'No sir. She ran back to the village. I'm here, and I intend to take her home.'

'I'm told she doesn't want to go. You better divorce her.'

'Sir, no. My house is empty, every night I come home and it's empty.'

'Why don't you have children?' asked Jaglani. 'Didn't you live with her as her husband?'

'In the beginning we tried. We had no luck.'

'That's grounds for divorce. I suggest you divorce her for being barren.'

'Please, Chaudrey Sahib, you and I grew up together in Dunyapur, we played together as children. I beg you, don't take what's mine. You have so much, and I so little.'

'I have so much because I took what I wanted. Go away.'

The husband said, 'Take her and be damned with her,' but Jaglani ignored him.

The next morning one of the farm accountants presented Aslam with some papers. Knowing the husband to be illiterate, and wishing to spare him further humiliation, the accountant assured him that the papers simply gave Zainab permission to live apart. Aslam left Dunyapur with a letter to the manager of the bank where he worked in Rawalpindi. In the letter Jaglani requested that the manager, a dependant of the Harounis, give Aslam a raise and watch over him.

A few weeks later Jaglani secretly married Zainab. The *maulvi* from the mosque came quietly into Chaudrey Sahib's house one morning, bringing with him one of the old managers to act as a witness. The villagers bullied the *maulvi*, a timid man with a scrawny beard. He blushed when he spoke, and would ask the cook in the *dera* for little treats from the common pot to take home for his wife, as his pay barely covered their thin monthly expenditure. The manager, by contrast, cuffed his men about and had a voice like a baying hound. Coming across the courtyard, under the blowing trees, the *maulvi* turned to the manager.

'Won't Jaglani's sons blame us for this?'

'Don't worry,' said the manager, 'there's not enough blood in their livers to clog the foot of a flea. Even when the big man dies they'll be afraid to cross him. And she can take care of herself, she's like a hatchet.'

When they entered the courtyard of the little house they found Jaglani sitting on a charpoy smoking his hookah. The two men sat down, and while the *maulvi* watched, Jaglani and the manager spoke of the September cane planting, just completed, and of the cotton just then developing bolls. The manager picked at a callus on his foot. After a few minutes the Register of Deeds, a man who owed his posting in the area to Jaglani, and who had collaborated in numerous dubious land transfers, entered with the marriage papers in a big ledger under his arm. He took from his pocket a gold pen worth several months of his official salary and began filling out the forms, writing in an elegant hand, and with a look of satisfaction on his face. He loved these forms, loved consummating rich transactions. Jaglani signed, the single witness signed, and then the *maulvi* rose and said a prayer, his hands cupped, speaking rapidly and with perfect memory. The other three required witnesses would sign later, if the need arose – the Register of Deeds had urged that they leave the document incomplete to this degree. Under the trees and with the birds calling, Jaglani felt extremely moved, felt his emotions to be like clear glass. He took the papers inside and Zainab affixed her thumbprint, leaning against him as they sat on the bed, her face soft. When he had insisted upon keeping the marriage secret she made only one stipulation – that they no longer would use birth control.

Zainab now slept the night in Jaglani's bed. She brought many of her things, clothes and jewellery, her make-up, and put them about the house. Seeing these little tokens of her presence made him happy, made him feel that he possessed her. She asked him to buy a buffalo, and twice a day, at dawn and at dusk, the villager who cared for the animal would bring a pail of the rich milk and leave it just inside the courtyard, covered with a cloth. She made ghee and butter, and if some were left over she sent it to Mustafa's house, or to the house of one of the poorer neighbours who couldn't afford to keep a buffalo. Only in the mornings, when Jaglani wanted to hold her, to lie in bed with her and talk quietly, or perhaps to make love, she still would not stay with him, but became restless and would get up, saying that she needed to begin the day. Although she did not like being touched, except when in bed, he found that now she tried to accept his caresses, tried not to be cold to him. When he came into the house and came behind her as she stood doing some household task, cupping her breasts in his hands, she became still and turned her head, smiling, and only after a moment would she disengage from him. Even then she would hold his hand and lead him outside, seating him on the charpoy and bringing his hookah. He became familiar with the smallest aspects of her body. She cut her toenails one day, but cut too far, into the quick, an inverted half moon, until one of the nails bled. He loved this wildness in her, evidence of hardness towards herself, contained violence.

She developed a urinary infection, and he took her into town. She rode in the back of his jeep, and as always her brother Mustafa drove. None of them spoke. She kept her head covered, and didn't look out of the window. Even this trip, their first together, became for him a significant memory. He wanted to take care of her, but often she would not allow him to. When he returned to Dunyapur after spending a few days in Firoza with his senior wife, as he drove towards the river he would feel a weight on his stomach. He feared Zainab, strangely enough, although he had made a career of fearing no one and of thereby dominating this lawless area. Sometimes he thought that it would be a relief to be rid of her, and yet his love kept increasing.

He became slightly complacent, finding her softer than he had imagined. After they made love she would lie next to him in the dark, tracing her fingers on his back and leaning down to kiss him. Before the marriage he always had been the one to caress her, while she lay with her back to him, curled into his body, her eyes open, rigid and seemingly resentful of having opened herself, not only physically but also emotionally, at least in the moments of sex.

She had blamed her husband for her failure to conceive. A year after her second marriage Jaglani arrived at dusk from Firoza. Mustafa drove the jeep into the *dera*, the headlights illuminating the banyan, the tractors standing in a row along the wall, ploughs and harrows and discs here and there. The watchman stood up, leaning on his long stick, and shielded his eyes with one hand. Another summer had passed, another monsoon. The jasmine planted along the high mud walls gave off its strong sweet smell. Jaglani liked flowers, and he also believed that the farm ran best when the roads were kept immaculate and smooth and the buildings whitewashed and adorned with flowers and trees. Order begat order.

Walking into the house he found the fire out and the light off, although he had sent word in the morning that he would be returning to the farm. Inside Zainab sat in the dark on the edge of the bed.

'Why no lights?' he asked, flipping the switch.

She had not dressed up, but wore wrinkled clothes.

'Do you know what day this is?'

'No.'

'The day we married, last year.' She paused. 'You know, I thought I didn't have children with Aslam because he couldn't. But it's me.' She almost began to cry, but then stopped herself. Her face became hard.

'I only married you because of that.'

Cut badly, he said, 'You had no choice. How long would your sister-in-law have treated you well? You came like a beggar.'

'I never begged, but now I'll beg from you. I'll bow down. I beg you, give me one of your sons' children to bring up. Shabir has three daughters. The little one, give me her. He has his sons, he'll still have them and the other girls. The little one is only a few months old, she won't even know that I'm not her real mother. Give her to me, I beg you, and I'll never ask for anything again.' She began to cry, through her teeth. 'I beg you, I beg you, I beg you. I've served you. I belong to you, you know I do. Give me the little girl. Shabir doesn't even want her, you know he doesn't.'

He refused. 'I can't, my family doesn't know we're married.'

That winter Jaglani decided to run for office, for the provincial assembly. The local powers, the people above him, the Makhdooms, hereditary saints who controlled huge areas of land nearby and who could hand out Muslim League tickets, sent people to Jaglani and offered to help get him elected. He went to Lahore and received

Yes, I would like to take out an annual subscription to *Granta* and receive a complimentary *Granta* special-edition **MOLESKINE**® notebook:

GIFT SUBSCRIPTION 1

Address:

FIRST NAME: LAST NAME:

ADDRESS:

CITY: STATE:

COUNTRY: ZIP CODE:

TELEPHONE:

EMAIL:

GIFT SUBSCRIPTION 2

Address:

FIRST NAME: LAST NAME:

ADDRESS:

CITY: STATE:

COUNTRY: ZIP CODE:

TELEPHONE:

EMAIL:

YOUR ADDRESS FOR BILLING

FIRST NAME: LAST NAME:

ADDRESS: CITY:

STATE: COUNTRY: ZIP CODE:

TELEPHONE: EMAIL:

NUMBER OF SUBSCRIPTIONS	DELIVERY REGION	PRICE	SAVINGS
☐	USA	$45.99	32%
☐	Canada	$57.99	32%
☐	Rest of World	$65.99	32%

I would like my subscription to start from: All prices include delivery

☐ the current issue   ☐ the next issue   GRANTA IS PUBLISHED QUARTERLY

PAYMENT DETAILS

☐ I enclose a check payable to '*Granta*' for $ _____ for _____ subscriptions to *Granta*

☐ Please charge my ☐ MASTERCARD ☐ VISA ☐ AMEX for £ _____ for _____ subscriptions

NUMBER ☐☐☐☐ ☐☐☐☐ ☐☐☐☐ ☐☐☐☐   SECURITY CODE ☐☐☐

EXPIRATION ☐☐ / ☐☐   SIGNED _____   DATE _____

☐ Please tick this box if you would like to receive special offers from *Granta*
☐ Please tick this box if you would like to receive offers from organizations selected by *Granta*

Please return this form to: **Granta Subscriptions, PO Box 359, Congers, NY 10920-0359, call Toll-free 1-866-438-6150** or go to **www.granta.com**

Please quote the following promotion code when ordering online: BUS104PG the blessing of K. K. Harouni. As a preliminary to the election, in order to prevent his opponent from using it against him, Jaglani disclosed the secret of his marriage to Zainab. He gave his wife and children no time to respond, he simply announced it to them. The villagers had already guessed, but now had it confirmed. Others found out. No one thought anything of it, he ruled his area in the old way, with force. He had the prerogative of taking a second wife, a chosen wife. Flushed with his power, Jaglani went further. He brought his son's infant daughter to Dunyapur and gave her to Zainab, to nurse and to bring up.

Another year passed. Jaglani had been elected to the provincial assembly by a wide margin, and thus spent his time either in Lahore attending sessions or at the farm, hearing the petitions and complaints of his constituents, the people from the area. His district ran along both sides of the Indus river, and the people on the far side came across on a wooden ferry, flat-bottomed and large enough to hold twenty people, pushed along on long sweeps by an old man, whose body had remained muscular, but whose skin hung off him wherever the muscles didn't extend.

One of Jaglani's first acts on entering office had been to move the ferry from another spot five miles downstream to a little bay on the river immediately next to Dunyapur, over the protests of those who found the original situation more convenient. The ferry had served the village of the man who stood against Jaglani in the election, and by moving it he showed the entire district his new powers. He had new bricked roads built to meet the ferry at each bank of the river, and these roads greatly increased the value of Jaglani's lands and the lands of his friends. Jaglani could order men arrested or released, could appoint them to government posts, could have government officers removed. He decided whose villages the new roads passed through, decided which areas got electricity, manipulated the flow of water through the canals. He could settle cases, even cases of murder, by imposing a reconciliation upon the two parties and ordering the police not to interfere. These new powers changed him. Because he had no higher ambitions, he became impartial. By temperament orderly, within this isolated area he sought to impose harmony and prosperity.

Coming into the house one afternoon, Jaglani did not find Zainab in the little kitchen preparing his food. He called.

'Where are you?'

'In my room,' she replied, speaking in her gentle voice, which he liked so much. 'Come in, come see.'

Jaglani walked through the room he shared with her and into her own quarters. Unlike the rest of the house, which was dark and crowded with furniture, Zainab's room had only a small low bed, padded with cotton, a chair and a plain wooden table, on which she had arranged her make-up and combs, with a mirror in front of it, and in one corner a crib. A small cotton dhurrie covered the centre of the brick floor. The high windows stood open, drawing light into the room, reflecting off the freshly whitewashed walls. The baby stood on the bed, waving her fat little arms, naked, her feet planted between Zainab's crossed legs. Zainab leaned against a pillow and, dipping a cloth into a bowl of warm water, gently washed the baby. The light from the windows reflected off the disturbed water in the brass bowl, throwing a pattern on to the walls.

'Watch,' said Zainab. She tickled the baby, whom she had renamed Saba, under the chin, holding her around the waist. He noticed the strength of Zainab's slender arm, on which the veins stood out, and he noticed the sureness with which his wife held this baby. The baby giggled. Zainab laid her on the bed and bent over her.

'Say it,' she whispered soothingly. Her pale manicured feet peeked out under her thighs, the soles reddened with henna. 'Say it, little bunny, my little Saba.'

The baby looked up at her, smiling, coral gums wet with spittle. She waved her chubby arms, fingers splayed. 'Ma,' she said.

'See?' said Zainab, turning to Jaglani, who sat on the little chair next to the table. Zainab had been worrying because the baby, nearly two years old, had not yet begun to speak.

Vulnerable, he watched the baby intently, smiling a shy smile, his features becoming gentle, the face of a sad boy, knowing and needy. 'If only the managers could see this smile,' she would say.

Zainab gestured. 'Come, bring your chair over by us.'

He carried the chair across the room and sat down, his elbows on his knees, looking into the little girl's face and at Zainab's hair, which fell over the baby.

For several months Jaglani had been feeling unwell. A few days after this little scene with the baby, Jaglani learned that he had bone cancer, and that he would be dead within six months. When he didn't visit the village for a week Zainab went to see her brother Mustafa, who spent each Friday night with his family in Dunyapur.

'You better come inside,' said Mustafa. He took her into a neat room, adorned with the fruits of his petty thefts, his inflated bills – a television and video player, a sewing machine covered with an embroidered cloth, a large garish clock with a plastic figure of a shepherdess that moved back and forth across the face – for like everyone else on the farm Mustafa trimmed out money where he could, a few rupees on the petrol, a bit of padding when he bought spare parts.

'What?' she said, as soon as her brother closed the door.

'He's dying.'

She sat down, almost falling, and hung her head. 'Oh my God. Of what? And now what do I do?'

'It's cancer. You better be sharp.'

'He hasn't come in a week,' she said.

'Don't count on anything anymore,' said Mustafa. 'His family's all around him now. He'll get weak fast. Don't forget, he owns twenty squares of land, just as a start. You'll be lucky to see him again, at least to see him alone.'

'He's tied to me,' she said, looking Mustafa in the eye. 'He'll come.'

Mustafa sat down and ran his hands over his face. 'What a mess. He's going tomorrow to Lahore. He's trying to make sure that Shabir wins the by-election. That won't happen, the boy barely has enough spine to stand upright. The big guys around here will eat him up once Jaglani's gone. No one reaches out very far from the grave.'

'You know what that means for me,' she said. Brother and sister understood the immensity of her loss, the failure of her preparations against abandonment. 'They're going to take Saba away from me, aren't they? She's too young, in a year she won't remember me. I'll get nothing.'

Jaglani faded away. Knowing how vulnerable his family would be to the enemies he had made in the course of a life in politics, he went to Lahore, seeking a sure seat in the Assembly for his son, the one who gave a daughter to Zainab, in the by-election that would follow his death.

The provincial party chief, a ward boss from Lahore who held the office of Punjab Chief Minister, received Jaglani just after sunset at his house, a large shabby building constructed on public land, formerly a park, which he had condemned and appropriated as soon as he attained office, throwing a wall around it.

Jaglani waited in the anteroom with twenty or thirty other supplicants, who gathered in circles or huddled together on grimy sofas, speaking in undertones, puffing cigarettes and whispering into cellphones tiny as jewels. Two pictures hung on a wall of the dirty, smoky room, one of the country's founder, the Quaid-e-Azam, and next to it, just slightly lower, a photo of the party's leader. The other men in the room, mostly provincial politicians risen from the business classes, held their phones in their hands when not speaking into them, displaying this new status symbol recently introduced in Lahore and the other big Pakistani cities.

Entering the immaculate office, ushered in by a sleek-looking steno, Jaglani approached the Chief Minister, who sat behind a desk covered with green baize, reading a file. He looked up, narrowed his eyes, and rose.

'Hello, hello Chaudrey Sahib.'

He walked from behind the desk, his Western clothes, a pinstriped suit and gold cufflinks and English shoes, distinguishing him from Jaglani and from most of the supplicants waiting in the anteroom. Taking Jaglani's hand and holding on to it, he sat them down next to each other on a sofa.

'You're looking well,' said the Chief Minister insincerely.

'Thanks to your honour.'

'And how is Mr K. K. Harouni?'

They began speaking of the political situation in Jaglani's district. The Chief Minister spoke little but listened, his face set in a shrewd expression, looking at the opposite wall and occasionally asking questions.

After ten minutes he looked at his watch.

'And how's everything else?'

'I've come with a request, sir. I regret to say I've been diagnosed with cancer.'

'Well, well, I'm so sorry,' said the Chief Minister, who knew all about it.

'Sir, I request that the party support my son in the by-election.'

'Nonsense, nonsense,' said the Minister. 'You're healthy as a horse. These doctors kill everyone off, everyone. You've still got twenty years ahead of you, bullying Dunyapur.'

'If something does happen to me, however, will you support the boy? He's capable, he knows the area, and he knows all the people. I've served the party for twenty-five years, in one way or another, and I've always voted in the Assembly the way you asked me to.' He played his only card. 'We go back a long way, Shujaat Sahib.'

'We'll have to put the boy forward. We'll plan that. Don't worry, it's done.'

'Will you call a meeting of the people from my area? We'll need to get them in line.'

The Chief Minister rose. 'Yes, yes. We'll have to do that.' Walking

Jaglani to the door and ushering the dying man out, the Minister said, shaking an upraised finger, 'Now remember, no more about this illness. You'll outlive us all, I know how you country people are, it's the food, it's the food.' He had this habit of repeating himself when telling lies.

Jaglani walked through the anteroom, down the dirty steps, and out the gate. Mustafa stood in a line of cars parked along the sidewalk. He had failed. He went back to Dunyapur without seeing any of his old friends and allies.

The city house in Firoza, with antimacassars and sofas covered with plastic liners and the constant smell of fried onions, depressed Jaglani, and yet its gloominess and air of resignation and finality seemed consistent with the great change coming over him. He felt the cancer as a tension in his stomach, a breeding knot that hurt sometimes but that never went away. He longed for the country and for Dunyapur, where he had been born and where he achieved all the successes that mattered to him now. He remembered the day when he became a manager, appointed by K. K. Harouni, who at that time still looked rich and clean and strong, different from anyone that Jaglani had ever known. Jaglani once went with him hunting ducks along the river, floating on a barge, and he remembered still the softness of the landowner's white shirt and the way in which his collar touched the brown hairs on his neck. Harouni had carried a beautiful shotgun, very light, slim, almost like a toy, but deadly.

Yet Dunyapur had been spoiled for him by the presence of Zainab. He minded very much that he had given his sons a stepmother of that class, a servant woman. He minded that he had insulted his first wife in that way, by marrying again, by marrying a servant, and then by keeping the marriage a secret. His senior wife had never reproached him, but after Jaglani told her she quickly became old. She prayed a great deal, spent much of her time in bed, stopped caring for herself. Her body became rounded like a hoop, not fat but fleshed uniformly all over, a body thrown away, throwing itself away, sitting all day in bed, dreaming, muttering perhaps when left alone. He reproached himself for taking his eldest son's daughter and giving her to Zainab, transplanting the little girl on to such different stock. Secretly, and most bitterly, he blamed himself for having been so weak as to love a woman who had never loved him. He made an idol of her, lavished himself upon her sexual body, gave himself to a woman who never gave back, except in the most practical terms. She blotted the cleanliness of his life trajectory, which he had always before believed in. She represented the culmination of his ascendancy, the reward of his virtue and striving, and showed him how little it all had been, his life and his ambitions. All of it he had thrown away, his manliness and strength, for a pair of legs that clasped his waist and a pair of eyes that pierced him and that yet had at bottom the deadness of foil.

One morning in April, three months after he had been diagnosed and condemned to die, Jaglani woke feeling better than usual. Walking now with a cane, his face gaunt and improved by it, he went to the veranda and without telling any of the people in the house ordered Mustafa to drive him to Dunyapur. They arrived in the *dera* just at the time when the sun began to pour down over the roofs of the sheds on to the bricked threshing floor. Chickens walked about picking at spilled grain, and the odour of burnt oil that had soaked into the dust added to the sleepiness of the scene, a sweetish baking scent.

Only a few people sat in the sun, two accountants, a watchman and one or two others, loafers sitting around drinking tea. On the far side of the large open square an old woman with bare feet hunched over and swept the floor, throwing up a cloud of dust in the sun. When the people sitting there saw the car they jumped up, saying, 'Chaudrey Sahib, Chaudrey Sahib,' as if they had something to hide.

Mustafa ran around to open the door, and Jaglani stepped painfully out, took his cane, and after receiving their obeisance went into his own house, without pausing to discuss business. The men had approached him not less deferentially than before but less fearfully. They knew he had come for the last time, and already their feelings about him were becoming sweeter and more genuinely respectful. With him an entire generation of men from Dunyapur would pass.

Jaglani had lived an opportunistic life, seizing power wherever he saw it available and unguarded, and therefore he had not developed sentimental attachments to the tokens of his power, land, possessions, or even men. Walking into the silent dark house, he felt, for the first time, that he would regret losing a place, these whitewashed walls, the little windows. He had aged greatly in the past weeks as the disease bit into him. He had never loved his wife, his children were fools and he had no friends. For him there had not been any great leave-takings, no farewells. He had spent his life among the farmers and peasants of the area, or among politicians. He liked some of them, liked their stories or their intelligence or cunning. Although he didn't laugh often, he played a part when the politicians or the strongmen from around Dunyapur gathered and talked. In the early years, Jaglani sat to one side, dark and acute, and in quiet moments added his intelligent remarks. Later, when he became important, he still mostly listened, but signalled to those around him that they could unwind and speak freely by making brief and slightly witty comments, speaking through lips almost clenched, resisting a smile. His social life had not extended beyond these diversions. He worked in concert with other men, or used them, or struggled against them. The rest did not interest him.

Going into the small living room, Jaglani saw a light in Zainab's room, and thought that she must be there with the baby. He wondered if someone in his household at Firoza had called and informed her of his arrival. He knew that she must have contacts among his servants in the city. She would want him to find her there, caring for the child. The darkness of the house, its dampness, the expectancy of the salt and pepper shakers carefully aligned on the table and the sadness of the toothpick holder, its pink plastic cover gleaming softly, waiting for his next visit and his next meal, reminded him of the days when he first realized that he loved Zainab, and she sensed that he loved her, and began to smile around him, to play as she served him dinner. He walked quietly to her bedroom. She lay on the white divan, with the baby next to her. He expected her to jump up, to make some reproach at his not having visited her for so long, but she put a finger to her lip, and then with gentle hands covered the baby with a tiny knitted blanket. She disengaged herself, rolled away, kissed the baby and stood up, smoothing her hair with one hand and arranging her headscarf.

'Salaam, Chaudrey Sahib,' she said quietly. 'Let me bring you some tea.' She showed no surprise at seeing him.

Without waiting for an answer she went out. He leaned on his cane, looking down at the baby lying splayed on its face, dressed too warmly, in socks, a sweater and a crocheted hat. Tiring, he sat down heavily on a chair. He loved her still, he realized, noting it, as if painfully writing something into a notebook. (Lately he often found himself doing this, inscribing his experiences and thoughts, his final record, in an invisible notebook, never able to find a pencil, holding the pad in the air and writing shakily, illegibly.) He had come here to abjure his great love, and he found just this – just a small room lit by a single bulb, chilly despite the sun outside, and the woman he loved sitting alone, putting to sleep this stolen child that he gave her. He finally understood that she lived a simple life, and a wave of pity came over him. He had imagined her moving quickly from task to task, and only now did he perceive how lonely she might have been, waiting for him in the past years, never knowing when he would arrive. She had made so little of his coming that it had not occurred to him that all her days must have been directed towards that moment.

She carried in the tea things, the milk in the pitcher steaming, the sugar bowl covered with an embroidered cloth. From the smugglers' market in Rawalpindi he had bought her this flowery tea set, kept unused on a shelf with her other good dishes. She was the only woman for whom he had ever brought presents. She placed the tray on a table by the bed, then sat down on the floor, at the edge of the carpet, with her knees drawn up and enclosed in her arms. She looked up at him, holding her chin on her knees. He noticed the kohl on her eyes.

'They tell me that you're dying,' she said quietly, as if smoothing it away between them.

'Probably.'

She rose up on her knees and poured him tea, sweetened it, and handed him the cup. Watching her settle back on her compact haunches, seated on the carpet, he understood that he would never again make love to her, never again hold her nor see her face when she woke in the morning. They talked of nothing, she told him of the baby's little tricks, asked him about the farm. It surprised him that she didn't ask about her own future, about property or money.

Finishing his tea, he rose, making an effort not to lean on the cane.

'Goodbye,' he said, looking at her. As he reached the door, leaving her sitting on the floor, he realized that he couldn't do this, that he must say more, although he had told himself that he wouldn't. He remembered the morning when he married her, quietly signing the papers while sitting under the mulberry tree in the little courtyard of this house, with the sounds of the village in the background, goats and a radio playing a song and tractors driving down the street.

'I've told the boys to give you something after I'm gone,' he said, without looking at her.

'Fine,' she replied, in a clipped voice.

Both of them knew that this meant nothing.

He walked out under the big banyan, where Mustafa toiled over the jeep, polishing it. The managers stood to one side, not speaking to each other. Jaglani got into the jeep and offhandedly said goodbye forever.

In the next few days Jaglani intended to do something for Zainab, to put a house in her name, for he had several in the city, or to give her a square of land. His children would anyway have so much, and after his death Zainab would be attacked from all sides, by the villagers and by his family. But his illness progressed very quickly, and the constant pain kept him from acting. He chose the path of least resistance, and his family ensured that this path always led to them and to the gratification of their interests. The papers ensuring their inheritance readily appeared whenever he had the impulse to sign them, whereas other documents, those that did not suit the two sons, were delayed indefinitely. The sons had agreed not to fight among themselves, but to divide the property equally. They also agreed to prevent their father from making any other disposition.

The servants moved Jaglani's bed into the living room of his house. They removed the furniture, except for one sofa, placing the bed in the middle, with a table covered with medicines next to it. On the floor stood a tin bucket, and then, contrastingly, two thin oxygen cylinders almost as tall as a man, with dented steel bodies, silver fittings and a profusion of clear tubes feeding him air through a cannula pinched on to his nose, the apparatus setting him apart from those who now surrounded him. Day and night, one or another of the servants would press his arms and legs. Often Jaglani grew angry with the servants, making cruel and untrue accusations, that they were hurting him, that they had always stolen from him. One of Jaglani's patrons, Makhdoom Talwan, paid a visit, a great landowner of the district, towards whom he had always been deferential. Now, when this man entered the room, Jaglani started up and told him to go to hell, began shrieking about stolen votes and stolen water, until he couldn't speak and lay panting. The family bustled the great man away.

Every day, at some moment when the room stood empty except for the servant on duty, Mustafa would come to pay his respects, one of the few people whom Jaglani looked on with kind eyes. Mustafa would remove his shoes and stand just inside the door with bare feet. Jaglani would call him forward, to stand beside the bed, and would say a few inconsequential words, asking about Dunyapur. Mustafa answered the questions very briefly and would stand beside him until he fell asleep.

Jaglani became weaker and angrier, until everyone wished he would die. One day he heard a commotion in the anteroom, raised voices and doors slamming. Zainab had come, taking a tonga from Dunyapur and then a bus, walking solitary up to the house, past the gatekeeper, who had become slack and who watched her without bothering even to get up from the chair where he sat smoking a hookah. He knew her, for like all the servants Jaglani had chosen him from the village.

The sick man heard her in the anteroom say to Shabir, the son, who had rushed to intercept her, 'Get your hands off me, you little piece of shit. I'm his wife. Don't touch me.' Jaglani reached painfully and rang the bell on a cord that lay by his pillow. Shabir came in, locking the door behind him.

'Tell her to go away,' said the dying man. 'I don't want to see her.' She had spoken in the most vulgar Punjabi, like women screaming over the common wall of their village huts.

Lying alone, unable to sleep, Jaglani had for days been renouncing Zainab. He had done wrong to his sons and to his senior wife, whom he didn't love, had never loved. His first wife and his sons belonged to another time, to his days of strength, when the world stood open to him. He remembered the river, the way it glittered in his youth and in his manhood. He married his first wife at seventeen, when he still earned a salary of only forty rupees, and she rose with him, made his meals, and now old, an image of his mother, wore smudged glasses and with teary eyes stood over him when he ate. She would die soon, would never again be happy. She hadn't been happy for years. Zainab would go on, she had life in her, vitality, many years ahead. He didn't want her to live on after him.

Mustafa took Zainab outside and walked her back through the gates of the compound and out into the busy street, where no one cared that Jaglani lay dying in the big house, or if they knew of it, thought only of the changes to come, new men up, old men down, Jaglani's adherents thrown down.

Zainab wept quietly and kept saying to herself, 'And they didn't even offer me a cup of tea.'

Two nights later Jaglani died. The cancer had spread to his lymph nodes and to his brain, and he died in great pain, despite the morphine. A woman from the city came and laid him out, bathing his body, tying his mouth shut with a strip of gauze. At the burial, held by custom before nightfall, the two sons stood next to Jaglani's patron, Makhdoom Talwan, the dominant landlord and politician in the district, a member of the National Assembly. Makhdoom Sahib said to Shabir, 'So now it's your seat to lose in the by-election.' Immediately after the burial his driver brought his big Land Cruiser jeep right up to the gates of the old cemetery, blocking the flow of mourners. Shaking hands with the two sons, looking with penetration at each of them, he drove away into the falling night, having said nothing more of the elections, offering no support.

Nevertheless, Shabir went to see the great man. Preparations for the by-election had begun in earnest, groups of men were gathering and going around together, forming alliances, bartering votes, but few people came to see Shabir, and the ones who did were bit players. The gatekeeper at Makhdoom Talwan's house leapt up on seeing Jaglani's car, but Shabir found that the further he penetrated into the sanctum the colder the reception he received. Talwan's personal assistant went so far as to suggest that Shabir should come back in the morning, at the time of general audience. Finally gaining admittance, Shabir was seated in a dark room and asked to wait. A servant brought him a glass of lemonade, then left him alone. Ten minutes later Makhdoom Sahib's enormous bulk pushed through the door, in an immaculate white kurta and a turban tied so that a flap hung down along the side of his head, fringed, like an egret's wing.

'Hello, young man,' he said rather casually, sitting down heavily with a little puffing exhalation, smoothing his hands down his belly, as if brushing away crumbs. 'So how are you? How are things settling out?'

He placidly asked a few questions, listened, seemed to approve when Shabir called him uncle. Then, at a pause in the conversation, just at the moment when Shabir was about to launch his plea, Makhdoom Sahib turned with a hard look.

'My boy, our friendly relations are one thing, politics are another. I want to give you an understanding of the position.' He paused to think. 'Let me tell you a story. You may remember Jam Rasheed, the famous Chief Minister of Sindh. He ran an entire province more strictly even than your father ran Dunyapur, with a whip made of good thick buffalo hide. Top to bottom everyone obeyed, and the ones who didn't died in police encounters or disappeared or lost their lands or their factories. Now, right at the height of his power, he arranged the wedding of his daughter. On his lands the public works people made a huge city of tents and pavilions for the guests – they spent crores of government money. Madam Noor Jahan came out of retirement, Nusrat played, everyone. The preparations were immense, on a royal scale.

'Jam Sahib had his creatures and creations, as such men do – freshly minted princes of industry and millionaire bureaucrats from humble families – and these gentlemen were made to understand that luxury vehicles, customized Mercedes limousines or the very latest models of jeep, would be acceptable gifts. The vehicles duly paraded in on the newly laid roads and were parked in a special compound, for all to see. Then, the second day into the festivities, while presiding over a magnificent dinner, Jam Sahib suddenly fell to the ground in front of the whole assembly. A stroke had left him incapable of speech and paralyzed on one side. That night, under cover of darkness, a strange procession slipped out from the tent city. The vehicles that had been brought as gifts crept away, never to be seen again by Jam Sahib or his daughter.'

Makhdoom Talwan stood up. 'Think about this story, and then think about your position. Your father is gone, but you're nevertheless a fortunate man, your father left you with a great deal of land and money. Enjoy what you have and learn to know your level. Most of all, don't let what now belongs to you be taken away. The first thing for you is to be safe. I'm speaking as your elder, and I offer you this counsel as repayment for the many years of support your father gave me. Goodbye.'

*

A few days later Makhdoom Talwan sent a group of lesser politicians to Shabir, requesting him to step aside during the by-election in favour of another man, a sleek lawyer from the city. They all promised to back Shabir in the next election, if he would just for now withdraw, and even prevailed upon him to take part in one of the lawyer's political meetings. The crowd, trucked in from the surrounding villages and in the mood for fun, munched on peanuts and sweets – for years on end the politicians ignored or abused the peasants, and then in election years the people abused the politicians. Called to the podium, removing his glasses from a case and putting them on, Shabir looked out on a shoal of grinning and unfriendly faces. He had barely begun his little speech, urging support for the lawyer, when someone in the back made a loud farting sound, silencing him. Two men, on far opposite sides of the crowd, began shouting back and forth to each other.

'Hello brother. What do you have there?' bellowed one of them.

The other man held up an enormous cucumber. 'Do you know what they say? The world is like a cucumber. Today it's in your hand, tomorrow it's up your ass.'

'Now that, my friend, is pure poetry. Kind of a metaphor – something you're sharing with the honourable speaker up on the stage, I suppose.'

The two went on in the same vein until finally the lawyer candidate stood up and took Shabir by the arm, hustling him off the podium and toward the cars, apologizing and saying they would definitely find out who had arranged this outrage, get to the bottom of it no matter where the trail led, and punish the guilty ones thoroughly.

As he was driven out of the stadium, Shabir's skin crawled with shame, his face itched, and in order to relieve the silence he drummed with his fingers on the windowsill. His eyes were unwillingly drawn to Mustafa's opaque expressionless face – this sole companion of his father's triumphs. 'First thing tomorrow,' he promised himself, 'I'm going to fire this man.' ∎

'JEST SHOOT IT!'

On my first acquaintance with coaches

Benjamin Markovits

My first recognizably sexual experience took place in the weight room of my junior high school, after class, during basketball practice. I say 'recognizably'; I'm not sure I recognized it at the time. We were working our way through various exercise stations, one of which required you to suspend yourself, with lifted legs, from two raised armrests; and I remember, as I closed my eyes with effort, the slow spread of strange sensations beginning to crowd the area between my thighs. It was basically a chemical reaction, nothing more, though I felt a little weak-kneed afterwards, and it may have been the same afternoon or another one, that a few of my teammates decided to make fun of the hair on my legs.

'Look at those man-legs,' somebody said, and I looked down at them and tried to work out if they were too hairy or not hairy enough. Then the other boys joined in. They might have been mocking me for their smoothness, and it seems typical of the age that I couldn't be sure and was simultaneously ashamed of being girlish and overdeveloped.

Sex talk, of course, was one of the things you had to learn to deal with in the locker room. On the basketball court, too. Practice is the only time in school a coach gets a class full of boys to himself, without any girls around to inhibit him.

'Been playin' with yourself last night?' one of our coaches would ask, whenever someone let a ball slip through his fingers.

General snickering. Coach Britten, we called him, though he was also the assistant principal and probably the first black man I had known in a position of authority. I was slightly terrified of him, of the shameful things he might accuse me of. Tall, straight-backed, he patrolled the baselines and sidelines in dark suits and well-shined shoes. Sometimes, when we had disappointed him, he would line us up against the wall of the gym and stand at centre court with a basketball in his hand.

'Stand still,' he called out. 'Keep still.'

Then he would take aim at one of our heads and we had to scatter out of the way. I don't remember anyone ever getting hit or hurt, though ball struck brick with terrific force. But he got his point across. Two points, really: sometimes you got to listen to me, and sometimes you got to trust your instincts. He considered it an important part of his job that he should teach us, among other things, to be men – in ways that teachers and parents couldn't or wouldn't. I've always assumed that one of the reasons I struggled in high-school sports is that I didn't learn.

Children who play sports go through a lot of coaches. I had soccer coaches and tennis coaches and basketball coaches, and not just one but several of each. I was a big kid. When I was four I played soccer on a team of six-year-olds. And before puberty hit, I could count on being as strong or fast as anyone I played against: middle-class white kids, mostly, more or less like me, whose parents signed them up to the YMCA leagues or the summer camp leagues and dropped them off in station wagons at the park or the gym, and picked them up afterwards. My own father, who has a talent for striking up conversations of mutual interest with salesmen and secretaries and strangers generally, often stayed late or came early to talk to my coaches. They talked about me.

In movies about American childhood it's common to show the bedroom bookcase of the teenage hero cluttered by marble trophies with gold-coloured statues on top. It isn't hard to win these trophies; sometimes you get them just for showing up. The marble is occasionally made out of stone, but the statues are always plastic and twisted into the uncomfortable-looking shape made by some kind of limb at the point of contact with some kind of ball. What they suggest, more than anything else, is a certain tone of voice: 'Well done!' 'You were great!' Whole childhoods filled with shiny encouragement.

Puberty hit in junior high. For two years, from the age of eleven to thirteen, I got bussed to school. Not that I knew I was being 'bussed'. Of course, I knew I had to catch a schoolbus in the morning, from a corner flanked by limestone columns just at the edge of my neighbourhood; and that I couldn't sleep much later than six if I wanted to make it. But I had no sense I was taking part in any kind of experiment with integration.

Construction on my junior high school, an ugly, pale brick, strangely windowless box built in east Austin next to a graveyard, finished shortly before I started going there: I was part of the first graduating class. The school was in the black part of town, which was separated by a highway from the centre, where we lived, and where the university campus was.

My bus passed under that highway, and then through some quiet residential neighbourhoods, made up of pretty, varied, Dutch-style timber houses like the houses I grew up among, but smaller and in worse repair, before it reached the artificial open spaces of the campus. I have a memory of looking out of the window and noticing, before we reached the school, things like rusting cars in the front yards and old tyres. But these strike me now as the kind of detail added afterwards by my imagination, for the sake of vividness. In any case, I never walked around these neighbourhoods and didn't know anybody who lived in them, at least not well.

A friend of mine, from my own neighbourhood, once described to me what he felt about going to school in east Austin: like salt in a pepper pot, he said. This sounds like something he might have heard and made use of, from an uncle or a friend of his father's; which isn't to say he didn't mean it. Probably he did mean it – why shouldn't he? I remember the line made me uncomfortable, maybe excessively uncomfortable, because I was shy as a kid about any kind of wrongdoing, which included all the varieties of wrong-feeling.

I think I tried to say something back that would make him feel my own discomfort, which might not have been the proper or even a useful thing to do. If I was unsympathetic, though, that was partly because I didn't feel what he felt – or rather, what he felt about going to a school with a majority of black kids I felt about going anywhere with a majority of any kind of kid. I should add that this friend of mine was a baseball fan and player, and it was still possible, in those days, to grow up playing and following American baseball without acquiring a fascination or admiration for, or envy of, black America; but I was a basketball kid and it wasn't possible for me.

On my seventh-grade basketball team, I was still one of the taller players, but something had changed about the rules of play. These weren't the boys I grew up with; I was a little scared of them. There were kids in that school with the kind of muscles you couldn't get without the drugs of puberty.

Our coach was an old football player named Schirpek. Texas is football-crazy, I mean the American kind, and most of the schools were too cheap to employ more than one guy to manage the boys' teams, and the people in power cared more about football than basketball, so they hired football guys. I mention this because football guys are different from basketball guys. They're shorter and bigger. Schirpek had the kind of shoulders you could run pulleys off. He looked a little stiff when he turned his head – like he needed oiling. When you're a skinny overgrown twelve-year-old boy you figure that men with real meat on them look down on boys without, as if the moral worth of any human being could best be calculated in pounds; and now that I'm a skinny overgrown thirty-four-year-old man, my sense is that that's probably true.

Schirpek had the same attitude to basketball that lots of people have towards art: I don't know anything about it, but I know what I like. He liked Pete Smith, a short, coffee-coloured boy who was the star of our team, because Pete could bully all the rest of us, and he could do it in games, too. Even in seventh grade, Pete had a kind of sullen temper that was not without its charms. He liked to indulge his own sense of dissatisfaction, and sometimes made a great show of being frustrated by life and the stupidity of the people around him – this is part of what made him our star. Whenever something went wrong he would make out that it was somebody else's fault, and after a while we couldn't help believing Pete was right.

I knew him for about six years, and played alongside him for four of those, but in all that time I probably had no more than a single conversation with him of any substance outside of a gym or a locker room. It's embarrassing, and maybe also shameful, how many of the black kids I got to know at school I got to know through basketball. How much of that had to do with what you might call a racial shyness, and how much with other kinds of shyness, I don't know.

My best friend on the team was a lanky, goofy boy named Lamont Melrose, whom I liked for two interconnected reasons: he spent about as much time as I did, during games, on the bench; and he did wonderful impersonations, including a pitch-perfect Bill Cosby at the dentist's office trying to feel his bottom lip. I say best friend: I was never invited to his house, and I'd be surprised if he remembers my name. But we sat on the bench and amused each other.

Lamont was a clown and Schirpek had no interest in clowns. Me he couldn't figure out. I was a tall kid, with quick feet and hands and a decent eye; obedient, too, and generally respectful, or at least quiet enough. I probably had a reputation as an honours student, conscientious about homework, good at tests, but I never amounted to much in the less predictable competitive environment of a game day. This puzzled him but did not worry him. Like many muscular middle-aged men, he seemed to carry around a certain amount of physical pain. Maybe that's why he didn't talk much, or talked reluctantly.

'Shoot!' he sometimes called out to me, during scrimmages, from his metal folding chair by the side of the court. 'Jest shoot it!'

So I shot it, and sometimes the ball went in and sometimes it didn't, and Schirpek would nod or shake his head accordingly.

I don't know why failure on the basketball court should have seemed to me more awful than other kinds of failure. My father may have had something to do with it; also, the fact that it was public. What was public, though, wasn't quite failure: I spent most games watching from the bench.

'You know what's wrong with this kid?' I could imagine Schirpek thinking. 'Psychology': as if it were a slightly dirty thing to have, like a top-shelf magazine.

All of this was a few years before the movie *White Men Can't Jump* came out, but I had grown up with the idea that dunking a basketball wasn't the kind of thing I could learn to do. It didn't seem very Jewish. I remember staring up at the rim, which is ten feet high, during practice, and thinking how impossible it was that I could ever do some of the things I had seen my teammates do. As it turns out, the psychological impossibilities were harder to overcome than the physical ones. By the time I was sixteen I could dunk a basketball comfortably enough, but I couldn't play my way into the starting line-up or perform under pressure when it counted.

My high-school coach, when I made the junior varsity team during my sophomore year, was a tall, tub-chested man named Don Caldwell. A light-skinned black man, another old football player, he taught Health and Driver's Ed and once smashed his fist up punching a kid's locker; he wore a cast for weeks. I sat in his class on the day the news broke that Magic Johnson had Aids. Caldwell abandoned the lesson and spent the hour discussing the announcement: he wanted us to know that something important had happened. Magic was one of the first black athletes to break the colour barrier of popular affection; for him to suffer this way struck Caldwell as a real setback.

I can't remember if he was proud of Magic for confessing to something he might have kept quiet about; or disappointed in him for being so promiscuously careless; or ashamed of him for other, harder to name reasons (there were rumours going around that Magic was gay). Coaches often treat health class as a kind of institutionally sanctioned pulpit from which to preach vague autobiographical 'life lessons', Caldwell among them. But I took from him the sense of a decent and solid view of what mattered in life and what didn't. He was a good high-school basketball coach: there can't be many jobs in America that give you so clear a perspective on youthful talent and the ways it runs to waste. I wanted him to like me. I also wanted him to think that I could play basketball.

The truth was, and this brings me to a part of the story that sets my modesty and my honesty at odds, I *could* play basketball. In the comfort of my backyard, on the tree-shaded half-court my father had built, I was a pretty decent player. I used to stay out, every day in summer and several hours after school, through the worst of the Texas heat and the sudden rope-thick downpours, working on my game. Basketball is one of those sports you can practise in isolation – almost everything you need to get good at you can get good at by yourself. But some things are lost in the transition from a private hobby to a public sport, and for most of my teenage years I suffered from the kind of humiliation you might expect of a forty-something-year-old who has been passed over for promotion at work. Really, I thought, I can do this job; you just need to give me a chance.

Coaches occupy a place in a boy's life somewhere between teacher and parent. They are partisan, as fathers are, but objective, too: it's their job to decide what you're worth and to put you to use. In some ways I was good at persuading people, but I couldn't persuade Caldwell that I could play. Race played a part in my shyness of him, I'm sure. There were also the physical facts: his arms were as thick as my legs; his legs as wide as my waist. He couldn't shoot a lick, and moved around the court, if forced for some reason into a demonstration, with the heavy, deliberate slowness of a vehicle that makes wide turns. But none of that mattered. There was something about his sheer size that suggested sober realism, as if he had decided, early on, that bulk and force were the qualities people most depend on in life, and worked decently to acquire them.

Game night was Friday night, which meant, for my father, a fifteen-minute drive by car to my high-school gym. There he would watch me, for two hours, amid the mild, sweaty, gossipy interest of a teenaged crowd, sit on the bench for two hours. Sometimes the league took us to remoter and more rural destinations, places like Del Valle and Copperas Cove, and high schools flying Confederate flags, where Pete Smith, among others, had to learn to put up with a certain amount of racial abuse. My father occasionally followed me even on these road trips, to sit with a few of the other dads; and I sat on the bench several rows beneath him, a little more nervous, watching what he watched: a high-school basketball game. Afterwards, when I couldn't face the ride home on the team bus, I asked permission to catch a lift from my father; and Caldwell let me go.

'Do you want me to talk to him?' my father asked me.

No, I said, no; and anyway, what could you possibly say?

He wanted to say his son just needed a chance to prove himself; that he had unrecognized talents. But this was a case his son needed to make for himself. It's possible, of course, that my father was basically right – that in spite of his bias, he saw me more clearly than Caldwell did, more intimately, certainly; and that a different coach could have put me to better use. I wonder now what Caldwell thought of me. My sense at the time was that he probably understood me well enough: that I was a 'good' kid, at least in terms of my schoolwork. A little nerdy, a little nervous; secretly, a bit of a complainer and coward. Even a snob. An impression no doubt confirmed when my father *did* talk to him, after practice one day, and suggested – I don't know what. Later that week Caldwell took me aside, gently and seriously.

'If you got something to say to me,' he said, 'you can say it yourself.'

I had failed even at complaining.

I have a memory from this period, of a Saturday afternoon; late summer, perhaps, before the school year started, amid the grassy and rundown neighbourhoods of east Austin. There might have been a pre-season tournament at my old junior high gym; maybe we just needed a place to practise. Caldwell took us around in his car, a big American car, I remember, with a bank of leather seats up front losing their stuffing; and we ate at a local diner I'd never been to, or got some food from a grocery store, and sat in the car or on the kerb of a residential street, fuelling up. His treat.

Most of that day is vague to me, and nothing of any significance seems to have happened, but the memory retains a few sharp glints of the real passage of time and I hoard it for that reason. I had never been out on a Saturday afternoon with these kids before, outside a gym; and we seemed to have so little to do that we pushed the hours along ourselves, telling jokes, eating junk, fooling around with a ball. We weren't winning or losing at anything, and so a few other qualities emerged. Probably the reason I remember this day is that I shed briefly some of the sense of difference that inhibited me.

Once, during my senior year, I ran into Pete Smith in the library after lunch, and we talked about university. All he hoped from basketball, he said, was a college education. I couldn't tell if this was something that he'd been taught to say; it might even have reflected what he'd been taught to feel. Pete was listed, in the high-school team sheet, at five feet eleven, and senior year is just about the peak of the selling season for a high-school talent. But if Pete reached five feet eleven, he was standing on tiptoe. He was also just about the quickest human being I've ever watched going past; not only quick, but comfortable in his speed, too, with all kinds of hesitation and misdirection at his disposal. He once made me fall back on my rear end just by standing in place, bouncing the ball, and pretending to commit to a first step.

I heard different stories about why he ended up where he did, at some east Texas university little known for its basketball programme. That he got in a fight in a public park, and bloodied some kid, scaring off major college interest. That his high-school sweetheart was pregnant with twins, so he decided to stick closer to home. I suspect, really, he was just a few inches short for the big time. Later, he drifted from one small college to another, chasing minutes; I don't know if he got his degree.

I mention this brief exchange as a context for the conversation that followed. At some point in my senior year I decided I'd had enough. What I had had enough of was the sense of my own daily failure, in practice and during games, a kind of frustration very intimate in its way and self-involving: you feel your own limits like you feel the tips of your fingers. I couldn't do what I knew I could do – this is the sort of line that used to run through my head like the rumble of a train on its track. The only problem with quitting was that I had to face Caldwell.

A month or so into the season I came to his office during school hours and knocked on his door. I had a strong, childish desire not to disappoint him. He was chewing peanuts when I walked in, reaching into his pocket and spitting the shells vaguely in the direction of the grey plastic standard-issue bin. Possibly part of an attempt to get off tobacco, I don't know: among the odd little life facts he explained to us, from the pulpit of his health class, was the right way to pronounce Pall Mall. I said I wanted to quit the basketball team. He asked me why. I had spent much of the week and the best part of the school day preparing an answer to this question. I said I wanted to concentrate on my college applications. Of course, I was partly hoping he would dissuade me, or try to; that he would tell me how much I mattered to the team, that he had big plans for me. But he nodded his head.

'Taking care of business,' he said, and palmed a few more nuts into his mouth. After spitting out the shells, he added that most of the guys on the team would do well to mind my example. 'That's what I tell them,' he repeated, 'you got to take care of business first. Knuckleheaded fools. They don't hear. They think they young forever.'

My excuse sounded, even to my ears, pretty thin; I was sure he'd see through it. College applications don't take up that much time, and the best thing I could have added to them was the fact that I played varsity basketball. I remember feeling, with something like relief, that he hadn't understood me after all – that he hadn't understood the dirty little secret of my 'psychology'. That my diffidence on court and in the locker room was only a kind of reserve, and not a particularly nice kind, either. That I was quitting out of cowardice. I couldn't stand up to the other boys, as I needed to, because of feelings that had something to do with class and might have had something to do with race. I was uncomfortable with any relations that didn't support my own sense of difference and superiority. This kind of arrogance was bad enough; what was really shameful, though, was that I didn't have the guts to act on it. At this distance, I can judge myself more sympathetically: it isn't easy being seventeen, and pride is sometimes the feeling you turn to for the relief of other, humbler feelings. I also suspect Caldwell understood me well enough. He thought I'd be fine; I wasn't the kind of kid he had to worry about, and he wished me well and told me to look in on him from time to time.

What happened over the next five months is still a source of regret. The high school I went to was a smallish, unremarkable state school in north Austin – the kind of high school that has the second worst football team in a city. But that year Pete Smith led the basketball squad to the state championships, and everybody went nuts for basketball. Players got recognized and approached in the school hallways, even those who never left the bench during games. When Caldwell complained about kids who thought they'd be young forever, this is what he meant by being young. There is a kind of celebrity high-school athletes can have which is more intense than any public celebrity. The world is smaller. The people curious about you see you in class; they know where your locker is. Not that all the publicity was confined to the school halls. Pete himself was named Central Texas Player of the Year. There was considerable media interest in him, and I heard, during cafeteria lunches, stories and rumours about his personal and home life. Meanwhile, I had my college applications to keep me busy.

In many American cities, sporting venues are the closest thing we have to civic monuments. The Frank Erwin Center in Austin looks like a great white upturned salad bowl and sits on top of a hill next to the larger and still grander football stadium. The semi-finals were held inside the salad bowl; it seats roughly twenty thousand. Twenty thousand people cheering you on: to be seventeen years old and a part of it. Instead, I sat with my friends in the upper decks and told whatever stories I could think of about playing with Pete Smith.

'Our' team, my old teammates, were clearly outmatched, but Pete himself was enough to keep us in contention, until a hard deliberate foul, late in the game, sent him on his back to the floor. For a minute nothing happened. We stood up, as if it was only a question of craning our necks to see, but all we could do was listen, and what we heard was the strange multitudinous unrest that is often described as a crowd collectively holding its breath. Then they dragged him to the side of the court and play continued. Caldwell had no one to turn to on the bench – it's possible, even, I might have been useful to him. By the time Pete came back on, to a sudden and vast and genuinely ecstatic applause, the game was out of reach.

A few years later, I saw Pete Smith again, in that same arena. His college was playing against Texas, the state university in Austin, which has plenty of money for sports, streaming in from rich alums and television contracts and sneaker deals. One of the major college programmes that had passed him over, coming out of high school. Sometimes the big state universities schedule games against minor local teams, as a kind of favour – it's an easy win for them and brings in a little TV revenue and national exposure for their opponents.

Pete looked very small beside the Texas players, as if he belonged to a different species. The game wasn't particularly close and the rows of empty stands had the cheap bright appearance of toys in an unused playroom. Few people stayed to the finish. But he still looked like the quickest player on the court, and I remember the feeling I used to have in high school, that there ought to be a better way of measuring talent than results, and another way of rewarding it, too.

After college, to put off the approach of ordinary adult life, I decided to try my hand at professional sports and spent a season in Germany playing basketball. This involves another, much longer story; but it's enough for me now to say that the season ended, and I went home to face the question I had postponed before. At some point I stopped by Coach Caldwell's office to say hello. I wanted to tell him that I had made it, in a small way, that I had overcome whatever it was that had held me back before. The truth is that professional sports left me with very much the same taste in my mouth as high-school sports: the taste of failure. (I wonder if I'm especially morbid, if in fact this isn't a general condition.) Regardless, I hoped to brag a little about what I had done – bragging was all it was good for.

Six years makes a great difference in a young man's life, but I remember him more or less unchanged: the same muscular, bald head and trunk-shaped arms. Perhaps he was even sitting on his office chair, chewing and spitting nuts. He was a little shorter than me – I noticed that when he stood up to take my hand. Maybe even a little shy of me. 'Is that so?' he said, when I gave him my news. 'Is that so?' Pleased; not especially surprised. He didn't often meet my eye. I was shy of him, too. It struck me it was really too late to impress him. There was a time it might have counted for something, but I had missed it, and there were other kids he had to worry about now. ■

Discover the
WRITER'S LIFE
in New York City

Over more than six decades of steady innovation, The New School has sustained a vital center for creative writing. Study writing and literature with The New School's renowned faculty of writers, critics, editors, and publishing professionals—in the heart of Greenwich Village.

Master of Fine Arts in Creative Writing
The New School's distinguished MFA program offers concentrations in fiction, poetry, nonfiction, and writing for children. Fellowships and financial aid are available.

Bachelor's Program in the Liberal Arts
Writing students seeking a BA may apply to the **Riggio Honors Program**. Students who are accepted into the program are eligible to receive a partial scholarship.

The Riggio Writing Honors Program is offered in conjunction with the Leonard and Louise Riggio Writing & Democracy initiative at The New School.

For more about the programs, call 212.229.5630 or visit us online.

www.newschool.edu/writing14

THE NEW SCHOOL

2008–2009

Director: Robert Polito

MFA FACULTY
Jeffery Renard Allen, Jonathan Ames, Robert Antoni, Susan Bell, Mark Bibbins, Susan Cheever, Elaine Equi, David Gates, Jennifer Michael Hecht, Ann Hood, Shelley Jackson, Zia Jaffrey, Hettie Jones, James Lasdun, David Lehman, Suzannah Lessard, David Levithan, Phillip Lopate, Patrick McGrath, Honor Moore, Sigrid Nunez, Meghan O'Rourke, Dale Peck, Darryl Pinckney, Robert Polito, Helen Schulman, Tor Seidler, Laurie Sheck, Darcey Steinke, Benjamin Taylor, Paul Violi, Sarah Weeks, Brenda Wineapple, Stephen Wright, Matthew Zapruder.

Associate Director: Jackson Taylor

MFA VISITING FACULTY
Max Blagg, Deborah Brodie, Patricia Carlin, Rosemary Deen, Marilyn Goldin, Vivian Gornick, Fannie Howe, Gary Indiana, Dave Johnson, Joyce Johnson, Mary Lee Kortez, Wendy Lesser, Sharon Mesmer, Marie Ponsot, David Prete, Lloyd Schwartz, Susan Shapiro, Frederic Tuten, Susan Van Metre, Vicky Wilson.

Associate Director: Luis Jaramillo

RIGGIO HONORS PROGRAM FACULTY
Jeffery Renard Allen, Catherine Barnett, Mark Bibbins, Patricia Carlin, Elizabeth Gaffney, Shelley Jackson, Zia Jaffrey, Suzannah Lessard, Greil Marcus, Sigrid Nunez, René Steinke, Lynne Tillman.

WRESTLERS

Photographs by Kevin Cummins

Words by John Naughton

Every six weeks or so, under the guidance of their leader, Andy Baker – or Scouse Lover to give him his ring moniker – the Runcorn Wrestling Academy puts on a show. They make little secret of the fact that the outcome is decided in advance – proceedings here more closely resemble a soap opera than a strict sporting contest. But that doesn't mean that events lack passion, either from the sell-out crowd of a couple of hundred locals, or among the wrestlers themselves. Nor is there any absence of skill, technique, pleasure or pain.

By day the members of the RWA resemble a typical cross-section of the labour force of this de-industrialized, service-driven area of Cheshire, in the north-west of England, best known for its bridge over the River Mersey and as the setting of the BBC sitcom, *Two Pints Of Lager & A Packet of Crisps*. Along with the unemployed, there are managers of KFC franchises, IT analysts, student hairdressers and IKEA employees.

But come showtime, they slip into spandex and assume their grappling alter egos, chosen carefully with the help of their drama coach, Melissa Reeves.

Soon, the makeshift ring at the Grangeway Community Centre echoes to the audience's catcalls at the falls of Element, Salvador Juan Disco, The Rocket Powered Love Machine and the current RWA champion, Party Time Angel D'Souza (Adam Foster to his friends).

Just as the wrestling is both real and fake, so too the RWA's approach combines the serious and the tongue-in-cheek. Their promotional videos for past contests such as 'A Midsummer's Night's Dream' or 'Dogs Of War' are a mixture of Shakespearean quotations and barely suppressed giggles as they beat the drum for the next showdown. For all their best attempts to terrify, this must be the friendliest assortment of assassins, pitbulls and beasts you could hope to meet. Baker, though, is adamant that they are more frightening on fight nights.

Their almost uniformly pallid skin and the occasional generous midriff is a far cry from the tanned and toned world of the American wrestling organization, World Wrestling Entertainment, which they hope to emulate. Nevertheless, this is one section of the sport that you can believe is free of steroids.

The glory days of British wrestling are behind us now. In the Seventies it was a fixture of ITV's *World of Sport* on Saturday afternoons and its practitioners could sell out venues twenty times the size of the modest hall where the RWA performs. Generations were introduced to a specialist vocabulary of wrestling holds: the suplex, the Boston crab and the full and half nelson. Men such as Kendo Nagasaki, Johnny Kwango, Big Daddy and the most feared hardman of them all, Les Kellet, were household names. The Queen watched them, Peter Blake painted them and Frank Sinatra told Martin Ruane, otherwise known as Giant Haystacks, that he thought that British wrestlers were the best entertainers in the world. But in December 1988 wrestling was axed from the schedules.

The one-time stars were cast adrift and audiences looked to America for an altogether more glamorous take on the sport, spearheaded by the World Wrestling Foundation. WWF (which subsequently had to change its name to WWE after it lost a court case with the World Wildlife Fund) was faster, bigger and louder. It quickly established its appeal in Britain. A 'Summerslam' at Wembley in 1992 was an 81,000 sell-out. Stars such as Hulk Hogan, Stone Cold Steve Austin and The Rock became global superstars.

Back in Runcorn, Andy Baker was sold. Inspired by the likes of the 'British Bulldog', the late Davey Boy Smith, a star of WWF born nearby in Golborne, he began wrestling as a teenager and in 2002 travelled to the United States to try his luck. After a spell in Kentucky at Ohio Valley Wrestling, putting on live shows and appearing in televised events, he returned to his hometown with the dream of founding his own academy. The Runcorn Wrestling Academy started up in September 2005.

'If it's something you love to do, it doesn't matter where you do it.'

Every Saturday he puts classes of children and adults through their paces, working on fitness, moves and what he calls ring psychology.

'You have to learn to tell a story when you're wrestling,' he explains. 'You're interacting with a crowd, learning to think on your feet when you're in there.'

His aim now is to find and fund RWA's own premises and to increase training to five days a week. At twenty-seven, he's young enough to try again in the States but seems happy enough with the progress he's making in Runcorn.

'Runcorn's not one of the poshest towns in Cheshire,' he admits, 'but this gives people the chance get fit, have fun and to live their dreams.'

'As soon as you come through that curtain you have to be a totally transformed person,' he reflects. 'Usually I'm laid back and dead quiet, but when I get out there I'm completely... different.' ■

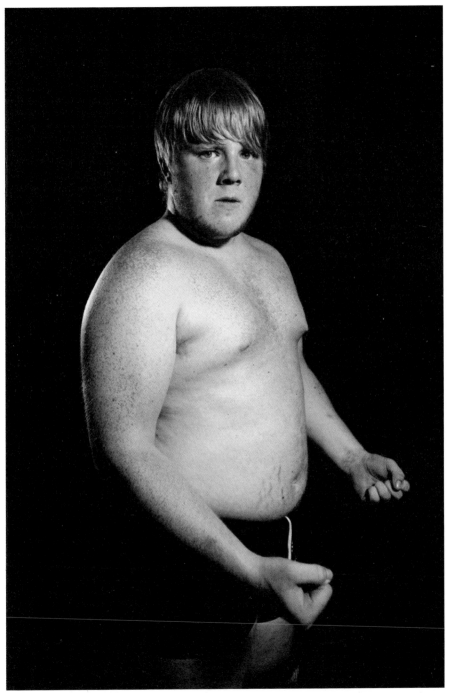

Greg Murray, 'Greg The Hatchet Hammond'

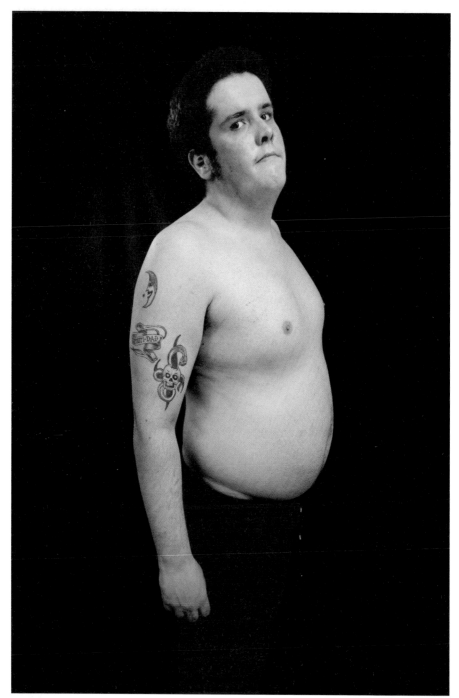

David Lowes, 'The Rocket-Powered Love Machine'

Justin Zane

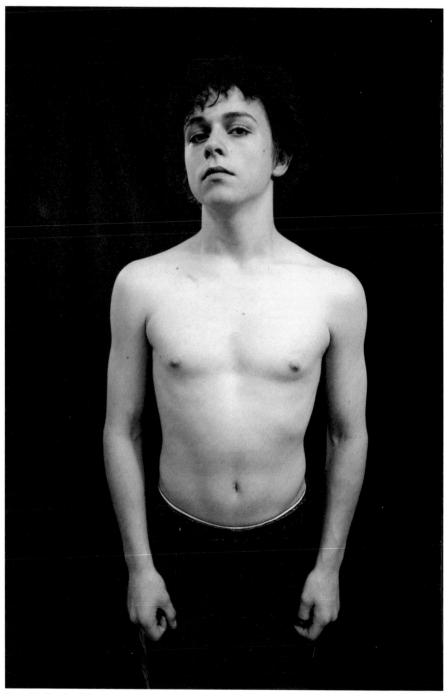

Troy McCarthy, 'Element'

Dan Evans, 'Heavy D'

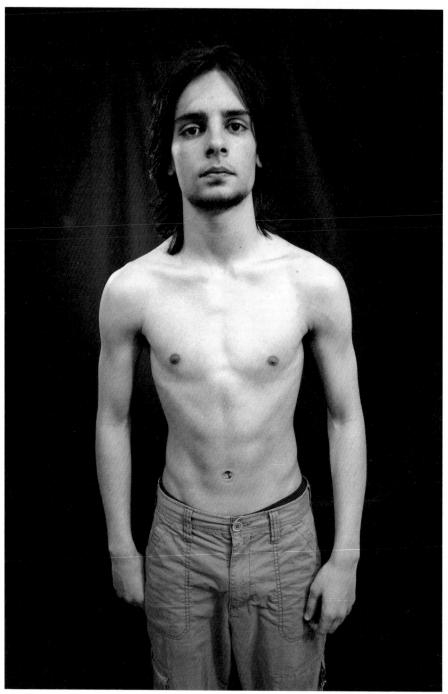

Chris Longmore

Adrian Cowan, 'A. C. Kage'

Andy Baker, 'Scouse Lover'

Evon Kirby, 'Purple Haze'

Sam Smitten-Downes, 'The Baby-Faced Pit Bull'

Daniel Brown, 'Paul Demo Gibson'

Steph Kinsh, 'Stacey K'

Daniel Kinsh, 'Deacon K'

Ryan Kinsh, 'Ricky F'

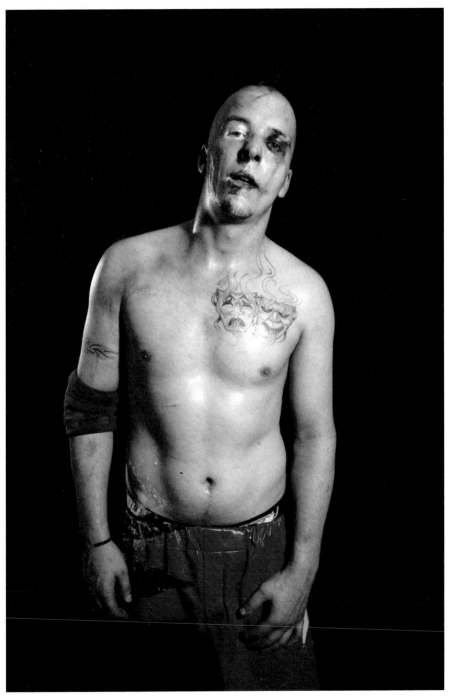

Richard Hearn, 'Joker Rico'

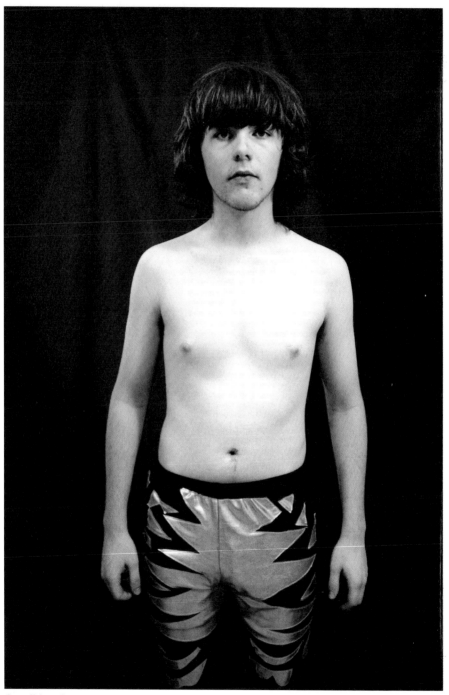

Cory Edwardson

Amy Watson, 'Pink Assassin'

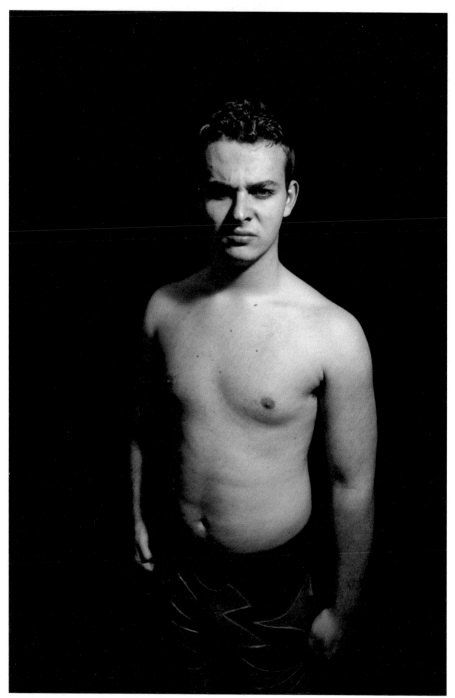

Chris Maguire, 'Reaper'

Troy McCarthy and Ryan Mounfield, 'DEMONi'

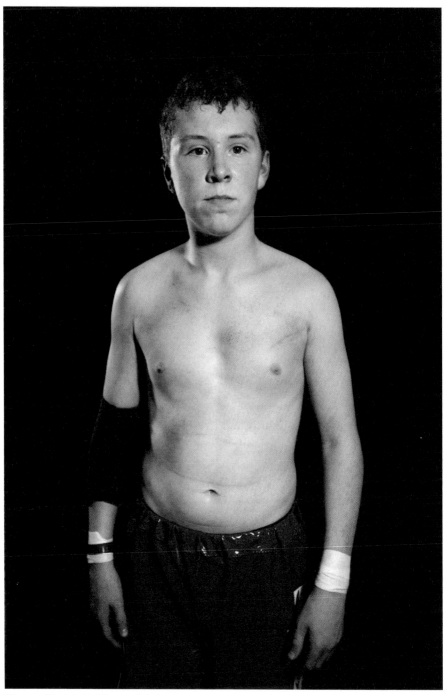

Thomas Hurdsfield, 'Tommy Ache'

Andrew Mason, 'Adrian Myers'

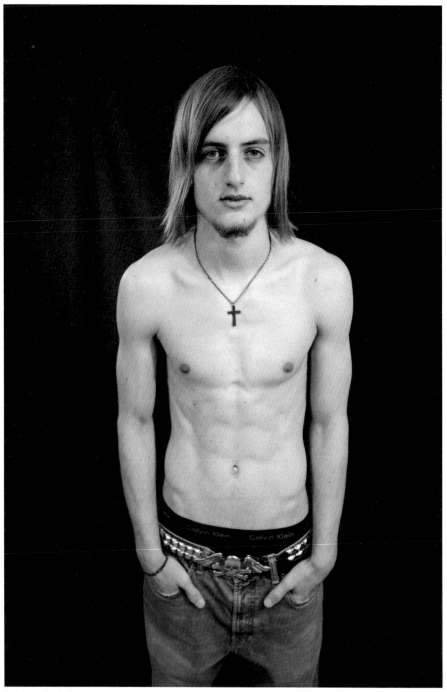

Jack Rea, 'Zak Diamond'

Adam Foster, 'Party Time Angel D'Souza'

WRITERLY BOOKS
From Chicago

The Writer as Migrant
Ha Jin

"In arguing for a literature that transcends language, Ha Jin challenges us to rethink the basics. How important are the words in which a work is written? What value ought we place on its translatability? Opinionated, provocative and poignant, *The Writer as Migrant* is real grist for the mill."—Gish Jen

Cloth $14.00

Obsession
A History
Lennard J. Davis

"From romantic obsessions to artistic obsessions to the neural underpinnings of obsessive-compulsive disorder, no aspect of the word or concept is left unexplored. Davis does not neglect the important question of why we medicate clinically obsessive people, yet laud those who are obsessed by their music, art, sports or other vocational calling. Beautifully written."
—*Kirkus Reviews*

Cloth $27.50

The Ancient Shore
Dispatches from Naples
Shirley Hazzard and Francis Steegmuller

"[Hazzard and Steegmuller] join in exquisite harmony to celebrate 'those of us who first came to Italy in the 1950s [and] were more than lucky; we were blessed.' Blessed, that is, with indelible impressions, for 'the day was an adventure of discoveries, mortal and immortal, inward or external, and occasionally somber.' A lovely book."—*Booklist*

Cloth $18.00

The Norman Maclean Reader
Edited and with an Introduction by O. Alan Weltzien

"This book introduces readers to Maclean's life and writing, collecting previously unpublished essays, stories, letters, and selections from his two books. . . . The man who emerges from these pages is funny, irreverent, and thoughtful. . . . This book will appeal to those who love good writing."
—*Library Journal*

Cloth $27.50

The University of Chicago Press　www.press.uchicago.edu

COMRADES

What life's like when you're the
last man standing

Michael Bywater

He denounced me for betraying him by getting a district nurse
in to dress his face where he'd torn it open falling over because
the lung cancer had moved to his brain. 'You've betrayed me,' he
roared, this tiny humped goblin, a skeleton in a skin, who still clung
to life with the toxic grip of a Komodo dragon on a tourist's leg.
'You betrayed me but I will *never* betray you! *Never*! I would *never*
tell Jane [my sister] about what you tried to make me do in my will!'
and then went on to outline, roaring at the top of his cracked and
tattered lungs, a scheme so subtle, so deceitful and vile, that my sister
didn't believe it and I wished I had thought of it.

He didn't close the window, though. It was already shut. All the
windows were shut, as if to keep the world out: black men, brown
men, Chinamen, women, people who had been to what he still called
'council schools', people who would ask him how he was and might
find out the answer was: *not too good; not too good at all.*

The orchard of dwarf apple trees and dwarf plums and dwarf pears
and full-sized crab apples, which are apparently dwarves at full size,

had gone: the one to which I had tied Dawn Fisher, and the one from which I had leapt on to Nigel Kenworthy, and the two (plums, one yellow and one red) behind which, at my seventh birthday party, I had shown Barbara Peake mine and she had shown me hers and I had been sent to my room and had to lie there as the May sunlight drifted through the curtains, listening to the sound of my own party from which I had been excluded. Nigel Widdowson and I had benefited from the clearance of these trees by making a giant bonfire on to which we had thrown several boxes of fireworks and three cans of hairspray before running like hell, which was precisely what erupted.

All gone. Only a faint singed pit from the hairspray bomb, and only then if you know where to look.

Garden levelled, like a war, then gone to couch grass and dandelions. Achingly redone houses over new firm fences, housing Asian general practitioners and well-to-do funeral directors, senior managers and men who had started with a lorry and now were in Logistics. It was all different.

But those weren't the differences my father saw, as the pressure on his brain slowly increased. He didn't see GPs, just like him but richer and browner-skinned, or the people who made their money from burying his mistakes. He saw terrible black men lurking. Gypsies lurking. Chinese drug fiends lurking. All lurking, to be in and out through an open window, cutting his throat and stealing the cat.

So the windows were closed, so he didn't have to shut them before he roared his rage at my betrayal, which was really his rage at his own death, finally inevitable, and at the cancers of his life. First, a malignant teratoma in his testis, which should have killed him at twenty-one, but they had it off and fired X-rays at him until he practically glowed, a hazard in the London wartime blackout where he was a medical student. Him and his best friend, Douglas Payne, a shrink who one day had a pop at my mother. She never forgave him (but never stopped talking about it either). But despite being an irradiated luminous glow visible to German bombers over the Thames Estuary, Dad went on to father two children and then, when we had left home, returned to the golf course and got his handicap back down to four again, when the prostate cancer got him. If it did; the day before the operation to remove his remaining ball, his PSA (which indicates prostate cancer) was 275. The day after, it was 2.75. The words 'decimal point' sprung into my mind and, I know, into his. But we didn't talk about it. What can you say?

And so he became a eunuch. And the loss of testosterone turned his bones into the bones of an old lady. He shrank. His vertebrae began to crumble. He became terrified in case, on the backswing, he simply split in two around the waist and missed an easy five-iron on to the green. And his hand curled into a claw: what laypeople like to call 'Dupuytren's contracture' and doctors 'Wanker's Hand'. 'What a waste,' he said. 'I can just slide my putter into my hand and it's fixed rigid. But it's no good. My golfing days are done.'

He said as much, at the last Freemasons' drinks party he went to. I accompanied him. He'd always been sad that I wouldn't join. 'You could be the organist,' he said, but I scorned the whole thing. 'I wouldn't be seen dead in the Freemasons,' I said. 'Idiots, with a trouser leg rolled up and bullshit aprons. It's not even a religion.' I was in my Roman Catholic phase, following my shadowy recusant ancestors in preference to my shadowy Jewish ones. Which gave me the right to sneer at my father: I hung out with a bunch of priests who wore not aprons but chasubles, and didn't even leaven things by rolling up their trousers.

I don't accuse myself of being a shit to my father because I think perhaps all men are shits to their fathers. That's our job. But when I went to the Freemasons' garden party – given in the grounds of a house once lived in by Byron, and now owned, I think, by a dentist and Byronista – I realized that these people were my father's friends. They seemed to like him. And indeed to respect him. He was *somebody*, and it had taken me forty-odd years to realize it. It had taken the death of my mother, about five months earlier, to make me have a look at my father.

So here he was with his friends, and there I was chatting to someone who was telling me what a fine fellow my old man was, and then I heard him talking to the organist, an ancient man with a bald sort of resurrected head like a benign Nosferatu and deaf as a brick (he died not long afterwards, leaving a vacancy which I could have made my father unspeakably proud by filling, except I wasn't a Freemason).

'Oh, not a lot,' my father was shouting to the organist. 'Of course, my wife passed away a few months ago but other than that, pretty fair, you know, pretty fair.'

It wasn't pretty fair, though, because he and my mother had had plans to travel – he'd worked until he was seventy to build up his pension – and they had already started having rows about where they were going when the hepatitis C got her. A doctor, and he couldn't save his wife. And then it was his turn, and the prostate cancer which he'd ignored because he was busy looking after his wife – a termagant with a failing liver transplant is no small handful; he even had to shut the windows for her, before she could yell at him about Vienna versus Las Vegas – and the testicle cancer from the war having had both his balls off him, his bones started to crumble and he stopped playing golf and stopped going to the Masonic lodge meetings because he didn't want people to see him like this.

As though it were going to get better.

As though they would care.

Friends are who you shouldn't mind seeing you...*like this*.

(But no they're not. The ones who you don't mind seeing you like this – however 'this' may be – aren't friends. They're comrades. That's different.)

And then the lung cancer got him. What he had left after his wife had died and the Masons had been given the go-by and the golf had to stop was fretting. And the tumour got into his brain and pressed down and the things he needed for fretting were semi-disabled. To fret, you need short-term memory. You need to make lists. You need to write things down to fret about them. The cancer got at the very part of his brain that he needed to do those things. All he could fret about was his inability to fret, and his inability to understand his inability to fret.

No wonder he denounced me. He must have been terrified. Shortly before this all came down upon him he said, *All my friends are dead and there's nobody to talk to. Gordon Griffin is dead and Derek Bussens is dead and old Basil Treece is dead and Richard Leighton is dead and the one I really miss is Douglas Payne.*

None to see him out. Last man standing, and that with difficulty. No wonder he roared.

O ne thing I sensed from earliest childhood was that friendship was *women's work*.

Each morning my father would leave the house, walk up the Park Steps, down the hill to East Circus Street and open up the surgery. This in itself was odd; not that he opened up the surgery, because he was a family doctor and it would have been peculiar if a family doctor *didn't* open up the surgery each morning, but because his partner was my grandfather, who lived above the shop but was a man of odd Victorian habits. He seldom rose before nine in the morning, breakfasted in his cavernous subterranean kitchen, shaved at his leisure (the bathroom cabinet was a health-and-safety nightmare, its shelves stacked with thousands of used razor blades piled precariously on worn-out stubs of Erasmic shaving sticks and lubricated with spillings of Violet Hair Oil) and seldom began to see his patients until gone ten. Until my grandfather retired, aged eighty, he had the Big Surgery and my father was relegated to a small room on a landing halfway down the kitchen stairs. There was a large bottle of mercury there, for some purpose I can't imagine – something, perhaps, to do with syphilis – which I was allowed to play with in slack periods; there was a desk and two chairs and a lash-up examination couch made out of a window seat in an alcove overlooking the sooty urban garden, in which the housekeeper's dog, a yellow mutt with a cankered ear, cavorted arthritically with lumps of anthracite from the coke pile beside its kennel.

This was my father's professional domain, while my grandfather, in the Big Surgery, occupied a room with a roll-top desk, a big partners' kneehole desk, a bentwood chair and a gas ring for sterilizing syringes. There were two corner cupboards stuffed with drug-peddlers' samples ('I think I may have just the thing for you, Mrs Beelby') and a letterhead embosser which I called The Djeeep because of the squeaking noise it made as it worked.

You didn't need much to be a doctor in those days, but my father and grandfather were minimalist even by the standards of the time. No practice nurse; no incentive schemes for encouraging patients to claim benefits, give up smoking, lose weight, get their blood pressure down, develop sexual continence, take exercise, attend regular Well Woman check-ups (let alone Well Man check-ups, which God forbid) or any of the other ruses of a well-meaning state which now seem increasingly sinister. You went to the doctor when you were ill and he decided if you were ill enough to see a proper doctor; and, if so, he wrote a brief note (Djeeeep!) saying something like 'Query leg?' and sent them up the hill to the Ropewalk (right) or the General Hospital (left) to see someone with whom he was invariably on first-name terms. Jimmy Neil, Gilroy Glass, Sheehan (who didn't seem to have a first name): these and their kind were the men in my father's life and whether they were friends or not was debatable. They were colleagues: professional men in the same line of work; required by their contracts to live within half a mile of the hospital, their lives naturally coincided both professionally and socially, whether at the regular meetings of the Medico-Chirurgical Society, where some visiting luminary would ventilate on sprue, *tabes dorsalis*, tube pedicles or malaria, or at the less regular but more formal Masonic assemblies of the Royal Sussex Lodge, to which most of them seemed to belong, accessorizing their professional broadcloth suits with a decorative pinafore and white gloves carried in a special little leather case, long and narrow.

Many years later, I lived near the great Masonic temple in Covent Garden and regularly saw otherwise unremarkable men walking along of an evening with their little cases, and instantly I would be carried back to my childhood: my father having an extra evening shave, then, later, coming back, mildly lit up, and creeping into my bedroom to kiss me goodnight, smelling of brandy and Havanas and handing me my customary souvenir, the aluminium tube of a Romeo y Julieta or a Partagas still heady with the scent of Cuban tobacco and the magical thin sheet of cedarwood which had wrapped and cosseted the cigar. Of these olfactory ghosts, my earliest memories of male friendship were formed; or, rather, not of friendship but of *sociability*. Even though I was quite incapable of rationalizing the distinction, I knew it was there. Male sociability was part of what, in the eighteenth century, they'd have called 'the conversible world'. It was something that involved food and drink and smoking, and a certain formality, and it was part not of the intimate world of family life, but of what men did during the day. It wasn't so much that men went out into the world but that the world, and being out in it, was where men *belonged*, and they came home in between.

Then there was the Royal Overseas League, 'the Overseas' for short. It occupied a splendid eighteenth-century house which stood alone beneath the shadow of the General Hospital with its great red-brick rotunda – circular wards so that nobody could get away with anything under the all-seeing eye of Sister, as I was to discover when, later, I was a regular visitor with footballing head-kicked-in episodes (I was myopic and played in goal, always good for a trip to casualty) and other childhood incidents like riding my bike smack into a tree in the garden, then, while showing Bryn Maltby and Richard Beardall how it had happened, riding smack into the even less yielding ironwork of my swing.

The Overseas stood alone because the houses surrounding it had been bombed during the Second World War and nobody had decided what to do about it. (I drove past the place recently and it was being turned into a student hostel; but it still stood alone. They had decided what to do about much of the rest of the city – destroy it – but perhaps the difficulty was that the Germans had destroyed that particular bit, and since destruction was the only shot in the council planners' locker, they had found themselves pre-empted and impotent.)

Every Sunday lunchtime, my mother and father would go to the Overseas, as would the others: the physicians and surgeons and lawyers and professional men, where they belonged: out of the house, clubbable, agents in the world. They all brought their wives but, in memory now, it seems to me that they brought their wives in the sense that women now bring their daughters to work, to see what mummy does during the day; this was an excursion for the wives, a continuation of life for the men.

The nose doesn't lie. When you smell something it passes straight into the brain without any intermediate processing. Unlike vision or hearing, olfaction is unmediated. It's the real thing, and it works both ways: just as a scent on the air can take us back in time instantaneously and often so overwhelmingly as to be disorienting, so memory can recall smells we had consciously forgotten, and when I think of the Overseas on a Sunday lunchtime I know in my olfactory memory that all those wives contributed a clamorous, heady accord, not just of Joy and Shocking de Schiaparelli and Chanel N° 5 and Chant d'Arômes and indeed (these being the days before Mum Rollette) of *women*…but all the same, what my mind's nose hurls back at me, brooking no debate, is the smell of beer and whisky, of potato crisps (them ones with the little twist of salt in waxed blue paper), of Player's cigarettes and Will's Whiffs and tarry Balkan tobacco, overlaid with the faintest hint of Old Spice and Imperial Leather and, indeed again, of *men*.

The Overseas was outside, in the world. It was for men.

For women, things were different. Even as a child I was aware (though I couldn't have explained it) that the process worked in the opposite direction. Women's external life, though it occupied less time, was somehow not only more intricate, a webwork of friends and acquaintances and gossip and precise calibrations and lookings-after and fallings-out, but also an extension of what they did at home.

My mother and her friends traded, not in fact or money, nor in Masonic ritual or the liturgies of the golf course, nor the law or the *materia medica*, but in *themselves*, and in their feelings and those of each other, just as they did with their children at home. When the men went out together, it was as though their friendship – their sociability, their *commensality* – somehow negated, temporarily, the very existence of their homes; as though, clustered round whatever it was they were clustered round (and men are always clustered round *something*), they were temporarily elevated to the status of a nomadic tribe, gloriously homeless. When I went out with my mother, and we met her friends in the coffee shop of Griffin & Spalding's department store, it was quite the opposite, as though the coffee shop became an aggregate of all their homes; as though these women (and looking back, they were young and pretty and moderately well-to-do women, none of them over thirty-five and all dressed up for the occasion) carried *Home* with them, like snails – powdered snails, in New Look dresses and Vitapointe hairdos – with an intricate but invisible shell.

And it was clear that they were friends in a way that the men, their husbands, were not. They were with each other without an agenda. And unlike the men their attention was not upon some common pursuit, but upon each other. The men were sending up signals, keeping on course; the women were doing what we'd now call *surfing*: travelling through an infinite network of intimate concerns, with no more goal than that of a man like me, now, putting off the business of getting words on paper by roaming around the Internet to see what I can see. Following the trail. Keeping an eye on things. Finding out how the network stitches together. Seeing what a remarkable world it is. The speculations of the net-surfer are as trivial yet simultaneously as diverting and as crucial as the conversation of those pretty women with their invisible home-shells, and if the proper study of mankind is man, then the wives knew something the husbands did not.

It's not what men do. Men go out to play, and the reason men go out to play is perhaps that men's friendships are about comradeship, not about friendship. Men united against a common enemy or in a common cause, and if there isn't one, we'll make one up: getting over the mountain pass in record time, going round in one under par, studying form and placing the bet, getting out there like the old men on the river in New Brunswick where I used to go salmon-fishing: rich old dudes in ancient Pendleton shirts with long built-cane rods and old English Hardy reels, men so rich they had heart conditions and the smokehouse didn't add salt. Men who would sit in the Canadian mists for hours at a stretch, silent in their canoes, at best monosyllabic, exchanging few words yet knowing each other as well as they knew their battered fishing rods or their ancient L. L. Bean duck boots.

Comrades.

My grandfather, it was said, had no friends. My mother, who could not abide him, said it was because he was a cantankerous bloody-minded evil self-centred snobbish egotistical old swine who, after a bit, she wasn't going to have in the house and she could see why his wife died early, leaving him alone for over a quarter of a century. My father expressed no opinion on the question. 'My mother did all that sort of thing,' he said, 'and there were plenty of friends when we were growing up. And after my mother died, Dad used to go and see a lot of his old patients.'

So he did. He would drive out to where his patients had retired to – little terraced houses in what would now be called slums, cleared for yuppies or for heavily patronized clients of the all-seeing state – and he would have tea, and they would tell him how the new doctor wasn't a patch on him, and then he would go for a walk: showerproof coat, Borsalino fedora (or, later on, as he became less aware of his appearance, a terrible Trevira faux-tweed golfing trilby), walking stick and, trotting at his heels, the ghosts of long-dead spaniels.

But *friends*? No. My mother used to say (though we have established her unreliability as a witness; even as a hostile witness, she was unreliable) that my grandparents' friends only tolerated them because of my grandmother – Euphemia May Vallance, of Morningside and Jenner's (the Edinburgh equivalent of Griffin & Spalding, where respectable Morningside ladies used to meet for coffee and the pleasures of mutual lip-pursing) – who was 'a saint'. She it was who would lure the friends around for dinner, though God knows how; my grandmother was a Good Plain Scottish Cook whose idea of a decent dinner was tripe and onions and mashed potato with white sauce on a white plate, and their cook looked up to my grandmother in the same way a short-order chef might look up to Jamie Oliver, except perhaps without the urge to punch the perky smug bastard in the cheeky grin.

And she it was, too, who would be on the telephone the following morning to apologize for my grandfather's behaviour. (In some re-tellings, the telephone would be replaced with trudging, and the trudging would take place in the snow, and my grandmother would become 'that little old lady' but articulated in an emphatic, *grand guignol* fashion that you will only ever hear from a Jewish woman articulating *someone else's* troubles. 'That. *Little*. OLD. *Lady*. Trudged...*five*. MILES. In the. *Snow*. Uphill To ap*OL*ogize. And then. She – trudged. *All the way*. Back. *UPHILL*. With her *leg*. Suchacantankerousswinehewaslikehitlergodknowshowshestoodithe broughthertoanearlygrave. *HE DID*. No Wonder He Had No Friends Not A Friend In The World.')

I never really listened to the last bit because, shamefully, I would be too preoccupied with imagining my grandmother trudging all the way back uphill *without* her leg. And then having to go back for it. Uphill. And it would have been my grandfather's fault.

Well now. I have misled you, and myself.

Long before feminism, we men occupied the moral low ground. It was just that men like my grandfather never quite realized it.

And probably he never realized he didn't have friends either. My father recently had all the old movies – back to the old Pathé nine-five, centre-sprocket films – transferred to DVD and they tell a different story. There is my grandfather, inconceivably young (though he must have been forty), imitating an Ouija mystic at the dining table, the family there, friends there ('Look! There's Olive Barclay! She's dead now, of course') laughing; there he is, filmed by my uncle, my father's older brother, who died before I was born: walking with friends, three of them, walking sticks swinging in unison, deep in conversation. There he is with Old Doctor Malkin, with whom they shared Parkie – Nanny Parkin – turn and turn about, according to who had an infant at the time. There he is: not an outcast at all. A man with friends.

But look a little closer and we're back to a version of the Overseas on a Sunday morning. The idea of a friendship passing the love of women would have been incomprehensible to him. It simply was not, I think, in his emotional repertoire. Laying down your life for your friends was something he saw plenty of – he was a Regimental Medical Officer in the Great War – but also something he thought foolish and in its way obscene. It was from him that I first heard Kipling's monstrous, scorching couplet from 'Epitaphs of the War', as violent as a Mills bomb in the face:

> If any question why we died,
> Tell them, because our fathers lied

… and that was all that needed to be said about it.

Otherwise he kept silent, except for once when a boy I was fond of at school (I am ashamed to admit I can no longer remember his name, though I can see his face clearly) died of leukaemia. 'You'll lose people,' he said. 'You know what it's like now. There's more of it to come and it gets harder.' Apart from that, he was like the Watchman who begins that greatest of tragedies, the *Oresteia* of Aeschylus, two and a half thousand years old: an old man on a wet roof in the dark, waiting for a signal, a beacon in the night. *There's an ox on my tongue…for them as knows, I'll speak; for the rest…I know nothing.*

He had lost his wife. He had lost his elder son. His younger son, my father, kept him company at work and outside work. And on he went. His friendships were an extension of work, and those that weren't (apart from the sightly gruesome curiosity of the hockey-team photograph, where he crossed out the faces of his old schoolfriends as they died), were an extension of family. My grandmother did that, and when she died, it stopped.

Women's work.

He ended his days in a nursing home with a room-mate, Mr Wise. Mr Wise was deaf and my grandfather blind. They argued like wolves over everything. You could hear the shouting as you approached their room. And when Mr Wise died, my grandfather pined for their rows, and within a few weeks was dead himself. It wasn't quite laying down your life for your friend, but it wasn't far off, either.

Something clicks, and it starts to make sense, and you realize you're rooming with a bugger and the bugger dies and then you do. Okay? Friendship or comradeship? Is this about us, or about some common cause, however imaginary it may be?

The more you think about it, the harder it gets to tell the two apart. ■

M y father set store by formal portraits like this one. In fact it looks positively stagey. The book under Dad's hand is certainly real (it has his name embossed on the spine), but looks more like an actor's prop than a professional resource. His gaze, stern but not inhuman, addresses the middle distance – the truth will not elude him. It's as if he was already contemplating the *Independent*'s verdict to come. Fair, but firm.

This photograph must stand in for another, taken when he was made a High Court Judge in 1969. The idea of a photo shoot for new judges has an element of comedy, as if this was a timid British version of the ecclesiastical fashion show in *Fellini's Roma*, but he approved of the resulting image. It became (as it were) his official photograph. He had many copies made and signed them in the white area created by his ermine cuff. Ava Gardner might have done something similar.

Dad loved his success and the status it brought. He was a rarity among High Court Judges at the time in not having been to public school. His father had been a farmer and local councillor in a small Denbighshire town (he also ran the Post Office). Dad spoke Welsh, but took care to shed any trace of a regional accent. He was christened William Lloyd Jones, but was persuaded by his father (who stumped up the fee) to add the family name of Mars by deed poll during the war. It was supposed to protect him through the dangers of Russian convoys. It certainly protected him after the war from having his name quickly forgotten at a time when lawyers were not allowed to advertise.

Dad loved the rituals of the law. His first years on the bench coincided with the passing away of the old system of courts, and he was the last judge to dispense justice in a number of small Welsh assizes. It was traditional in some assize towns, if there were no criminal cases on the list, to present the judge with a pair of white kid gloves. One courtroom was so small that the defendant could have leaned out of the dock and pinched the judge's nose.

At Christmas Dad gave a copy of his official photograph, framed and signed, to each of his sons. We mocked Dad's egotism among ourselves. I certainly felt that I didn't need to be reminded what he

The Honourable Sir William Mars-Jones

looked like, since I was still living under his roof. I put my trophy on a high shelf, and at some stage laid it face down.

Dad's identification with his role was wholehearted. He referred to his fellow judges as his 'brothers' ('my brother Aubrey was saying…'), and didn't respond to our pretended puzzlement ('but Dad, isn't your brother called David…?'). He was once heard on the phone negotiating with American Express about how many of his honorifics – MBE, LLB – could be crammed on to his Gold Card. After tough negotiation he agreed to surgery on his first name and became Sir Wm. Very few people would see the form of words on that Gold Card – that wasn't the point. His first name he had been given. Those qualifications had been earned.

What he liked about roles was exactly what other people dislike: the way they fix relations. He preferred formal occasions to intimate ones, and a staged portrait like this one to anything a snapshot might reveal.

There were times when he employed one of his sons as his Marshal, supposedly so that we could witness the workings of the law. He enjoyed being addressed as 'Judge', and indicated that there was no real reason to revert to 'Dad' when the working week was over.

He had enough of a sense of humour to relish the cheeky headline in a North Wales newspaper (LOCAL BOY MAKES BARD) when he was made a member of the Gorsedd at the National Eisteddfod one year. He thought us merely callow when we pointed out that one of his sister Bards that year was Mary Hopkin, honoured for her services to warbling, and that the wet-weather regalia for Druids included natty white shorty Wellingtons.

As an experienced lawyer Dad knew the value of surprise in an argument, and it was during a wrangle over something quite different that he announced he had found my copy of the signed photograph in its disgraced position and had confiscated it. I rather think I begged for its return, but he told me he had given it to someone who would appreciate it more. I was too mortified to call his bluff, though as the signature on that creamy cuff was 'Dad' there were only so many places it could go. ∎

MAN AND BOY

Emma Donoghue

O ff your tuck this morning, aren't you? That's not like you. It's
the chill, perhaps. These March winds come straight from the
Urals, up the Thames, or so they say. No, that's not your favourite
Horse Guards playing, can't fool you; you never like it when they
change the band. Fancy a bun? You'll feel the better for a good
breakfast. Come along, have a couple of buns… Please yourself, then.
Maybe later, after your bath.

I had some unpleasantness with the Superintendent this morning.
Yes, over you, my boy, need you ask? He's applied to the Trustees for
permission to buy a gun.

Calm down, no one's going to shoot you, or my name's not
Matthew Scott. But let it be a warning. I don't mean to lay blame,
but this is what comes of tantrums. (*Demented rampages*, the
Superintendent calls them.) Look at this old patched wall here; who
was it that stove it in? To err is human and all that, but it still don't
excuse such an exhibition. You only went and hurt yourself, and
you're still not the better for that abscess.

Jumbo. at the Zoo. Barnum's famous elephant.

Jumbo at London Zoo, early 1880s

Anyway, the Superintendent has an iddy-fix that you're a danger to the kiddies, now you're a man, as it were. Oh, you know and I know that's all my eye, you dote on the smalls. You don't care for confinement, that's all, and who can blame you? I can always settle you with a little wander round the Gardens to meet your friends. But the Superintendent says, 'What if you're off the premises, Scott, when the musth next comes on Jumbo? No other keeper here can handle him; every time I assign you an assistant, the creature terrorizes him and sends him packing. It's a most irregular state of affairs, not to mention the pungency, and stains, and…well, engorgement. That Member's wife almost fainted when she caught sight!'

I pointed out you could hardly help that.

'Besides, bull Africans are known for killing their keepers,' he lectured me. 'In one of his furies, he could swat you down with his little tail, then crush you with his skull.'

'Not this elephant,' I said, 'nor this keeper.'

Then he went off on a gory story about a crazed elephant he saw gunned down in the Strand when he was knee-high, 152 bullets it took, he's never been the same since. Well, that explains a lot about the Superintendent.

I assure you, my boy, I stood up for you. I looked the old man in the watery eye and said, 'We all have our off days. But Jumbo's a cleanly, hard-working fellow, as a rule. I have never felt afraid of him for one moment in the seventeen years he's been in my care.'

He muttered something impertinent about that proving my arrogance rather than your safety. 'I believe it's gone to your head, Scott.'

'What has, Superintendent?'

'Jumbo's fame. You fancy yourself the cock of the walk.'

I drew myself up. 'If I enjoy a certain position in this establishment, if I was awarded a medal back in '66, that is due to having bred, nursed and reared more exotic animals and birds than any other living man.'

He pursed his lips. 'Not to mention the fortune you pocket from those tuppenny rides— '

The nerve! 'Aren't I the one who helps the kiddies up the ladder, and leads Jumbo round the Gardens, and makes sure they don't topple off?' (By rights the cash should be half yours, lad, but what use would it be to you? You like to mouth the coins with your trunk and slip them into my pocket.)

The Superintendent plucked at his beard. 'Be that as it may, it's inequitable; bad for morale. You're all charm when it earns you tips, Scott, but flagrantly rude to your superiors in this Society, and as for your fellow keepers, they're nervous of saying a word to you these days.'

That crew of ignorami!

'I have plenty of conversation,' I told him, 'but I save it for those as appreciate it.'

'They call you a tyrant.'

Well, I laughed. After all, I'm the fifteenth child of seventeen, no silver spoons in *my* infant mouth, a humble son of toil who's made good in a precarious profession, and I need apologize to nobody. We don't mind the piddling tiddlers of this world, do we, boy? We just avert our gaze.

There's a crate sitting outside on the grass this morning. Pitch-pine planking, girded with iron, on a kind of trolley with wheels. Gives me a funny feeling. It's twelve feet high, as near as I can guess; that's just half a foot more than you. Nobody's said a word to me about it. Best to mind my own business I suppose. This place – there's too much gossip and interference already.

It'll be time to stretch a leg soon, boy. The kiddies will be lined up outside in their dozens. They missed you yesterday, when it was raining. Here, kneel down and we'll get your howdah on. Yes, yes, I'll remember to put a double fold of blanket under the corner where it was rubbing. Aren't your toenails looking pearly after that scrub I gave them?

There's two men out there by the crate now, setting up some kind of ramp. I don't like the looks of this at all. If this is what I think it is, it's too blooming much—

I'm off to the Superintendent's office, none of this *Please make an appointment*. Here's a sack of oats to be getting on with. Oh don't take on, hush your bellowing, I'll be back before you miss me.

Well, Jumbo, I could bloody spit! Pardon my French, but there are moments in a man's life on this miserable earth—

And to think, the Superintendent didn't give me so much as a word of warning. Just fancy, after all these years of working at the Society together – after the perils he and I have run, sawing off that rhinoceros's deformed horn and whatnot – it makes me shudder, the perfidiousness of it. 'I'll thank you,' says I, 'to tell me what's afoot in the matter of my elephant.'

'*Yours*, Scott?' says he with a curl of the lip.

'Figure of speech,' says I. 'As keeper here thirty-one years, man and boy, I take a natural interest in all property of the Society.'

He was all stuff and bluster, I'd got him on the wrong foot. 'Since you inquire,' says he, 'I must inform you that Jumbo is now the property of another party.'

Didn't I stare! 'Which other party?'

His beard began to tremble. 'Mr P. T. Barnum.'

'The Yankee showman?'

He couldn't deny it. Then wasn't there a row, not half. My dear boy, I can hardly get the words out, but he's only been and gone and sold you to the circus!

It's a shocking smirch on the good name of the London Zoological Society, that's what I say. Such sneaking, double-dealing treachery behind closed doors. In the best interests of the British public, my hat! Two thousand pounds, that's the price the Superintendent put on you, though it's not as if they need the funds, and who's the chief draw but the Children's Pal, the Beloved Pachydermic Behemoth, as the papers call you? Why, you may be the most magnificent elephant the world has ever seen, due to falling so fortuitously young into my hands as a crusty little stray, to be nursed back from the edge of the grave and fed up proper. And who's to say how long your poor tribe will last, with ivory so fashionable? The special friend of our dear Queen as well as generations of young Britons born and unborn, and yet the Society has flogged you off like horse meat, and all because of a few whiffs and tantrums!

Oh, Jumbo. You might just settle down now. Your feelings do you credit and all that, but there's no good in such displays. You must be a brave boy. You've got through worse before, haven't you? When the traders gunned down your whole kin in front of you—

Hush now, my mouth, I shouldn't bring up painful recollections. Going into exile in America can't be half as bad, that's all I mean. Worse things happen. Come to think of it, if I hadn't rescued you from that wretched Jardin des Plantes, you'd have got eaten by hungry Frogs during the Siege of '71! So best to put a brave face on.

I just hope you don't get seasick. I reminded the Superintendent you'd need two hundred pounds of hay a day on the voyage to New York, not to speak of sweet biscuits, potatoes, loaves, figs and onions, your favourite... You'll be joining the Greatest Show on Earth, I suppose that has a sort of ring to it, if a vulgar one. (The Superintendent claims travel may calm your rages, or if it doesn't then such a huge circus will have 'facilities for seclusion', though I don't like the sound of that.) No tricks to learn, I made sure of that much: you'll be announced as 'The Most Enormous Land Animal in Captivity' and walk round the ring, that's all. I was worried you'd have to tramp across the whole United States, but you'll tour in your own comfy railway carriage, fancy that! The old millionaire's got twenty other elephants but you'll be the king. Oh, and rats, I said to pass on word that you're tormented by the sight of a rat, ever since they half ate your feet when you were a nipper.

Of course you'll miss England, and giving the kiddies rides, that's only to be expected. And doing headstands in the Pool, wandering down the Parrot Walk, the Carnivora Terrace, all the old sights. You'll find those American winters a trial to your spirits, I shouldn't wonder. And I expect once in a while you'll spare a thought for your old pa—

When you came to London, a filthy baby no taller than me, you used to wake screaming at night and sucking your trunk for comfort, and I'd give you a cuddle and you'd start to leak behind the ears...

Pardon me, boy, I'm overcome.

Today's the evil day, Jumbo, I believe you know it. You're all ashiver, and your trunk hovers in front of my face as if to take me in. It's like some tree turned hairy snake, puffing warm wet air on me. There, there. Have a bit of gingerbread. Let me give your leg a good hard pat. Will I blow into your trunk, give your tongue a last little rub?

Come along, bad form to keep anyone waiting, I suppose, even a jumped-up Yankee animal handler like this 'Elephant Bill' Newman. (Oh, those little watery eyes of yours, lashes like a ballet dancer – I can hardly look you in the face.) That's a boy; down this passage to the left; I know it's not the usual way but a change is as good as a rest, don't they say? This way, now. Up the little ramp and into the crate you go. Plenty of room in there, if you put your head down. Go on.

Ah now, let's have no nonsense. Into your crate this minute. What good will it do to plunge and bellow? No, stop it, don't lie down. Up, boy, up. Bad boy. Jumbo!

You're all right, don't take on so. You're back in your quarters for the moment; it's getting dark out. Such a to-do! They're only chains. I know you dislike the weight of them, but they're temporary. No, I can't take them off tonight or this Elephant Bill will raise a stink. He says we must try you again first thing tomorrow. The chains are for securing you inside the crate, till the crane hoists you on board the steamer. No, calm down, boy. Enough of that roaring. Drink your scotch. Oi! Pick up my bowler and give it back. Thank you.

The Yankee, Elephant Bill, has some cheek. He began by informing me that Barnum's agents tried to secure the captured King of the Zulus for exhibition, and then the cottage where Shakespeare was born; you're only their third choice of British treasures. Well, I bristled, you can imagine.

When you wouldn't walk into the crate no matter how we urged and pushed, even after he took the whip to your poor saggy posterior – when I'd led you round the corner and tried again half a dozen times – he rolled his eyes, said it was clear as day you'd been spoiled.

'Spoiled?' I repeated.

'Made half pet, half human,' says the American, 'by all these treats and pattings and chit-chat. Is it true what the other fellows say, Scott, that you share a bottle of whisky with the beast every night, and caterwaul like sweethearts, curled up together in his stall?'

Well, I didn't want to dignify that kind of impertinence with a reply. But then I thought of how you whine like a naughty child if I don't come back from the pub by bedtime, and a dreadful thought occurred to me. 'Elephants are family-minded creatures, you must know that much,' I told him. 'I hope you don't mean to leave Jumbo alone at night? He only sleeps two or three hours, on and off; he'll need company when he wakes.'

A snort from the Yank. 'I don't bed down with nobody but human females.'

Which shows the coarseness of the man.

Settle down, Jumbo, it's only three in the morning. No, I can't sleep neither. I haven't had a decent kip since that blooming crate arrived. Don't those new violet-bottomed mandrills make an awful racket?

Over 7,000 visitors counted at the turnstile today. All because of you, Jumbo. Your sale's been in the papers; you'd hardly credit what a fuss it's making. Heartbroken letters from kiddies, denunciations of the Trustees, offers to raise a subscription to ransom you back. It's said the Prince of Wales has voiced his objections, and Mr Ruskin, and some Fellows of the Society are going to court to prove the sale illegal!

I wish you could read some of the letters you're getting every day now, from grown-ups as well as kiddies. Money enclosed, and gingerbread, not to mention cigars. (I ate the couple of dozen oysters, as I knew you wouldn't fancy them.) A bun stuck with pins; that's some sot's idea of a joke. And look at this huge floral wreath for you to wear, with a banner that says A TROPHY OF TRIUMPH OVER THE AMERICAN SLAVERS. I've had letters myself, some offering me bribes to 'do something to prevent this', others calling me a Judas. If they only knew the mortifications of my position!

Oh dear, I did think today's attempt would have gone better. It was my own idea, that since you'd taken against the very sight of the crate, it should be removed from view. I told this Elephant Bill I'd lead you through the streets, the full six miles, and surely by the time you reached the docks you'd be glad to go into your crate for a rest.

But you saw right through me, didn't you, artful dodger? No, no tongue massage for you tonight, Badness! You somehow knew this wasn't an ordinary stroll. Not an inch beyond the gates of the Gardens but you dropped to your knees. Playing to the crowd, rather, I thought, and how they whooped at the sight of you on all fours like some plucky martyr for the British cause. The public's gone berserk over your *sit-down strike*, you wouldn't believe the papers.

I almost lost my temper with you today at the gates, boy, when you wouldn't get up for me, and yet I couldn't help but feel a sort of pride, to see you put up such a good fight.

That Yank is a nasty piece of work. When I pointed out that it might prove impossible to force you on to that ship, he muttered about putting you on low rations to damp your spirit, or even bull hooks to the ears and hot irons.

'I'll have you know, we don't stand for that kind of barbarism in this country,' I told him, and he grinned and said the English were more squeamish about beating their animals than their children. He showed me a gun he carries and drawled something about getting you to New York dead or alive.

The lout was just trying to put the wind up me, of course.

Primitive tactics. 'Jumbo won't be of much use to your employer if he's in the former state,' says I coldly.

Elephant Bill shrugged, and said he didn't know about that, Barnum could always stuff your hide and tour it as 'The Conquered Briton'.

That left me speechless.

Will we take a stroll round the Gardens this morning before the gates open? Over eighteen thousand visitors yesterday, and as many expected today, to catch what might be a last glimpse of you. Such queues for the rides! We could charge a guinea apiece if we chose, not that we would.

Let's you and me go and take a look at your crate. It's nothing to be afraid of, idiot boy; only a big box. Look, some fresh writing since yesterday: *Jumbo don't go*, that's kind. More flowers. Dollies, books, even. See that woman on her knees outside the gates? A lunatic, but the civil kind. She's handing out leaflets and praying for divine intervention to stop your departure.

But the thing is, lad, you're going to have to go sooner or later. You know that, don't you? There comes a time in every man's life when he must knuckle down and do the necessary. The judge has ruled your sale was legal. Barnum's told the *Daily Telegraph* he won't reconsider, not for a hundred thousand pounds. So the cruel fact is that our days together are numbered. Why not step on into your crate now, this very minute, get the wrench of parting over, since it must come to that in the end? Quick, now, as a favour to your sorrowful pa? Argh! Be that way, then; suit yourself, but don't blame me if the Yank comes at you with hooks and irons.

It's like trying to move a mountain, sometimes. Am I your master or your servant, that's what I want to know? It's a queer business.

That Superintendent! To think I used to be amused by his little ways, almost fond of the old gent. Well, a colder fish I never met. Sits there in his dusty top hat and frock coat flecked with hippopotamuses's whatsits, tells me he's giving me a little holiday.

'A holiday?' I was taken aback, as you can imagine. I haven't taken a day off in years, you'd never stand for it.

He fixes me with his yellowing eyes and tells me that my temporary removal will allow Mr Newman to accustom himself to the elephant's habits and tastes before departure.

'You know Jumbo's tastes already,' I protest. 'He can't stand that Yank. And if the fellow dares to try cruel measures, word will get out and you'll have the police down on you like a shot, spark off riots, I shouldn't wonder.'

Which sends the Superintendent off on a rant about how I've been conspicuously unwilling to get you into that crate.

'Oh I like that,' says I. 'I've only loaded the unfortunate creature with shackles, pushed and roared to drive all six and a half tons of him into that blooming trap, so how is it my fault if he won't go?'

He fixes me with a stare. 'Mr Newman informs me that you must be engaging in sabotage, by giving the elephant secret signals. I suspected as much when I sent you perfectly competent assistants and Jumbo ran amok and knocked them down like ninepins.'

'Secret signals?' I repeat, flabbergasted.

'All I know is that your hold over that beast is uncanny,' says the Superintendent between his teeth.

Uncanny? What's uncanny about it? Nothing more natural than that you'd have a certain regard for your pa, after he's seen to all your little wants day and night for the last seventeen years. *Why does the lamb love Mary so*, and all that rot.

Well, boy, at that moment I hear a little click in my head. It's like at the halls when a scene flies up and another one descends. I suddenly say – prepare yourself, lad – I say, 'Then why don't you send a telegraph to this Barnum and tell him to take me too?'

The Superintendent blinks.

'I'm offering my services as Jumbo's keeper,' says I, 'as long as his terms are liberal.'

'What makes you imagine Mr Barnum would hire such a

stubborn devil as you, Scott?'

That threw me, but only for a second. 'Because he must be a stubborn devil himself to have paid two thousand pounds for an elephant he can't get on to the ship.'

A long stare, and the Superintendent says, 'I knew I was right. You have been thwarting me all along, using covert devices to keep Jumbo in the Zoo.'

I smirked, letting him believe it. Covert devices, my eye! To the impure, all things are impure. 'Just you send that telegraph,' I told him, 'and you'll be soon rid of both of us.'

Now now, boy, let me explain. Doesn't it strike you that we've had enough of England? Whoa! No chucking your filth on the walls, that's a low habit. Hear me out. I know what a patriotic heart you've got, but how have you been repaid? Yes, the plain people dote on you, but it strikes me that you've grown out of these cramped quarters. If the Society's condemned you to transportation for smashing a few walls and shocking a few Member's wives, why then – let's up stakes and be off to pastures new, I say. You're not twenty-one yet, and I'm not fifty. We're self-made prodigies, come up from nothing and now headline news. We can make a fresh start in *the land of the free and home of the brave*. We'll be ten times as famous, and won't England feel the loss of us, won't Victoria weep!

I expect the Superintendent will call me in right after lunch, the wonders of modern telegraphy being what they are. (Whatever Barnum offers me, I'll accept it. The Society can kiss my you-know-exactly-what-I-mean.) I'll come straight back here and lead you out to the crate. Now whatever you do, Jumbo, don't make a liar of me. I don't have any secret signals or hidden powers; all I can think to do is to walk into the crate first, and turn, and open my arms and call you. Trust me, dearest boy, and I'll see you safe across the ocean, and stay by your side for better for worse, and take a father and mother's care of you till the end. Are you with me?

Note

The struggle to get Jumbo into his travel crate lasted three weeks, until March 11, 1882 – but the controversy, nicknamed 'Jumbomania' or 'the Jumbo movement', lingered for several months on both sides of the Atlantic. It included songs, poems, jokes, cartoons, advertisements, and 'Jumbo' cigars, collars, fans, earrings, perfume and ice cream; as a pop culture phenomenon it was unmatched until the Beatles.

Once in North America, Jumbo toured very successfully for four seasons, and his reclusive keeper seems to have relished life on the road as 'Jumbo Scott' (as the crowds called him). In 1885, as Matthew Scott led his charge across a railway track after a performance in St Thomas, Ontario, Jumbo was killed by an unscheduled freight train. The circus rehired the shattered Scott for one more season to stand beside Jumbo's stuffed hide and skeleton and tell stories about him. Despite being put under pressure to return to England, Scott seems to have hung on near the circus's winter HQ in Bridgeport, Connecticut, where he died in 1914 in the almshouse, aged around eighty. Jumbo's bones lie in storage at the American Museum of Natural History.

My main sources for 'Man and Boy' were reports in *The Times* between January and April 1882, the slim, ghostwritten *Autobiography of Matthew Scott, Jumbo's Keeper* (1885), and Superintendent Abraham Bartlett's memoir *Wild Animals in Captivity* (1898). Other details come from *Jumbo: The Greatest Elephant in the World* (2007) by Paul Chambers, the fullest account of this strange partnership. ∎

I didn't see my father much when I was growing up. He came to the house, though, by way of the radio and the television set: *Hancock's Half Hour*, featuring Sidney Balmoral James. Even now when I look at Tony Hancock's face I have the oddest sensation of Sidness. It's as if the two men have been momentarily shuffled together, my double dad.

Imagining their own dead fathers revived and mobile, people say, 'Doesn't it upset you, watching him on TV?' Not me, mate. I love watching him; I've always loved watching him. It's the screen that binds us. The night he died, I switched over to the nine o'clock news and saw his face, not knowing that he'd collapsed on stage barely an hour before.

I've got four stills, four images of us together. In the earliest, he's walnut-faced and thirty-four. He holds the baby me up to the camera and I curve towards him, reaching for his cheek; we're both beaming. He's only been in England for nine months and he's already made three films. We live in Kensington and their marriage is up the Swanee.

In the next one, I'm a year older. He's holding me again. We're in a line, my mother on the left with her eyes closed, caught by the camera in mid-blink. I'm in the middle: white socks, button shoes, white dress, my hands wrapped round Dad's finger. He's in a white shirt and a thin tie. He's making more films, he's on in the West End, he's still smiling. I'm still smiling. Everybody's smiling because there's a camera pointing at us but there's not much time left, they'll be separated within the year.

Then I'm five, the au pair's bridesmaid in white satin and tulle. Dad's in a suit and knitted waistcoat, a wedding guest, and we're sitting on my bed. His arm's round my back, he's holding an earthenware dish and I'm feeding him a crisp, staring up at his face. They're divorced. I look as if I can't quite believe he's there.

The last photograph: my first marriage. I'm seventeen. There are two long lines of family and friends and he's centre stage. He's mugging for the photographer, so am I. He's made over a hundred films, he's in the *Carry-On*s, he's a star. 'If it doesn't work out, darling,' he says, in a rare stab at paternal counsel, 'you can always leave.' No Sid chuckle, no wink. Not funny. ■

Sid James with his daughter Reina James, aged five, in 1952

Shivkumar Joshi, c.1972

TRACING PUPPA

Shadow-boxing, drive-chatting and three slaps

Ruchir Joshi

This is a story I've heard. I've no way of knowing for sure, but I think it's true.

1946. Calcutta is a city ripped apart like an old sari. Hindus and Muslims are hacking into each other, the attacks coming in uneven wave and counter-wave. All the authorities can do is clamp down a citywide curfew, allowing people a window of two or three hours to get their supplies. On a hot day, during the hours when movement is allowed, a man of about thirty goes out to meet a friend who lives nearby. On his way back through the deserted streets, he sees two teenage boys pelting out of a side street, leaving a trail of blood behind them. The boys see him too, and start with terror. Then they see that he is alone, that he isn't about to chase them. They take a chance. 'Please sahab, please save us!' The man is a middle-class Hindu, you can tell from his dress: a white dhoti flowing out from under the long, loose shirt called a kurta. The boys are Muslim and poor, you can tell from the simple, checked lungis wrapped around their waists. Whatever they were wearing on their upper bodies is torn to shreds, and there are fresh wounds bleeding. One of them is limping from where a blade has caught his foot.

The man tells them to stay close and walk behind him. He knows there is a hospital half a mile away where they are taking in riot victims from both sides. He also knows that the half-mile is completely Hindu and Sikh territory – it's his own neighbourhood. He walks forward, hoping nothing will happen, and the boys follow.

The man is a Gujarati, from the west of the country, and he has settled in this part of town, which has a shared concentration of Gujaratis and Sikhs – immigrants too, but from the north-west of India. The two communities have in common their strict vegetarianism and a willingness to leave home and go anywhere on the planet to make a living. What sets them apart, however, is important: the Gujaratis are mainly businessmen who go to great lengths to avoid physical labour and physical altercation while the Sikhs, the Sardars, are from peasant stock, not shy of hard manual work, and belong to a religion that was forced to give primacy to the sword; as they see themselves and as the world sees them, if ever a man was born to be a warrior it was a Sardar. There is a joke: just as a Sikh is supposed to have his kirpan – his religious dagger – with him at all times, so a Gujarati never lets his accounts book stray too far from hand.

As the man and his wards cross a street of mechanics' garages, their worst fears suddenly become reality. Five Sikhs are walking towards them, two of them with long swords, the rest with their kirpans on their belts. The boys look to run but they know they are trapped. The leader of the Sardars comes up to the man in the white dhoti.

'*Babuji*, where are you taking these vermin?'

'To the hospital. You can see they are hurt.'

'Please move aside, *Babuji*. These two are not going to need a hospital.'

The word 'Babuji' implies all the class-respect a taxi driver or car mechanic would give a middle-class customer, but there's no mistaking that the Sardar means business.

The man stands his ground. As the Sardar starts to go around him,

he steps sideways, keeping himself between the Sardar and the boys.
'They are hurt badly enough. Now stop. All this has to stop.'
'It will stop when they are all dead. Each and every one of these
dogs. Then we will stop.'
'No. You will stop now.'
'*Babuji*, I will kill you if I have to, but there is no saving these dogs.'
'You will have to kill me first.'

The words are out of the man's mouth before he knows what he
is saying, but they only define what his body is already doing. It is
near noon and the shadows are small, hard, black puddles around the
men's feet. The two boys are clutching each other and shaking, and
their shadows are joined together over the blood they've smeared on
the road.

The Sardar's calm demeanour explodes. The postcards describing
what's been happening back in western Punjab, in Lahore, in Sialkot
and Rawalpindi catch fire in his eyes – the raped girls, the slaughtered
cousins, the burned farms. In his mind, only the Sikhs have suffered,
and the Hindus; in his mind there is not a single Muslim woman
dishonoured, not a single Muslim baby skewered and thrown into a
well. As the other four spread out to catch the boys when they run,
the leader's sword arm goes around and up, as if he's about to hit a
hard backhand in tennis. The sword is not new or shiny – it is dull
even when it catches the sun – but it looks sharp enough.

'Move, I tell you!' The Sardar is shouting now, all respect gone for
this man who would protect these poisonous creatures over his own
sisters. Two dead or three, the sword wouldn't know the difference; one
Hindu but then two of them, the sword would feel no guilt; one more
swing of the arm in these endless days and nights of many strikes, his
arm will feel no more tired than if it was just the two boy-rats.

The sword quivers for the last time, sucking up the energy it
needs to come slicing down. The man straightens his back, looking
for the right kind of final prayer. Every time I hear the story, I start
to pray too: *God, please don't let him bring the sword down, please don't
let him kill the man who will become my father.*

With my mother, the story would often start backwards. When the man who had not yet even imagined me got the boys to the hospital on Elgin Road, he took them to where they were keeping the Muslim wounded. The section was as far away as possible from where they were keeping the Hindus. As the boys ran into the compound, the man in the dhoti waited to see if they were going to be looked after. I don't think he was waiting for any gratitude from the boys, his own thanksgiving at still being alive was crowding his head. What he didn't expect in the haze of relief was what the two boys actually did, for them to turn around and point to him, shouting 'Saala Hindu hai! He's a Hindu! Get him!' It took the man a few precious seconds to overcome the shock as the crowd surged towards him, but he managed to escape.

If there was any trace of self-gifted heroism in my father's recounting it would always be leavened by this last kick in the tail – how stupid could he have been, why couldn't he have just turned away at the hospital gate and left the two bleeding boys to their fate? How naive could he have been about what was going on? He would have understood if they had run into the Muslim section and disappeared without a backward look, they had barely escaped with their lives; but where did they find the reservoir of hatred, the energy to turn around and try and get people to attack him, the man who had just risked his own life to save theirs?

'Ek laafo maarva nu munn thhaay!' – 'One really feels like giving them a slap!' my mother would say, when she actually meant she felt like killing them.

A mixed neighbourhood of Gujaratis and Sikhs. An older Gujarati lady looks down and sees someone she knows, Shivkumar Joshi, a nice young Gujarati man, about to be beheaded by the Sikh owner of a car-repair garage, a man she also knows.

'Ei Sardarji! What are you doing? He is like my brother!'

My father always described it as a lifesaving shriek. Maybe it was a scream, maybe actually a calm, strong calling out. Whatever it was, it worked. The woman, for whom my father was like a brother, was also 'like a mother' to the man holding the sword. So he stopped, and so did the others. With the greatest reluctance they let the two boys go, along with the fool protecting them.

'I still don't see why Puppa needed to do that!' After all those years, my mother was still angry with my father for having risked his life. 'It's fine to be brave, but really, your father was actually saved by Ma Durga herself, coming in through that lady. Those Sikhs can be very violent – they would have killed him for sure!'

'Don't you want to slap them as well?' I would ask, gleefully imagining my mother laying into five strapping Sardars.

When I was a kid, parents regularly slapped their children. It was a standard mode of discipline and chastisement, sealed off from any deep thought or excessive premeditation. Like Eskimos with their thirty-two names for snow, we had many different names for aggressive hand-to-face contact, the variations and degrees demanding precision: for instance, the mild finger-flick was a '*lappad*', a proper palm landing on cheek was a '*laafo*' or a '*thhappad*', whereas a full-force forehand catching someone on the ear and sending them flying was, in my parents' language, Gujarati, a '*dhhawl*'.

The time was the 1960s and the slap was a kind of behavioural coin of the realm. Heroes in films slapped villains, employers slapped servants, cops slapped rickshaw-pullers for traffic infringements, teachers smacked students, husbands lit into wives and parents hit children. India was only a few years old then and it was a country trying to slap itself into becoming a nation. The slapping was the mildest tip of the iceberg, of a whole, immovable Arctic shelf of violence that lay under the pictures of Mahatma Gandhi and the pomp and ceremony of a state that proudly proclaimed its non-violent antecedents while still trying to stem the deep wounds of the mass bloodletting that had been the price of independence.

A vague awareness of the larger violence taking place all around didn't help much while dealing with the daily danger of assault from parents or teachers. When I was six, I witnessed a teacher draw blood

Satyavati and Shivkumar Joshi, early 1960s

when she flung a wooden duster and caught the kid next to me on
the forehead; she apologized profusely to his parents and went back
to plain slapping and spanking the next day. Most teachers hit us, but
at home things were different. Boys usually caught it from their
fathers and went running to their mothers for comfort. In my family
of three, however, the main turbine for generating punishment was
my mother. Any mischief would be met with a ticking-off, any
escalation then countered with a *lappad* or a *thhappad*; the dangers
of having sporting equipment lying around were also brought home
to me when my mother once deployed a hockey stick, and another
time a cricket stump.

In the first ten years of my life, my mother did ninety-nine per
cent of the hitting but also most of the loving. My father slapped me
exactly three times and I remember feeling like I'd deserved it. They
were hard slaps, *thhappad* but dangerously close to *dhhawl*, and they
hurt like mad, but there was no residue of rancour and so they didn't
fester in me like my mother's punishments.

With my mother a slap had as many meanings as it had names: there was a fear of losing control, there was frustration at the actual loss of it, there was an anger towards the world in general and there was sometimes a sense of betrayal, when the love she gave me wasn't reciprocated as she wanted. On the other hand, the three slaps escaped from my father despite himself. It wasn't as if there was a whole army of them simmering inside him; I'd crossed a line beyond tolerably annoying and got whacked, and that was it, it was over, with both of us equally shocked. Afterwards, I could see he deeply regretted hitting me; what I could not see was that he was saving his anger and fight for other things, things that mattered, things that could not be sorted with a slap.

Both my parents were blessed with warm, loving hands. I was their only child and they made sure I knew just how wanted I was and how loved. I still can't figure out how that love communicated itself through touch, or how that touch has managed to live on inside me. Equally, I can't understand how my father managed to be both affectionate and yet distant; why there is such a distinct difference between my mother's touch and my father's in my sensory memory.

Though we didn't talk much in my early childhood, I was very physical with my father. We'd hug, we'd shadow-box, we'd wrestle. Once, when horsing around, I flailed at him with my foot and took out a front tooth – there was hell to pay, but entirely from my mother shouting at the two of us while my father defended me through a cloth held to his bleeding mouth. I still remember him coming home, grinning, with the gold replacement, and my mother berating me about how much the dentistry had cost. I didn't pay it much mind. It was only Puppa, after all, and not some vengeful teacher that I'd kicked, and it was only Mummi, who shouted a lot anyway.

Because he'd told me a few stories, I knew that as a teenager Puppa had worked out on a '*malkhamb*', wrestled and played tennis. The *malkhamb* was a smooth, iron pillar you found sticking out of the sand in traditional Indian gymnasiums, usually about ten feet high and about three and a half feet in circumference. The idea was to strip down to the barest loin-covering, oil yourself all over and use muscle and speed to twist up to the rounded head of the pillar; once on top, you did slidy, oily gymnastics before working your way down again. This crazy *malkhamb* and the wrestling gave my father muscles that he retained well into his fifties. For me the curious thing was that along with the hard muscles went a deep adherence to Gandhi's philosophy; whether the country did or not, my father certainly took the idea of non-violence very seriously. Whereas a lot of his earlier gym-mates had turned into Hindu fascists with grandiose and vicious ideas of Hindu supremacy, my father had become a Gandhi-ite, thrown away his Brahman's sacred thread and tried to stick as far as possible to the Mahatma's creed.

For my father, non-violence meant avoiding violence as a first, second or even third choice but not always and under any circumstances. As I grew to know him, I saw that courage and immovable quality as central to his being. But as a kid I was confused by him. He was mild-mannered and yet solid. He lost his temper only about once a year, usually with a shout that could have shattered wood, causing everybody to dive for cover. Otherwise, he had infinite patience and great tolerance of all kinds of stupidities that would send me or my mother over the edge. Even the solidity was leavened by the way the man held himself, by his grace and by the way he dressed.

He was an unusual father in many ways and this was reflected in his appearance. At home, Puppa would wear the normal loose kurta and pyjama worn by a lot of Indian men. It was the going-out clothes that were different.

Most other fathers wore 'shirt-pants', the ubiquitous 1960s combo of bush shirt and trousers and, from the late 1970s, the ghastly safari suit, the power-dress favoured by everyone from industrialists to Indira Gandhi's 'Black Cat' security detail; some daddies who worked for foreign companies wore proper suits, some wore shorts on days off and made like they were in Israel or Virginia. My father's own business was totally dependent on the aspirational and affluent urban Indian male's desire to dress like a Westerner; he was the representative in eastern India of textile mills on the other side of the country that manufactured 'terelene', 'tericot' and other cloth made with polyester yarn content. Though he spent a lifetime selling it, my father hardly ever let that synthetic stuff touch his skin – on most days he wore a crisp dhoti and kurta made from the roughest khadi, the handspun cotton cloth Gandhi had made legendary. The dhoti would take a full three minutes to put on, with the different folds and layers being wrapped around his legs and then the final pleating making a fan that flowed down the middle to the ground. The *ganji* – the sleeveless vest – also made of khadi, would go on next, and then the starched white kurta. Within minutes the ironed kurta sleeves would be rolled up but the rest of the creases remained intact throughout the hot, fetid Calcutta days, coming back remarkably unscathed from one of the few workplaces in Badabazar market still without air conditioning.

In the line-up of adults in my head, there were women, who all wore saris, there were men whose signature was the shirt and pants, and then there was Puppa. Even though I saw my father as a 'tough guy', to my mind this dhoti and kurta were not a fighter's clothes. Western film-warriors wore pants and hats and gun belts; Indian mythological figures did have dhotis but they were tightly wound around the legs so that they were almost trousers, nothing that would get in the way of drawing sword from scabbard. My father's dhoti-kurta undercut all this in ways I couldn't figure out – he somehow managed to look feminine, graceful and manly all at the same time; no matter what others thought, he was completely assured in his own definition of masculinity and Indianness.

When I heard stories of his generation facing the policemen deployed by the Raj, I often wondered how these 'freedom-fighters' managed to avoid tear-gas canisters, run, jump across roofs and escape from cops in proper battlegear; but by the time I was about eight or nine I noticed the agility people like my parents had while dancing the traditional Gujarati dances of *garbo* and *raas*. My father was very active on the Calcutta stage, directing plays in Gujarati and Hindi, and during rehearsals I saw how quick-footed he could be, leaping from the front aisle on to the stage to make an adjustment to the blocking or the set, all wearing the same dhoti-kurta.

As a privileged child of modern India, wearing my shorts and sports shoes, and later my bell-bottomed jeans, it was difficult for me to understand, but gradually I began to accept that the dhoti-kurta was part and parcel of my father, that any other dress would be wrong. Whenever I'd ask him about his clothes, he'd reply: 'These are the clothes in which I'm happy. You shouldn't change your nature to suit fashion.' His trousered friends would rib him about the irony of a man in traditional khadi trying to convince people to buy polyester suitings but it wouldn't make any difference – business was just business, to stand in for religion my father had other passions.

Written in English, 'Mummy' and 'Papa' don't convey the actual names I called them.

There were, of course, many different names for 'mother' and 'father', and each set came embedded with morals and social weight, usually explained to me by Mummi. There was the commonly used '*maa*' and '*baap*', which worked equally in Gujarati and Hindi and cut across all classes – even the poor had one each; there was the Bengali '*ma*' and '*baba*' (confusing, because 'baba' was also the Gujarati/Hindi word for 'baby' and 'child'); there was the slang we used among us kids, lifted straight from American comics, 'Mom' and 'Pop' (amusing in the family, but God help you if you used either before visiting relatives); and then there was the super-formal, Sanskrit '*matru*' and '*pitru*'.

What I called my mother was a very Gujarati '*Mumm-ii*'. The 'Puppa', too, was an address typical of modern, urban Gujaratis and not the Anglo-Saxon/French 'pa pa' nor the Italian/Punjabi 'paa-pp-a', but '*Pupp-paah*', the first syllable more or less the same as the word for baby dogs. The names came with a hierarchy that was instilled early and it remained unchanged: even though both my parents are gone, 'Puppa' is still attached to a respectful and formal '*tamhey*', while 'Mummi' is always locked to a familiar '*tu*'.

I questioned this ranking early on and I remember yet again coming under the wheels of Mummi's inexorable rule-chariot. 'That's just the way it is. No you *cannot* call Puppa "tu"! And you call me "tu" because I am your *maa* and you love me!' It did not occur to me to ask whether I loved Puppa. Clearly, mummis were for loving while puppas were chiefly there to be respected.

It was my mother's job, as Comptroller of All Seriousness, to pass on to me the basic cultural building blocks Hindus call '*sanskaar*'. The word means, simultaneously, traditions, morals, graces, manners; a kind of cultural sixth sense that needs to be both hard-wired and programmed into one's child. It was always my mother's project to imprint upon my being the strictest *sanskaars* she could – nothing less would befit a child of her and my father's lineage. A *sanskaar* could include basic instruction – dos and don'ts, sayings or Sanskrit *shlokas* (specific chants meant to be incanted at different ceremonies). One that my mother repeated often, especially when I was cheeky or rude to her, was '*Matru Deivo Bhavaha… Pitru Deivo Bhavaha…*' – 'Treat thy mother as a god, as a god treat thou thy father…'

Besides trying to convince me to treat her and my father like gods, my mother also took recourse to English sayings and phrases to bolster my fledgling character. 'Your father is the Head of the Family,' was one she would repeat, when I could plainly see this was not true. My mother was not designed to be bossed by anyone and it was probably one of the main qualities that had attracted my father. Throughout my childhood, Mummi took all the decisions: she didn't drive but she was the one who decided about buying our first car; she never took photographs but she deployed the money to get my father an expensive Nikon; she controlled all the toys and books I had; she managed all food and household help; she had initiating powers and final veto on holidays. Puppa may have been the titular head of the family the three of us made up but, in the day-to-day, Mummi was the General Officer Commanding.

Though he had very clear ideas about *sanskaar* himself, my father never tried to drill them into me. By the time I turned twelve, the usefulness of slaps and *dhhawls* was long over, not that Puppa had much favoured these; by that time he had watched my mother's frustration smash against the rocks of my intransigence for nearly ten years and he had drawn his own conclusions. When it was his turn to take charge, he was smart. He was also a straight-talker, so there was no attempt at those favourite parental techniques, subterfuge and manipulation. He decided I was old enough and he began a conversation with me.

'It says in the old texts that a son is a child from birth till the age of eight and you should treat him gently. Then, from eight to the age of sixteen he is your son and should be treated firmly, but with love. From sixteen he is no longer your son but your friend – if a man is wise, he should have turned his son into a friend by the time he reaches sixteen.'

It was a pretty bold laying out of what he wanted. As far as I knew, none of my friends' fathers had ever said anything like this to them. It did away with all the smoke and mirrors of patriarchal power and it was a softly-spoken challenge both to me and to himself – let's try this, because it's the only thing that will give us a relationship worth the name.

But then my father had experience of other models that hadn't worked, models laced with violence that wasn't always physical. His own father, my *Dadaji*, was a scary figure who cracked the whip over a huge family; in my mind, he competed for the Cruelty Cup with other psychopathic Heads of Families who ruled that class and caste in early twentieth-century Ahmedabad. My father was the fourth of eight children who hardly seem to have spoken to the man they all called 'Mohta Bhai', literally, 'Big Brother'. If a child was reported for a misdemeanour, serious naughtiness, a bad school report or having been caught at the cinema, Mohta Bhai would call down from his study:

'Shivkumar!'

'Yes, Mohta Bhai.'
'Come up here.'
'Yes, Mohta Bhai.'
'And bring the cane with you.'

And so my father would have to climb up the stairs to the landing where the cane was prominently suspended, take it off the wall and carry it up to his father. The canings hurt but having to deliver and then take away your own instrument of punishment seemed to have left a deeper wound. This strict 'discipline' left scars, but they were nothing compared to what followed. Coupled with the gross despotism in my grandfather was a disdain for any feelings and desires his children might have: their life-pairings were decided well before they reached anywhere near the supposed Age of Friendship. By the time they were eleven or twelve, my father and his siblings, both older and younger, were committed to marriages with equally prepubescent spouses, chosen according to precise sub-caste and in terms of strategic societal alliances. My father and most of my aunts and uncles were forced into disastrous marriages with failure, tragedy and oppression cemented deep into the foundations; my father's youngest sister was the one exception, with a long and happy marriage; my father was the only one who eventually escaped, fighting and scrapping his way out of this self-perpetuating trap of dutiful, deadly matrimony.

My grandmother died when she was forty-two, sixteen pregnancies (including eight miscarriages) taking their toll. When my grandfather, then in his fifties, took a sixteen-year-old for a second wife, my father was the one who protested. Mohta Bhai's retaliation was to pull the educational rug from under Puppa and send him to coventry in Calcutta, away from Ahmedabad and away from the girl he loved, Satyavati – Satu – who would one day, nevertheless, manage to become my mother.

My father did marry Sunanda, the girl he was ordered to, but not without a fight. He asked her first to release him from the agreement (as if she had a say) and, when she refused, informed her she would be marrying the equivalent of a corpse. He was eighteen then and she was probably no more than fourteen or fifteen; they married when they were a bit older. After the marriage, Shivkumar spent most of his time in Calcutta, working in his uncle's business. For a few years, he refused to join his wife in bed. Whenever he needed to return to Ahmedabad he would sleep on the veranda of the large house Dadaji's whole family occupied.

The one thing my father looked forward to on those trips back to Ahmedabad was meeting my mother. They would snatch time cycling on the streets or talking in tea shops. If my father was imprisoned in his marriage, my mother too was trapped in her life, supporting her mother and brother by tutoring rich mill-owners' wives and daughters as she put herself through college and started a career as a teacher. By the time she was twenty-seven she had become the principal of the most prestigious girls' school in Ahmedabad.

Much later, when I was in my twenties, I summoned up the courage to ask my father the one question I'd always been scared to approach: 'So, Puppa, if you were so determined not to consummate your marriage with Sunandaben, how did you end up having children with her?' Puppa laughed and said, 'Ask Satu.' The answer Mummi gave me was stunningly simple: 'Sunanda came to me and asked me for help. I told Puppa he had to stop being stubborn and accept his marriage.'

The acceptance led to three children, my sister and my two older brothers. It also, I suspect, sharpened the reality for both my parents that this was the wrong marriage. After nearly twelve years of longing, twelve years when my father was mostly in Calcutta while my mother was nearly two thousand miles away to the west in Ahmedabad, the gap bridged by fragile and frequent letters, my parents decided to take a leap. In an operation involving great secrecy, double bluffs, early cross-country airline services and a small camera to capture documentary proof of the ceremony, with a sole friend as guest and witness, they pulled off their long overdue wedding. The year was 1952, and their marriage just squeaked in under the wire being laid down by Parliament – the Marriage Act – which forbade Hindu men from having more than one wife where previously they'd been allowed two.

There was no question of a divorce; Sunandaben wouldn't hear of it, and in those days, there were no unilateral grounds for the nullification of a fully consummated marriage with three 'issues' as evidence. Neither would my father's family, in whose business he was embroiled, stand for it, my grandfather's own shenanigans notwithstanding; and my mother, now being a school principal and a paragon of morality and virtue, wouldn't be able to retain her job. All of Gujarati society would see it as a scandal. QED, a proper marriage it had to be, both in the beady eyes of the law and the all-seeing eyes of the gods and goddesses, but it also had to be a union that was kept secret for the time being.

Whatever the status of his second marriage, it's now clear to me that my father minimized his interaction with his first wife after their third child was born. Shivkumar would meet his children on his visits to Ahmedabad, which were twice or thrice a year, and sometimes they would visit us, but for about two decades he completely stopped talking to their mother. There was a small apartment he'd bought them, and their daily life and education were all paid for by him, but there was little of the kind of contact I, his fourth and 'only' child, took for granted. I remember watching his exchanges with my sister and brothers, by then all in their twenties, and they were of a quiet, affectionate but basically distant nature. They called him not 'Puppa' but by the name his whole family used: 'Sara Bhai', which means 'Good Brother'. It was a direct link to the dreaded Mohta Bhai and his moats of formality, and traces of that patriarchal distance were clearly visible to me as I grew older and understood how privileged and rare my own relationship was with my father.

Despite his rejection of the way his own father brought him up, Puppa had been incapable of making himself the kind of father he wanted to be for his first three children. This is all conjecture, of course, but my guess is that my father's default mode of parenting was an extremely benign version of my grandfather's. Neither Mummi nor Puppa are around to contradict me, nor too many of the friends who were witness to our family at the time, but examining my memories of the first decade of my life tells me that the odd bout of wrestling and clowning around were counter-intuitive. He was fighting his own programming.

I didn't buy any of the *Pitru deivo bhavaha* stuff, but as a young boy I did see that there were actually three or four Puppas. One was the crumpled pyjama-kurta man who read the newspaper, drove to the market and helped me with my arithmetic; one was the man who dressed, went to the office and made money; one was the man who was into theatre and laughed and joked with friends; and then there was the well-known Gujarati writer, the man who gave speeches, attended conferences, won awards and was respected by all sorts of strangers in Calcutta's literary circles, and much more widely on our visits to Bombay and Ahmedabad.

The crumpled-kurta Puppa would sit at home, hugging his desk, rapidly scratching away with his thick-nibbed fountain pen; the small, square, unlined notebooks would pile up until there were ten, twelve or fifteen of them and then copied into 'fair'; then packed in cloth, sealed with wax and sent off to Bombay via the '*dadukias*', the traditional business couriers used by Gujaratis, who carried anything – cash, bonds, jewellery, documents and deeds – no questions asked, no delivery ever failing. The publishers employed one man whose chief job was to decipher the handwriting of a Shivkumar Joshi manuscript when it arrived. This man would transfer the text to hand-run typesetting and letterpress, and the proofs would duly come back for my father to correct. One day a big brick wrapped in thick brown or white paper would arrive; my father would tear open the wrapping and present my mother with the first copy of his latest book and my mother would proffer the book to her picture of Krishna. From this activity came the man everyone knew as the '*lekhhak*' – the writer – Shivkumar Joshi, who sometimes stood on stages to speak and to receive garlands, a formal shawl draped over his shoulder. By the time he died, my father had published over ninety books (many quite slim, a few quite fat, as I divided them then), of novels, short stories, plays, essays and travelogues.

When he was young, my father had wanted to be a painter but Mohta Bhai would have none of it. 'No son of mine is going to become a paint-slave!' Gujarati is probably the only language to have a derogatory word for 'painter', the word my grandfather actually used – *chitaaro*. My father did paint occasionally, but the regular hunger to produce images transferred to his photography; the many narratives he saw and lived started to come out in words, soon after his secret marriage to my mother. By the time I became aware of him, Shivkumar Joshi was already an established writer in Gujarati, but an odd one, living and writing from Calcutta, from Bengal, on the other side of the country from where most of his readership lived.

That readership was mainly in Gujarat and Bombay but it also spread across Pakistan, East Africa, Britain, America and Canada; wherever there was a sizeable Gujarati community. Despite this, the books never earned much; there was no question of being able to give up the textile business and write full-time. He took himself quite seriously, and he took the art and craft of literature very seriously indeed, but there was no room to indulge in myths of sculpting masterpieces while starving in garrets. Both my parents had to work and earn because there were three families to support: ours, the one from his first marriage and my mother's brother's children, who were also in Ahmedabad. It was a hard-won bit of luck that the business allowed him the time to read and think and produce what he considered his real work.

Puppa would point out that Mohta Bhai had done him a huge favour by forcing him to leave for Calcutta. It would have been fairly easy for a spirited young man to establish himself in Ahmedabad as a painter or a man of letters; instead, Shivkumar was obliged to leave a backwater for the centre of the known universe. When my father arrived in Calcutta in the late 1930s, it was the only Indian city that was truly cosmopolitan. It was also the thriving, undisputed cultural capital of what we now call South Asia: Rabindranath Tagore was still alive, the great cultural movement of the Bengal Renaissance was yet to become supernova; without trying too hard, Shivkumar found himself thrown into a crowded melee of artists, writers, playwrights and musicians, not to mention ongoing political upheavals. Joining his uncle in the family business was unavoidable torture – it felt then like the end of his life – but the move to Calcutta was actually the making of him.

In our house, writing was never seen as an isolated activity. Yes, literature was privileged, as was Gujarati (not unimportantly also the language my mother taught in her college), but on our little first-floor island we were surrounded by the huge ocean of Bengali clashing with the seas of three Hindis and four or five kinds of English; we lived in a neighbourhood that had a reasonable scattering of eccentric painters and graphic designers; acting in plays and directing them was a central pleasure of life, as was photography; the best cinema being produced in India lurked all around, just out of frame. Ours was a fairly small apartment but with very few of the knick-knacks and souvenirs you often found in middle-class houses: most of the shelf-space was devoted to books, piles of *Encounter* and *Plays & Players*, translations of Sartre, Ionesco, Lorca and Mishima, and many art books full of reproductions to satiate the unfulfilled *chitaaro* in my father.

The writer in Shivkumar eventually allowed the *chitaaro* to go to Europe and America to see his favourite paintings in the original. In 1969, my father was invited to a PEN theatre conference in Budapest and so, at the age of fifty-five, he finally went abroad. Using the paid-for Hungarian leg as a booster, Puppa organized a round-the-world journey that would take him via Beirut to Europe, and through the United States to Japan before depositing him back with us after four long months.

The trip meant that yet another Puppa emerged before my eyes, adding to the three or four already there. Normally, the few Western clothes my father possessed would come out of mothballs only when we were headed for the coldest of hill stations. Now the trousers, shirts and sweater acquired a suit as well (though no tie, it was a Nehru jacket), as he planned how to tackle the different latitudes. I remember being very uncomfortable seeing him try out that Western costume before departure.

I realize now that it had taken me some effort to get used to the stares, sniggers and unspoken taunts of my peers whenever my dhoti-kurta'ed father appeared in school or playground; their inaudible question hanging – 'Why is your pop in that funny village get-up? Can't he afford proper clothes?' Once I'd accepted and internalized his look, the defiant attire he presented to the world, it was hard for me to see him in any other clothes. Now, he became somehow ordinary, diminished, reduced to the level of all those other fathers, suddenly a middle-aged *Indian* man, the Indianness of his body starkly revealed, the paunch under control but now visible where it had been hidden by the flow of the kurta; the height suddenly short, *only* five feet six inches as opposed to all of nearly five feet seven; the shirt not sitting right, the collar bringing out his jowls, whereas the round neck of the kurtas normally mitigated them; the trousers all wrong – slightly flared at my insistence but still ultra square – and his legs, which didn't know quite how to stand in them, looking even odder ending in shoes.

Watching him try out the suit, I found myself worrying about him – it was as if the warrior had divested himself of his armour. It was as if the world was going to claim him and take him away from me. My discomfort came out in bad jokes.

'Ha, ha, Puppa, you look like a *villyunn*, you look like Pran!' I said, naming the dapper alpha baddie of Hindi cinema. But, just as he was unconcerned about people's reactions to his normal dhoti-kurta, he remained completely untouched by my jeering, even hamming up the villain as he checked himself out in the mirror. My father was a man who could laugh at himself – not a quality commonly found in middle-class Indian Heads of Families at the time. Also, at core, he was a theatre man, an actor, and he had the confidence of the genuine performer – 'life makes you go through many roles and you have to act them with style!'

Around the time I was eleven or twelve, my relationship with my mother was hit by a meteorite. Looking back, it was actually more like a twin-strike, her menopause probably peaking at the same time my teenage hormones decided to kick down the door. There was nothing Mummi and I could say without setting each other off; everything I did was wrong, everything she did was stupid, and vice versa.

I realize now that this was the one thing that knocked my father's self-assurance: he could handle the worlds he had chosen to enter but he could not tough it out when faced with a schism at the heart of his universe. He watched with growing alarm as my mother and I began to repel each other like two large, ill-matched magnets; the model they had tried to construct, the nuclear family living far away from the imprisoning maze of the joint-family, the three of us united and free from the constant, multi-level attrition of traditional kinship, was coming apart. As my mother chose to put it, many of the things I did felt like a slap in her face.

On the other hand, on a parallel track, Puppa began to communicate with me in a way he had not done before.

When I was around the age of nine or so, someone had presented me with a box of poster colours (gouache, as I learned to call them much later) and I'd begun to mess around. Rapidly, this brush-and-colour stuff became addictive. I'd come back from school and get in some painting before going down to play; I'd wake up in the morning and paint instead of fooling around or doing last-minute homework; my punishments in school began to come because I was caught doodling in class rather than throwing paper arrows or chatting; my choice of presents began to move from toys to art materials.

Puppa talked to a proper painter friend in our neighbourhood who gave him the best advice imaginable – just let the kid paint, don't

Shivkumar with Ruchir, 1971

interfere, buy him all the colours and paper he wants and then let him be. Puppa was very attentive but also very hands-off: he never told me what to paint or how to paint, he never picked up a brush to show me how, he never stopped me from making mistakes; all he would occasionally do is bring into play Picasso's great axiom: 'Every painter needs someone to stand behind him and knock him out when he has done enough.'

Mummi was as proud of my painting as she was of Puppa's writing. In the creativity of 'her creation' – me – she saw a fulfilment of all the hopes of her marriage. She didn't mind if I pursued art as long as it wasn't my main profession, just as, later, she didn't mind that I got obsessed with films as long as I didn't shove everything else aside to jump into film-making (which, or course, I did). She wanted me to make money, sure, but it wasn't even about that; there were a few respectable professions – economist, professor of literature, architect, writer – that she would have chosen any time over me being a businessman-millionaire, say. But it was the edgy, rootless, riskily bohemian ways of life she hated. As I got deeper into the spin of adolescence, somewhere Mummi sensed that this 'creativity' of mine would mean going against the straight and narrow, not just in education or profession but also in my personal life, and it was a prospect that scared a woman otherwise not easily frightened.

Around this time was also the closest I saw my father come to being frightened himself. At thirteen, I made a choice to go to a boarding school in Rajasthan, right across the country. It was hard for mummi-puppa to afford but somehow they managed – the alternative was the constant trouble in my day school with the attendant fear of expulsion. When I started coming home for vacations, Puppa invented the ritual of the morning drive, where he and I would take the car and go sit by the big lake not far from our house. One reason for these morning trips was for him to start teaching me how to drive, but they also became his hour to talk to me, to negotiate various truces between me and my mother, to try and understand whatever was going on in my hormone-hounded head.

One time I came back for holidays from my boarding school and Puppa and I went for our drive. Sitting by the lakes near our flat, I decided to get it off my chest.

'Puppa, I have to tell you something.'

'Yes?'

'Me and my friend Sudeep went to a restaurant before catching the train.'

'Yes. So?'

'Well, Sudeep ordered a mutton burger and I tried it.'

'Did you…like eating it?'

'Yes, so I ordered a whole one for myself. And one for Sudeep because I'd eaten half of his.'

Puppa ducked his head, almost smacking the steering wheel. Then he composed himself.

'Well…it doesn't come as a surprise. If we send you out into the world this is a risk we take.'

'Yeah, I guess…'

'But. Please don't tell your mother. On no account must she find out.'

'Why, what will happen?'

'One of you will have to leave the house. It's as simple as that. Since you're still a child, she will go. And I can't have that.'

The problem was, Mummi's adherence to strictures wasn't just confined to food. There were models of purity, notions of cleanliness, certain ideas of god and morality, all forming a grid inside her and therefore directly applicable to me as well. As she got older, this grid became more inflexible. Luckily for me, Puppa understood that things couldn't stay so clean, that tangling with art was an inherently messy, prickly, anti-bourgeois, anti-Brahmanical business. He knew it meant immersion in reality, no matter how unpalatable, he knew it meant dirtying yourself with commitment so that you didn't soil yourself with compromise. It meant breaking sacred eggs and tasting strange omelettes. It meant risking the wrath of the gods.

Our drive-chats began when I was fourteen and Puppa was approaching fifty-eight. It still baffles me how he managed, at that age, to take on all the concerns of a difficult teenager. While my mother tried to deny its existence, my father understood sexual desire. He was an open, sensual man, but my guess is he never managed to live a full and happy sexual life. He had been at odds with his first marriage and young with it; in his second one it was his wife who was at an angle with the whole business; for all her huge tactile sense, my mother always had a hard time connecting love, of which she was a great champion, with lust, around which she was forever a vigilante. My father was never capable of being unfaithful and the different hands that life dealt him meant he had to sublimate his natural instincts into his writing. He wrote freely about sex – too freely, in my mother's opinion – but he knew acutely what it meant to people, to others, and most importantly to me as I navigated my teens.

Puppa also understood rebelliousness. Both he and my mother had been rebels, they had both bucked the system at various points, first as young volunteers in the independence movement and then again with their marriage. In the conservative Gujarati society of Calcutta, mostly driven by business, our family radiated subversion. But where my mother's feistiness didn't cross over to support mine, my father's did. While she worried about what would happen to a kid who fought the powers, especially in ways she didn't agree with or understand, my father acknowledged that they had brought me up to question things, which inevitably meant also questioning the rules and principles they, mummi-puppa, had laid down; he had enough of a memory of his own growing up and a supple enough imagination to realize that he wouldn't always understand why I did what I was doing.

M ay and June 1975 found us all travelling acround Europe and the United States. Puppa and I got to Paris a few days earlier than Mummi. As he watched, I took in all the imagery the city had to throw at a fifteen-year-old. We visited the Louvre, spending a lot of time in the Impressionist wing, and we paid our respects to Picasso and Matisse. Just like Puppa six years earlier, I was happy to see the originals of all my favourite paintings at long last. But when it came to buying reproductions on our limited budget my eyes immediately reached for some posters of soft-focus nudes, sub-Degasian nymphets photographed by David Hamilton. My father gently pushed me into buying one or two of the smaller postcards, it remaining clear that Madame Joshi, when she arrived, was not to have her sensibility assaulted by these 'art' photographs.

There was, however, no avoiding the newspaper that was waiting to assault us all in an Indian restaurant in New York. INDIRA GANDHI DECLARES EMERGENCY! said the main headline. FREEDOM OF SPEECH SUSPENDED cried the subheader.

By the time we returned to India, the crackdown was in full force – arrests, censorship, the infamous '20-point Programme', slogans of loyalty on the walls and billboards, all of it. I got it that things weren't good, but I returned to my boarding school still excited by my new T-shirts and all the small soft-porn pictures and books I'd picked up behind my mother's back. It was only when I came back for the Christmas holidays that I really began to understand what was happening: most political opponents of Indira Gandhi's regime were in jail, civil liberties were gone, the right to criticize the government in print was indefinitely suspended, the poor were being rounded up and relocated from their slums, working-class men were being rounded up and sterilized, the country was – no mistaking it – under a dictatorship.

My father showed no sensible fear or caution. Probably the one thing that kept him out of jail was that he wasn't affiliated with any political party, having had no time for any of them after 1947. Once he had assessed what was happening, he began writing against Indira and her son, publishing his columns every week in a big Gujarati daily in Bombay. The only nod to strategy was that he called Indira and her son by the names of mythological demons, a reference so thinly veiled it was almost more insulting. After a while, the editor in Bombay was pressured into stopping the columns. All that did was make my father all the more determined.

The Emergency lasted for a little more than a year and a half. On my visits back home, I could see the fight-light in my father's eyes. It was a quiet change of energy, but it was palpable all the same: the warrior was back at war. He was deeply angry about what was happening to his country, but in terms of his personal situation he couldn't have been more acutely focussed. It was as if he'd cleared his emotional desk to make himself ready for battle. He had always talked to me about important things, but now, on our morning drives, he made an extra effort to be very clear about why he believed what he did, why he was doing what he was doing. It was perhaps a function of my age that I was worried but mainly proud, whereas it may also have been to do with her age that my mother was proud but mainly worried.

When the Emergency was at its peak, my father attended a meeting PEN had called in Calcutta. The idea was for writers and journalists to meet and have a dialogue with Yashpal Kapoor, then Mrs Gandhi's chief public relations henchman. While most other writers fudged and shuffled, Shivkumar Joshi stood up and let the Safari-Suit know in no uncertain terms what he thought of the Emergency and the suspension of free speech. It was after this evening that my mother's anxiety really mounted. Nothing happened though, no knock came on the door, no summons, no jail. Puppa's reading was that the situation was already getting out of hand for Mrs G and her cohorts. He was right.

When the end came, it was quick. I finished with school just before a confident Indira declared national elections. For the duration of the elections, people were again allowed to write what they wanted. Many had lost the habit of free speech but many more, including my father, had not. People spoke out, people campaigned, people wrote passionately and incisively. Indira Gandhi and her Congress were swept away in a landslide. I shared my parents' elation and I felt as if it was my own triumph as much as anyone else's.

On our morning drives, Puppa and I went back to discussing art.

U nlike me, my father didn't drink, didn't smoke and never ate meat. He had survived jumping across Ahmedabad rooftops, running from the police, he had survived the Sardar's sword, and he had survived the Emergency. I imagined he would last forever but, typically, it was my grandfather, Mohta Bhai, who did that, outliving several of his children and one or two grandchildren before dying at the age of one hundred and one. My father died two years before Dadaji, going far too early at the age of seventy-one.

Sometimes I find myself doing strange time calculations when looking back, as if working stuff out mathematically will yield something I've missed.

In the matrix of marriage and childbearing from which my parents emerged, my mother should have been an older aunt to a child born in early 1960 and my father a young grand-uncle. They themselves were both born in the heavy penumbra of the nineteenth century –

which always seems to have left India later than many other places –
and yet they both ended up dealing with a twenty-something son who
hammered their ears with Iggy Pop, Talking Heads and Pere Ubu. In
the last few years we had together, my father saw me struggle with
drawings, photographs and film that had far more to do with people
such as Joseph Beuys, Robert Rauschenberg and Jean-Luc Godard
than they did with his favourite Cartier-Bresson and Matisse.

In the aggregate of time, there is a massive 'only' attached to the
seventy-one years he lived and this gets magnified when I do further
sums and come to the result that we were close only for fifteen or so
of the twenty-eight years I had with him; of those, I was away and
out of his life for about seven, and living my own adult life while
co-habiting with my parents for the last six.

Trying to flip to his point of view, I entered his life when he had
already lived two-thirds of it, though he was not to know that then.
He had many friends, but he had a closeness with me that he had
with very few of his contemporaries, and in some ways I know that I
was the one closest to him. It may have surprised him, the friendship
he forged with this unexpected late child; he was used to the idea of
unconditional love, of missing it, of fighting for a space where it could
exist, of seeing it mutate and evaporate. I think what might have
really surprised him was being able to express that love and find it
reciprocated from this strange, usually adversarial quarter.

Not everybody I know has had difficult or disastrous fathers, but
far too many of them did or do. A very few of my friends have
brilliant, nourishing relationships with them, but most of them don't
– there was often this odd look I'd get when speaking warmly of my
old man, as if I'd ordered steak in a vegan restaurant. Now that he's
gone this has lessened to some degree, praise for the departed being
harder to censure.

It's difficult to explain the huge span of time my father covered.
Again, it's not about the figures. It's not about the hardware either,
though this man born under gas-lamps enjoyed his technology – one
of my big regrets is that he missed home computers and the Web by

only a few years. The span of time Puppa gave me has to do with him being able to share with me his whole store of memory, with keeping it sharp and yet supple and on the whole free of bitterness, with being able to analyze his experience with an open heart. This 'time' I received from him also has to do with him being receptive to a future he could not know. He knew the external world would soon change beyond all recognition and that he would probably not live to see many of the changes. It was with the internal world he realized he could most help me, by giving me the deepest, most genuine *sanskaars* I would need to handle what was coming.

I remember thinking when he died that he'd somehow managed to stay genuinely young, for himself and for me. I remember this again and again as I watch others' parents get old and as I watch my own friends starting to become set in their ways and their thinking.

In the devastation of his going, I remember feeling inexpressible gratitude. In the middle of that pain, I also remember feeling sharp relief that I myself, at least, would never have to face the challenge of being a father. ∎

THE FATHER

Kirsty Gunn

The father said he'd take them down to the beach to go swimming but he never took them. Cassie went into his room three times to see. First time, that he would take them. Second time, to say that they were ready now. Third time, to just remind him that he'd said that he would take them. But all three times the father was asleep.

Seemed all he wanted to do, the father, was stay in that old room and in the dark. Outside it was sunny and Aunt P said they could all get down there to the water on their own. That Bill knew the little sea path over the cliffs, she said, that he could lead the girls safely on their way.

'But the father said he'd take us,' Ailsa said. 'He picked me up in his big arms and he told me and we all believed.' Then she started to cry.

Ailsa was just four though. What would she know? That's what Bill said later, when he and Cassie went down the path alone, their swimming things on underneath their clothes and Bill with a picnic in a bag. 'If you're only four,' said Bill, 'you believe all the lies that grown-ups tell. That father of my mother…' He swung the bag around and banged it on the grass. 'He just makes up stories. That's what I heard my mum say. Your mum said it too.'

'Did she?' said Cassie. It was like she was wanting to be certain but seeing in her mind already that of course her mum would be agreeing. Laughing, kind of. It was the way her mum and Aunt Pammy were together all the time, laughing and telling secrets like they were in love. *Go away now…* That was all her mother ever said when they came up here on holidays. *I need time with my sister, Cass. You'll be the same with Ailsa one day. Your Aunt and I have things we need to talk about. Remember? We don't see each other through the year and now's our only chance…*

'Yeah,' Cassie said to Bill now. 'I think she did say that. My mum listens to everything your mum says.'

'My mum says the father's strokey,' said Bill, heaving the picnic bag from one shoulder to the other. 'That ever since Granny died he's gone funny in the head.' Then he ran down the rest of the hill ahead of her and Cassie saw him on the little beach where Ailsa and the father should also have been, flinging down the bag with the sandwiches and juice and pulling off his clothes in the light and lovely Highland sun.

Cassie loved it coming up here to see Bill and Aunt P. And her mum did and Ailsa and their granny too when she used to visit sometimes and they would all be together and so it was strange having someone else among them, in their private and special world. They never had people who could be fathers here before. *We don't do men…* she heard her mother say once, when they were in the village and someone was asking Cassie where her 'daddy' was. Truth tell: she'd never had a daddy nor Bill either. There'd been daddies once, her mum and Aunty Pammy told them, but that was a long time ago when the children were very little and Ailsa was a tiny baby. Bill said he could just remember his. Something to do with a blue jersey. But Cassie couldn't see a thing when she tried to picture what a father was.

Only here was one suddenly come in among them this summer. Her mum and Aunty Pam's own daddy come all the way over from the west in his funny car. And he used to be married to Granny all the years from when she was a bride and they never knew that too. No one talking about him, thinking about him. Then one day just arriving, driving up the road that afternoon *out of the blue...* That was the sentence Cassie kept hearing her mother say. Remembering every time she remembers it with a shock the look on her mother's face when the car came down the little road leading to the house.

Everything felt changed then, from that moment. *Out of the blue.* The way her mother's face changed, how she put her hands up to her mouth when she saw the funny car as if to stop herself from screaming... Then running inside to find Aunty Pam and them both holding each other like they were little girls and Aunty Pam saying over and over, 'Don't worry, Susan. We're grown-ups now. We'll find out what this is all about. Money, probably. We'll give him something and he'll go away.'

But that was at the beginning of the holidays, nearly, and now they were halfway through. And nothing had been found out, had it? And he hadn't gone away. The father just stayed in his room or then in the evening came out and sat, started talking, asking questions like he was waiting for something, a glass in his hand, a bottle on a little table beside him. Bill said the father was an alky as well as someone with a stroke and that meant he was a strange kind of dad. He'd heard his mum say that, Bill said, when he couldn't get to sleep one night and he'd heard his mum and Cassie's mum whispering in the kitchen after the father had gone to bed.

'He drinks whisky and beer and then he can't talk any more,' said Bill to Cassie next day, after he'd been up in the middle of the night listening at the door. 'I know everything now,' he said. 'Why he's come. Why my mum and your mum left home when they were little children and never saw him again.'

But what did that mean though, 'everything'? That's what Cassie wanted to know. If Bill knew everything, and the mothers did, then why did everything just stay the same?

In the end no one seemed to know that much at all. Why the father had arrived when they didn't even know their mothers had a father. Why her mum and her aunt should have a daddy of their own and never tell.

When she asked her mum about it her mum just said, 'Shhh. Doesn't matter darling.' She'd be doing dishes or pinning washing out on the line with Aunty P and talking... Always those two sisters had so much to say. And the father in his room, pretty much all the time, but then he came out in the late afternoon and he started talking too, sitting in the sofa in the sunny sitting room, stretching out his legs like he'd been living there all his life. 'I want around me all my grandchildren,' he'd say then. 'What'll we do tomorrow, eh? Tell me. What would all you little ones like to do?'

So that's how it had come up, that Ailsa had said would he take them swimming, because in the books about families that's the kind of thing the fathers do. They take picnics to the cliffs and they walk down from the cliffs like giants, holding the children's hands and taking bags and tents and things to make fires, all the way to the sea. Helping the children when they fall. Swinging the mighty bags and calling out, 'This way! This way! Follow me!' And the father had said that yes he'd take them. And not just any kind of swimming. That he'd take them out to the rock in the sea where the seals sometimes came, that he'd help them swim all that way, and it would be easy too, he'd show them how to do it, he'd show them the way. 'We'll get a plastic bag for a picnic and I'll strap it to my back,' Cassie remembers to this day him saying. He'd sat there with them all around him, making shapes in the air with his hands, to show them how it would be. What they'd do when they got there, to the beach and the rock and the cold, cold blue... All the loveliness of the project gathered there in the patterns shaped in the afternoon sun by his thin white hands, in the dream of them all together for that moment, the sun in the room, the two mothers standing in the doorway like they couldn't quite dare to let themselves enter more fully in but still even they were smiling, they were smiling.

'I'll swim with each of you out on to the rock and we'll stay there all day, make friends with seals and meet a mermaid or two… We might even spend the night, build a fire, have a camp…'

'And all of that from swimming?' Ailsa said.

'All of that,' the father said. 'Come here, my darling…' And that's when he took my sister up into his arms and made her laugh and swung her in the air. It's when we believed. ∎

On the top shelf of my closet, there's a box of plastic action figures which has survived five moves across the country spanning a fifteen-year period. A few original Star Wars figures remain: Yoda sans cloth robe and pet snake; C3PO minus an arm; a scuffed, stickerless R2D2. Gone is the special edition Emperor, which my older brother got in the mail for complaining to the Kenner toy company about our defective X-wing fighter. And I'll never know what became of 'The Burned Luke', so christened when his severed head was melted back on to his body by my father in what felt like a mystical healing ceremony by the light of the kitchen stove.

What predominates in that dusty box are my Masters of the Universe 'He-man' figures, which I disingenuously tell myself I'm holding on to for my own son. I know I'm not alone in my fondness for toys. There's been a trend in the last decade of fine artists, designers and even otherwise 'literary-minded' cartoonists producing dizzying, fantastical moulded vinyl figurines based on their characters. Though this more 'serious' autobiographical genre in comics that I work in is usually thought of as an antidote to the power fantasy which dominates the rest of the medium, there's still an element of power play in our work. In my case, I found it incredibly empowering to shrink my parents down to less than an inch tall and control their movements and thoughts in my carefully structured, remembered narratives.

A few years ago, before a particular comics convention, I was seized with the idea of making a toy to sell. But what would the toy be? A toy version of myself? The thought of literally selling myself at one of those little folding tables was too pathetic for words. No, the obvious choice was my dad – the sad, broken little man who couldn't conquer his own problems, let alone the ones plaguing the rest of the universe. He's always been my anti-hero. I packaged each of my little toy dads into his fitted vinyl sleeve and stapled on the tag. $99. Priced to move. Before they went on sale, I made sure to give one to my dad on Father's Day. Would you believe he loved it? ■

Erich and Francesca Segal, Israel, 1982

IN MY FATHER'S FOOTSTEPS

Francesca Segal

A s his parents' apartment building did not permit pets or children, my father spent the first six years of his life living with his grandparents at 800 St Marks Avenue, a neat neo-Georgian mansion in Brooklyn's Bedford-Stuyvesant. For much of the time, he was sequestered in the nursery on the top floor and tended to by a shifting cast of starched and white-capped nannies. Down the hall, preserved in all its nineteenth-century splendour, was the ballroom, with high vaulted ceilings and a grand theatre stage at the far end. This was a home more suited to the lifestyle of an old East Coast family than to that of aspirant Polish immigrants, but it was a house his family were proud of, a clear sign that they had made it – that they were right to cross oceans and that America, for those who worked hard enough, was indeed a land of opportunity.

With an ailing grandmother trapped downstairs and an absent, driven grandfather running his fabric store in Manhattan, my father's earliest memories are of performing on that stage to an invented crowd; filling a solitary world with companions from his imagination.

He wrote plays and performed them, emoting to an echoing and empty theatre. Inventing people became a powerful defence against loneliness, and later an even more powerful tool for engaging the attention of real people. In those evenings at the top of the house he would wait anxiously for his mother's visits and would continue the storytelling for her, spurred into creativity by his desperation to produce a cliffhanger that would entice her to come back again the next night. From the earliest years of his life, fiction served the dual purpose of creating a cast of characters he cared about, and making the cast of his own life care more about him. It is little wonder that at Harvard he was drawn to the fantasy and melodrama of the Greek and Roman myths, still less surprising that he became a writer. A little boy playing alone on an empty stage has a heightened drama of its own and those years of isolation led, in their way, to *Love Story*.

My father wrote *Love Story* in a white heat, when he was thirty-two years old. At the time he was a professor of classics at Yale University, on the verge of tenure and beloved by his students who would pile into the 600-seat Stirling Law auditorium to hear his lectures. At Harvard in 1958 he had written *The Hasty Pudding Review* with composer Joe Raposo and they had gone on to have some success with a musical, *Sing, Muse!*, which ran for thirty-nine performances off Broadway and won my father the attentions of an agent. Since then he'd had a successful secondary career writing musicals in New York and film scripts in Hollywood, work he relished as an escape from the suffocating atmosphere that he had always felt pervaded academia.

Love Story was the product of a Christmas break, inspired by a true story he'd heard that had captured his imagination. His agent begged him to put it aside, convinced it would ruin his reputation as a writer of macho action screenplays. But it had poured from him in what felt like a single sitting and, although he could not have known to what extent, he knew it was worth fighting for. *Love Story* altered everything. By the end of 1970, the combined success of the novel and the film had made him a household name – and face. He was a born performer and his publishers exploited his love of public speaking, honed at the lectern, by sending him on late-night talk shows again and again. He was their most powerful advertisement. When the film wasn't doing as well as expected in Japan, for example, the solution was to 'send Erich' and sales skyrocketed. For better or for worse, he was brought out from behind his desk and turned into a celebrity to rival the stars of his movies and, almost overnight, he became a world-famous author.

M y earliest memories of my father are inextricably linked with his identity as a writer. Our games all had language at their core – limericks and wordplay, reciting poetry, composing songs and recording interviews with one another for hours on his Dictaphone. My mother has boxes of tiny unlabelled tapes that summon these moments – aged two and a half, whenever I entered my father's office, no matter what he had been doing when I arrived, he would raise a small black Dictaphone to my lips and ask, 'Miss Segal. Any comments?' He was a sage and focused interviewer, probing my thoughts on nursery school, on the weather, on my plans for the afternoon, on the well-being of my imaginary friend, Latty. I was striving to emulate my father long before I was old enough to write – Latty was a secretary whose predominant responsibility was to take my dictation. I knew nothing else. He was always in his office, always writing, and when he wasn't in his office he was reading to me.

He chose our reading material from the canon, but dismissed squadrons of poets for being 'boring' – no one ever made me recite 'On Westminster Bridge'. My bedtime stories were Robert Frost, Edgar Allan Poe, Ogden Nash, e e cummings. From cummings he taught me that children are apt to forget to remember; from Poe the word 'tintinnabulation' and the magical concept of onomatopoeia. From Nash he taught me that ever-useful adage that candy is dandy but liquor is almost always quicker. These recitations would make my mother laugh, as did the dirty limericks he taught me, relishing my glee at the rude words, but most of all relishing my engagement with rhyme and rhythm. Writing was the centre of our family, the language we spoke, and the love between my parents. Identical ring binders open on their knees, they were often together on the sofa, arguing about sentences, exchanging strings of synonyms as if they were endearments. My father the writer, my mother the editor – theirs are the only skills to which I've ever aspired.

When I tell Americans that my father is from Brooklyn they nod. It makes sense – that's where New York Jews of his generation grew up, if not on the Lower East Side. When I tell them that he was raised in Bedford-Stuyvesant, they laugh. It is a deeply improbable place for him to be from.

The area achieved its notoriety because it is by far one of the most impoverished and troubled in the country. Only Los Angeles' Watts ghetto could rival it for violence, drug crime and homicide. 'Bed-Stuy – Do or Die' has been the motto for many decades now. As early as the 1950s, its reputation was anything but salubrious and from then on it got worse, not better. Rappers such as Jay Z, brought up in Bed-Stuy's infamous Marcy Houses, Busta Rhymes, Lil' Kim and Mos Def have raised its profile in recent years. Notorious B.I.G. is another famous Bed-Stuy alumnus, and one of almost innumerable young men murdered in its gang rivalries. Through these artists and through Spike Lee's iconic film *Do the Right Thing*, almost everyone in America has now heard of it. But it isn't a place that five-foot-seven, Jewish, middle-class, romantic-novel-writing classicists are actually *from*.

In the 1980s, when I was growing up in London and innocently boasting of my own family history, Bed-Stuy was known as nothing but a vast and seething slum, a violent district rife with crack dens, whorehouses and crumbling abandoned buildings, a place where once-proud family homes were divided repeatedly until they became rabbit warrens; tiny rental properties that were still barely affordable to the transient and indigent population of hookers, dealers, pimps, illegal immigrants and the terrified elderly who had come to the area in the first half of the century in search of a better life and who were now just as frightened in Bed-Stuy as they'd been in Alabama. The first public housing in Bedford-Stuyvesant was built in 1941 and throughout the 1960s enormous project towers were erected, an attempt to address the vast influx of low-income newcomers to the area and constructed in a way that, with hindsight, seems designed to maximize the dehumanization of their occupants. By the early 1970s, the majority of the reported rapes took place in the elevators and corridors of these projects – also a favoured haunt for robbers, muggers and murderers. Infant mortality, that most brutal index of social disadvantage, is more than double the national average in the district.

My parents settled in London, where I grew up, in 1984, and when we visited America, we spent our time on the West Coast. Though he has always been very much a New Yorker in both humour and character, my father seemed to feel no pull to return; no nostalgia whatsoever for the place where he grew up. On the contrary, we spent as little time there as possible, stopping only for a night, now and again, to break up the long flight to Los Angeles. He used to tell my mother that he couldn't sleep in New York City. But before the onward flight to LA there was usually one free morning, just long enough to take us to his old neighbourhood, had he wanted to. He was always resolute, though – it was too dangerous, and in any case, even if he had agreed, no cab driver would be willing to make the journey.

And that was it. In the 1980s Bedford-Stuyvesant was forbidden and impossibly tantalizing – half an hour, but half a world, away. All I knew was that he'd grown up there and that it was too unsafe for us to visit. And so with no concept of eras, of demographic shifts or social change, I re-imagined my father's life in the 'hood; gang wars raging in the street below as he sat in his room toiling over his Hebrew homework. I studded their middle-class brownstone with bullet holes; made paupers of my comfortable and successful immigrant family. It was a confusing and, as it would turn out, anachronistic fantasy. I had mangled history, combining the relative prosperity of the 1940s with the absolute brutality of the 1960s into a nonsensical hybrid. The truth was that Bed-Stuy had begun its descent before my father was born, but it wasn't until about the time he left for Manhattan in 1950 that it mutated, driven by a combination of civic neglect and racial prejudice, from a ghetto into a fully-fledged slum.

The first time I was in New York alone was in 1998. I was eighteen and I called my mother to ask for my father's childhood address.

'For God's sake don't tell her,' I heard him say in the background, 'or she'll go.'

Until scuppered, that had of course been my plan. It seemed impossible to me that there was anywhere that you really, truly shouldn't go. Maybe not at night, maybe not in a short skirt, maybe not wearing jewellery. But a no-go area was incomprehensible to me. I was an idiot. In 1990 there was a murder in Bedford-Stuyvesant every three days, a rape every two and a half days and ten robberies, six burglaries and four car thefts a day – and those are merely the reported crimes. By 1998 it was scarcely better. And so it wasn't until 2004 that I finally got my wish. I was in New York catching up with old friends, and when it came up in conversation that my father was from Bed-Stuy they looked askance. Again.

'But it's getting better,' Cassim assured me and, as he is an urban planner, I presumed he should know. 'It's not like it was. We could go now, if we don't get out of the car.'

With that endorsement, I called my parents and was finally granted the classified information once I'd promised that I would be accompanied and that, in keeping with the traditions of the neighbourhood, we would merely do a drive-by.

Neither Cassim, an intrepid architecture enthusiast and long-time Brooklyn resident, nor Alex, a born-and-bred New Yorker, had ever been there. It was early evening but already deep in winter dark and, as we dug Cassim's car out of a snowdrift, I was nervous with excitement. For a long time the car was stuck, ice clinging high around the wheel arches, but we persevered. It was now or never.

Do or Die. That first visit lasted seconds. We found the block on St Marks Avenue and we cruised down it slowly, blackened banks of ploughed snow standing high between street and sidewalk, thick, frozen mist hanging low in the air. We didn't even stop, but it was enough for me then. The cold had chased people indoors and the block was empty, off duty. I had no sense of a neighbourhood, a culture, a community, just row after row of brownstones. But at least I'd finally been. And on the way back, Cassim told me its story.

Bedford was established by the Dutch West India Company in 1662, remaining largely rural until the beginning of the nineteenth century, when Dutch farmers began selling land to other settlers. In a matter of decades it became predominantly residential, a desirable town for the rich, white, middle classes.

But free African-American settlements in the area go back almost as far. In 1838 a black stevedore named James Weeks bought land in southern Bedford, selling it on to other African-Americans in what would become Weeksville. Freedom then was of a complicated kind – finding a landlord willing to rent to black tenants was tremendously difficult and it was harder still to buy land. In reality there were few places that the newly freed blacks were actually free to go, and successful black landowners such as Weeks provided a lifeline.

During the 1860s and 1870s, the railways improved access to Manhattan and wealthy white New Yorkers continued to populate the area. Rows of sturdy terraced houses sprang up clad in the fashionable brownstone that is now so characteristic of Brooklyn, considered far more sophisticated than the red brick that it concealed. The buildings of Bedford-Stuyvesant were, without question, constructed for the rich. The affluence of the community during this period has left an extraordinary architectural legacy, with Bedford-Stuyvesant now home to the most brownstones in the City of New York.

The beginnings of Bed-Stuy's decline began, as with so many other neighbourhoods and institutions, with the Great Depression.

As real estate value dropped, working-class immigrant families – Irish, Jewish, black and Italian – began to move in, but the real shift, the transformation of a once privileged enclave into a vast and raging slum, was wrought by a force powerful throughout American history – racism. Blockbusting is the illegal practice of buying homes cheaply from white families nervous of incipient demographic changes, and selling them on to impoverished black families at an extortionate markup, exploiting their desperation to own a home and their limited options elsewhere.

In the early part of the twentieth century, when anti-black prejudice was endemic, white flight from a neighbourhood gathered momentum with great speed. And at the same time there were many black arrivals from the still-troubled South, economic migrants drawn to the area by the historic presence of communities such as Weeksville. For the chance to buy in Bedford, black owners were forced to rent out every square inch of their new property to as many tenants as possible, carving their precious family homes into flophouses simply to keep up mortgage repayments. Most of these black owners struggled along in this manner until the Depression and then, last hired and first fired, the true crisis began. The social consequences of the vast numbers of ensuing foreclosures on these homes, bought with sub-prime mortgages, have particular resonances now.

But during my father's childhood Bedford-Stuyvesant was not yet an unusual place for a Jewish boy to grow up, although it was certainly not common, unlike the very Jewish Crown Heights or Williamsburg. Few people wanted Jews next door any more than they wanted a black family. But friends of my father's from later life who grew up in other areas have no memories of fleeing from tough Irish schoolboys for the simple reason, they told me, that they never crossed paths. For my father, on the other hand, to walk home from yeshiva to St Marks Avenue, from Crown Heights to Bedford-Stuyvesant, was to venture into treacherous territory. It was twelve blocks, and each evening he would stuff his yarmulke into his pocket, deciding whether he wanted to risk a beating from the black boys in one direction or the Irish boys at St Gregory's in the other. In his novel *Acts of Faith*, my father explored Brooklyn's Jewish-Irish tensions, although he cast a rather more romantic light on the subject than was there in reality – in his recollection, every encounter he had with the local Catholic boys was suffused with pure terror. Thus self-preservation played a role in the tendency of all Brooklyn's immigrant communities to stick to their own when they settled, the Jews as much as the blacks.

A few of the houses on my father's block were still, like his grandparents', single-family homes, and a few were also Jewish. But if it was a detached home you wanted, better to move with the others to Long Island, where the loss in architectural beauty might be compensated for by a big backyard and the offer of a more homogeneous, less troubled community. The years in which my father lived there were ones of seismic social change for Bedford-Stuyvesant, and so I've long been fascinated by the neighbourhood. But it's only recently that I've been able to admit to myself that my curiosity was less about understanding the mechanics of an urban history, and more about understanding my relationship with my father.

I was eighteen months old when my father was diagnosed with Parkinson's disease, a name that would become as familiar within our family as any of our own. It was part of him but eventually, inevitably, it would become part of all of us. The two monoliths that dominated my father's identity – the peak and the trough of his life – were *Love Story* and Parkinson's disease.

I am now twenty-eight, and my father has been seriously ill for all of my conscious memory. I know nothing else and it is impossible for me to look with any real perspective at how it has affected me. For a long time I believed that I had accepted it. But lately I have begun to realize that my long-standing coping mechanisms are failing me, and that the denial of his illness, in which I have operated for most of my life, is causing more damage than it prevents.

I had separated who he was in my childhood from who he is now; compartmentalizing so I had both a relatively healthy father for whom I felt a constant, powerful nostalgia and a fiercely protective pride, and someone else entirely; a father I love equally who is battling with a vicious neurological disease. It was too painful for me to face the reality that one had become the other, and until very recently I fought to keep the first uncontaminated by the second. But the right way to honour him, both who he was and who he is, was to bring them together.

I had no idea how to effect that integration, but going back to his beginnings seemed a good place to start. And so in the summer of 2008 I went to Bedford-Stuyvesant, to try to understand where he came from and where I came from. I wanted to be able to see him clearly again, to rediscover him, even if it hurt.

CROWN HEIGHTS

M y first morning in Brooklyn, I have arranged to join a regular, organized walking tour of Jewish Crown Heights, the neighbouring district to Bedford-Stuyvesant and the area where my father went to school. Since he left Brooklyn in 1950, the Jewish community in Crown Heights has changed character significantly, but I'm unsure where else to begin. Here at least I'll have a tour guide of whom I can ask my questions, even if he might not have the answers.

The son of a rabbi, my father was raised in Conservative Judaism, a movement that, despite its misleading name, is founded on modern and progressive ideals – committed to tolerance, liberalism and intellectual engagement. This is the movement, together with Reform Judaism, with which the majority of America's lapsed, shellfish-eating Jews would identify. In the 1940s Crown Heights was predominantly Conservative, and my father walked the six blocks to attend the movement's kindergarten. But the Conservative Jews of Crown Heights have long since vanished, moving on to Manhattan or the suburbs, following an upward trajectory from hard-working immigrant grandparent to assimilated, white-collar grandson. And in their wake have come the Lubavitch Hasidim, the 'black hats', replacing once progressive organizations with the institutions and mores of the old world.

It's difficult to emphasize just how enormous the shift has been. The Conservative Jews encompassed the socialists and communists, campaigned for sexual and racial equality, kept a casual sort of kosher, went to the movies on Sabbath, sang workers' anthems, learned modern, spoken Hebrew and raised money to plant trees in what they hoped would become the state of Israel. Casting off the antiquated restrictions inherent in any ancient religion, the movement was about looking forwards. The Hasidim, committed to maintaining law and lore, look back to the past.

In 1997 the Conservative Brooklyn Jewish Center closed its doors for good. The community had gone and there was no one now to use the banqueting halls, swimming pool, gymnasium, school and synagogue that had been built to be the social hub of a vibrant, living community. This had been my father's kindergarten, where as early as the 1940s the gaggle of boys and girls, schooled together, had worn blue jeans, studied a curriculum based on levelling, socialist, egalitarian ideals, written plays about Zionism and sung black freedom songs in Prospect Park.

When the building was sold, the buyers were the Lubavitch, whose rapidly expanding community made excellent use of the space. Girls were evicted from the classrooms. Neither could the Conservative Crown Heights Yeshiva, where my father had later studied, fill its spaces and it moved to Flatbush – the building it once occupied was also bought by the Lubavitch and turned into a religious girls' school. All the significant institutions of my father's childhood are now occupied by seats of Orthodox Jewish learning. If only to gain access to the buildings in which my father once studied, the Lubavitch seemed as good a place as any to begin.

The international centre of the Lubavitch Hasidic movement is at 770 Eastern Parkway, in the heart of Crown Heights. The majority of the non-Hasidic residents of the area are black – and, indeed, they are the majority of the residents. Right next door to Bedford-Stuyvesant, Crown Heights is another complex and conflicted community with an entirely different symphony of tensions. But one thing that it is, unlike many other areas, is a mixed community – the Lubavitch, as one rabbi explained to me, do not feel the need to flee when a black family moves in upstairs.

To an outsider, the Lubavitch are indistinguishable from any other brand of Orthodox Jew. They wear black hats and sidecurls, speak Yiddish and obey the 613 commandments handed down to Moses on Mount Sinai. Men and women study separately, work separately and a man is forbidden even to shake the hand of a woman who is not his wife. In their belief that modesty is paramount, the men all dress the same, a sombre garb of black and white, and women, often well into their eighth, ninth or tenth pregnancies, cover their bodies almost completely in long skirts and long sleeves. Hair is believed to be a significant source of female beauty and thus married women wear wigs called *sheitels*, preserving the sexually stimulating sight of their real tresses for their husbands alone. In all of this, the Lubavitch are no different from any other Orthodox Hasidic Jewish community. Where they differ is in their attitudes to the outside world.

Proselytizing is strictly forbidden in Judaism, which explains why across the centuries it has remained tiny compared to other monotheistic religions. A common anti-Semitic belief holds that there are hundreds of millions of Jews worldwide merely biding their time before they attempt world domination – in reality, the religion is comparatively small. There are roughly 14 million Jews in the world, compared with nearly 2 billion Christians and more than a billion Muslims. Clearly, a prohibition against evangelical practice doesn't help the numbers.

But what is not forbidden, and what remains at the core of Lubavitch philosophy, is outreach to people precisely like myself –

non-practising Jews for whom cultural and intellectual identification has become more important than religious practice. Other Orthodox groups have no interest in adding to their ranks and might even be hostile to lapsed Jews wanting in, but the Lubavitch would like nothing more than to see me shed my jeans and don a long wool skirt in their place. They'd help, they'd celebrate, they'd drink whisky, and then they'd find me a husband who'd had a similar awakening. Thus they are actively engaged with the secular world – visiting Jewish students in universities, running open-door Sabbath dinners in far-flung parts of the globe where Jewish travellers might be struck by nostalgia, and driving brightly painted vans through lower Manhattan every winter, blasting out Hanukkah songs from roof-mounted speakers while distributing kosher doughnuts. And because so many of them were raised in secular homes before their own religious rediscoveries, they know about the world.

I'm staying with my friend Cassim again, with whom I began this exploration, and decide to walk from his apartment near Park Slope along Eastern Parkway to the corner where I am due to meet the group for the Crown Heights walking tour. Park Slope is the apotheosis of Brooklyn's white gentrification – filled with shops that sell handmade glycerine soaps studded with dried rosebuds, gem-encrusted photo frames, eight-dollar greetings cards and raw-silk scarves – indulgent indicators of a large disposable income. After twenty minutes, the change in demographic is unmistakable. The tree-shaded benches that squat beside the path are filled only with black men – old men sitting alone and enjoying the shade, young men lounging in small groups who suck their teeth or hiss at me as I pass. The third time it happens I notice why – it's eighty degrees and I am in a vest top, but mine is the only white skin on display. The women walking past are all white, and all swaddled in the common dress of the Hasidim – square-shouldered, high-collared houndstooth jackets with matching mid-calf skirts, accompanied by a pushchair and multiple toddlers, and heavy wigs and woollen tights, despite the rising and oppressive humidity. By the time I approach the junction of Eastern Parkway and Kingston Avenue everyone is eyeing me with curiosity – white but in jeans; in jeans but white. Already overheating, I feel compelled to put on a sweater.

On Kingston it would be impossible to imagine that the Lubavitch are the minority in this community. Every store displays one of two flags, either the Stars and Stripes or a bright yellow flag depicting the deceased Lubavitch Rebbe or chief rabbi, who, many in the community believe, was the Messiah. ('The fact that he died,' I'm told later, 'doesn't necessarily disqualify him.') Judaica World stands next to Weinstein's Hardware, a kosher deli on the other side. The clothing shop next door sells a variety of *tichels* (headscarves). Barbie is nowhere to be seen and instead the toystore sells plastic figures of *Zaidy* and *Bubbe* ('Grandpa' and 'Grandma' in Yiddish), he with a grey beard, she with her plastic hair modestly hidden beneath a plastic *sheitel*. I can't resist buying Jewish Superheroes!, a card game that seems modelled on Happy Families. Outside I hesitate, then return for *Zaidy* and *Bubbe*.

Emerging from the toystore, I can immediately see my fellow tourists from down the block, for they stick out, if possible, even more than I do. Two plump and faintly confused-looking Chinese women are standing on the corner with backpacks, stocky and ostentatiously pale legs emerging from matching army shorts. Mrs Chen and her daughter Alex are here from San Francisco, it transpires, celebrating Alex's sixteenth birthday. Why Alex Chen might want to spend the day traipsing around an American shtetl is not immediately obvious to me, and from the look on her face it is not immediately obvious to her either. But Mrs Chen is brimming with enthusiasm.

Our guide, Rabbi Epstein, appears, detaching himself from the crowds of identically clothed men and ushering us downstairs to a library, brandishing a carton of kosher chocolate soy milk in one hand and a box of *rugelach*, small knots of sticky chocolate pastry, in the other. 'I can't talk unless y'all are eatin'!' he bellows in a languorous, and deeply incongruous, Tennessee drawl. Mrs Chen moves to shake his hand and he steps back with a booming laugh, hands raised as though in a hold-up. 'Men are men and women are women, y'know what I'm sayin'?' Mrs Chen obviously does not know what he's saying, but she gamely accepts the box of *rugelach* that he thrusts into her hand in compensation.

The next few hours are some of the more surreal that I will spend in Brooklyn. Rabbi Epstein's yeehaw Southern inflection and frequent use of the phrase 'to touch pinkies' as a euphemism for sex mean I am in constant danger of giggling; the block looks as if it could be in eighteenth-century Eastern Europe, but there are many reminders that this is merely a mini-community within a larger – and very different – majority whenever the street shakes with the boom of dance-hall music, blasting out of the cars at stop lights. Poland meets Jamaica.

Before we start, Rabbi Epstein gives us some background. As he talks he swings on his chair, fedora pushed back at a jaunty angle as he explains that the study of the soul is at the heart of Lubavitch philosophy. 'I'm into soul, baby!' he shouts at one point. 'Know what I'm sayin'?' Mrs Chen asks a series of increasingly perplexed questions. Alex Chen adopts the pose most beloved of awkward teenagers and slumps, staring miserably at the floor. And then we're off on our tour – into the closed heart of a Jewish community utterly unlike my own, and unlike my father's, though the architecture is the same. We visit huge segregated synagogues where women are sequestered behind walls to keep the men from unholy thoughts during prayer; baths for ritual cleansing; and workshops where Torah scrolls are repaired by earnest students who ignore us and break only to speak into mobile phones in rapid Yiddish. Three hours pass, then four, and Alex Chen is throwing a tantrum. This is their last day in New York, she was meant to be meeting people and this is *boring*. Unfazed, the rabbi is sympathetic and immediately commands that her friends join us for lunch.

We are the only customers in the kosher Chinese restaurant, and so there is little problem that our party has expanded. A waiter pushes some tables together and then announces the unholy trinity of dishes on the 'authentic' menu – lo mein noodles, pastrami and pickle on rye, or an American hamburger. Mrs Chen instructs us in the correct pronunciation of 'lo mein'.

After we've ordered, an overweight black teenager appears in the restaurant and begins studying us from beneath his baseball cap, hands twisted behind him in discomfort. An equally overweight Dominican girl joins him moments later.

'Calvin?' asks Alex Chen, perking up. The boy nods. The rabbi leaps to his feet to shake his hand – the first man of the day provides an opportunity for effusive and compensatory handshaking.

Calvin and his friend are from Harlem, it transpires, and know Alex Chen from the Internet. They are avid fans of a 2D role-playing game called Maple Story ('I call it Maple Stupid,' says Mrs Chen tartly) and have never met in real life, but soon fall into low mumbles. I take the opportunity to ask the rabbi about my father's old yeshiva and delight in the familiar names he reels off, characters who have long featured in my family mythology – one former classmate of my father's whose parents ran a kosher chocolate factory and who was allergic to almost every ingredient in a chocolate bar; the headmaster who once beat my father when he caught him drawing a picture, inexplicably, of a ham. The stories were so oft-repeated that it is hard to believe they actually featured real people, and yet nearly sixty years after they crossed paths with my father I am back in Crown Heights with a rabbi who seems to know them all.

BED-STUY

It takes me several days to find the courage to visit Bedford-Stuyvesant properly. I hadn't realized how anxious I was about it, how resistant I would be to embarking on the journey that I've wanted to make for so long. But it feels daunting, and complicated, and in the meantime I find myself drawn to red herrings, exploring the rich African-American history of the area; going to the Weeksville

An abandoned building in Bedford-Stuyvesant, 1968

Museum, immersing myself in a heritage that, while fascinating, shares merely a geographical coincidence with my own. Time after time I postpone the confrontation with the particulars of my father's childhood.

The first day I go to Bedford-Stuyvesant itself I begin in the now familiar Crown Heights, walking north on Utica Avenue to watch the neighbourhoods change. North of Eastern Parkway already has a different sense – there are still several Orthodox Jews on the streets but many fewer, and just streets away from the Lubavitch centre the dominant ethnicity has changed completely. Almost an entire block is taken up with tiny, storefront churches: the Baptist Church; Eglesias Pentecostal; the New Jerusalem Temple; St Martin's Southern Baptist Church; the Holy Church of Prayer; St Paul's Baptist Church. Tall crosses hang where the shop awnings would be. Only six blocks south, each store displayed its loyalty to the Lubavitch Rebbe; now each proclaims: 'We Preach Christ and Him Crucified!' The wig shops and Yiddish bookstores have been replaced by nail bars and African hair-braiding salons offering custom-cut weaves and synthetic dreadlocks; alongside the plums and apples, the displays outside the grocery stores now contain tall sugar cane, cut watermelons, fat pineapples.

Although this southern part of Bedford-Stuyvesant is known to be the least troubled by a significant margin, it doesn't take long before one senses the deprivation of the area. The deeper I walk into Bed-Stuy, the more common a sight it becomes to see that the iron bars on ground-floor windows, thick as prison railings, have been prised away and hang loosely; that in place of curtains almost every one of these windows is blocked with graffitied chipboard, and that the many vacant lots are littered with television sets with shattered screens, flat on their backs and filled with rainwater like small ponds, ripped mattresses, mangled engine parts and sacks of rotting household waste. Each lot is piled so high with garbage that it conceals the rusting sign declaring DO NOT THROW YOUR GARBAGE HERE!

On Malcolm X Boulevard, the Magic Soul Food Restaurant Inc. looks as if it might once have been relatively high-end, offering a classy interpretation of traditional Southern fare. The sign, now cracked, is more elaborate than anything else I've seen here, in a swirling white font that looks as if it ought to belong to an East Village bakery or an organic cafe. Clearly the locals agreed that it was in the wrong place – every pane of glass in its frontage is smashed, and the broken furniture inside has been heaped in the centre of the restaurant so that it appears as if someone is getting ready for a bonfire. Across the street, the New Sun Lee Chinese Takeout seems better prepared. Still operational, it boasts a bullet-proof shield between the customers and the staff. It's like ordering noodles in a bank.

For the next week I walk the streets and my days take the same pattern, boarding the C train and watching, bemused, as the subway sheds white people and collects black, so that each morning I am the only white woman disembarking at Nostrand Avenue. I have never been so racially aware and I realize that I have never had to be – I have never before been the one who stands out. I become used to occasional looks of suspicion and hostility, and to the more frequent glances of straightforward surprise at my presence here. Swathes of time go by every day during which I pass hundreds of people on busy streets, and still no one else is white. And I'm sure I would stop noticing, were it not for the expressions on the faces around me, which make it difficult to forget.

But for all the time I've spent here, I've not yet been to my father's house. It's only on my third day in the neighbourhood that I even become aware I am procrastinating, postponing an experience that I already understand is likely to be empty of the significance I had hoped for. There has been nothing of my father on these streets, and I'm frightened that I won't find him anywhere here, even in his own landmarks. Finally I force myself to go, arriving on the block on which my father grew up – St Marks, between New York and Brooklyn Avenues.

But 800 St Marks Avenue no longer exists. In its place is the red-brick Marcus Garvey Residents' Home, an old people's facility that takes up a quarter of the block, rap music blasting from its windows so loudly that it can only come from a professional sound system. The pavement outside vibrates with the subwoofer. His house is the only one that's gone – every other on that side of the block remains standing; neat, identical homes just like the one my father spent the first six years of his life in. I study the house next door for meaning, finding little. Eventually I cross the street to number 825, the more modest brownstone almost directly opposite to which my father moved when he was in grade school, home to the ground-floor apartment where, aged six, he lived with his mother and father for the first time. I stand on the sidewalk staring through its windows, unsure of what I should be feeling.

As I'm taking photographs of the brownstone a battered van pulls up beside me and one of the blacked-out windows rolls down.

'How much you askin'?' the driver shouts. Behind him another man is visible in the passenger seat, craning to hear my reply. I genuinely have no idea whether they think I'm a prostitute or a real estate agent but in either case, it's time to leave.

The next person to approach me is a workman on a construction site across the street, when I regret my swift departure and return later to take a photograph of the rows of neo-Georgian mansions that are still there. They are all identical to one another – it seems unlikely that 800 was any different. As I take out my camera he sets down a drill, leans on the chain-link fence and shouts, 'You tinkin' of buying dat house?'

I have been shouted at a lot on the streets of Bed-Stuy, and this is the first time it has happened without a trace of hostility. I cross the street and explain why I'm here. It surprises me how grateful I feel talking to him – his West Indian accent sounds like London to me, and I instantly feel safer. His name is Gary, and he's been a builder in New York since he left Jamaica twenty years ago.

'They rob me too many times here. But, ah...' He turns and

gestures behind him, gazing up at the half-renovated house. '*Look* at this architecture. It's marvellous.'

And it is. The buildings in Bedford-Stuyvesant are more beautiful than anything I've seen in Manhattan. Thick, rough-cut brownstone has a glow when it's clean; there is a grandeur to the buildings here that seeps through, even when the sidewalks are cracked and swollen and filled with trash, even when windows are boarded up with damp and rotting plywood, when pointless scrawls of blood-red, spray-painted graffiti coat every inch of the cladding and razor wire encircles everything, shredded plastic bags snagged and snapping on its teeth. The buildings remain extraordinary, all the more so for their sheer volume – street after street of faded beauty.

Gary is worried about me being here, and concerned I might encounter some of the 'elements' that he is keen to see removed from the area. 'Jus' don' get in their way. You can do your research here if you mus', but know who you're talking to. Because they will target you too. Always be on your guard, watch your back, don't go hinterfering.' Before he lets me go, he teaches me how to 'hidentify' gang members – their clothes, colours, gestures and territories. 'This is Bed-Stuy,' he calls after me as I leave, as though that says it all.

Talking to Gary is heartening. After twenty years in New York, he tells me, he's ready to go home to Jamaica. 'But you got to weigh the opportunity costs. My oldest son is in college here, studying to be an engineer, my second son is going to do law, and so I have to stay for them, make sure I go through the rough time with them, you know? I need to cushion them until they're grown.'

His explanation brings a tightness to my throat, and after I leave I attempt to gauge my reaction. A lack of available father figures is at the core of social disintegration here – almost everyone I speak to acknowledges that the gangs are substitute families, and that older gang members often provide the only male role models available to teenage boys. Single-parent families are the majority and make the boys particularly vulnerable, one of many reasons that the streets of Bedford-Stuyvesant are a treacherous place for a young black man to grow up. Their models are the hustlers and drug dealers – the few men in the neighbourhood who have more money than merely a welfare cheque.

But it also touches me because my own father is constantly on my mind, present in my thoughts and yet absent from the streets. I can't feel him here, can't picture his life, and I'm frustrated that what physical monuments remain of his childhood – the houses, the block, his school – should evoke so little for me. And the depth of Gary's desire to protect his children, that most fundamental drive of fatherhood, makes me miss my father desperately. I know that for my whole life he has wanted to shield me from his illness, and it feels terribly painful to acknowledge how much it must hurt him that he couldn't cushion me until I was grown.

From St Marks Avenue I walk back down to Fulton Street, the main shopping area and the place, at the junction with Nostrand Avenue, where the infamous riots and looting began in the 1960s. I stop suddenly outside a shop, my eye caught by a hideous grinning Jewish caricature on the cover of a DVD displayed prominently in the window. It's all there – hooked nose, knowing smirk, black hat branded with the Star of David. *The Illegitimacy of a People Called Jews* appears to be one of the lessons of Supreme Wisdom put out by the Nation of Islam, and is but one in a series. I go inside.

The current vendors seem to be squatters in the establishment, a dusty, ill-lit space that I later discover was once the concession area of the now-defunct Slave Theater One next door, on whose stage a young Al Sharpton honed his oratorical skills. On sale are framed quotations by Reverend Louis Farrakhan and a variety of black supremacists, on subjects ranging from marriage and women to violence, repression and the evildoings of the white man. The neglect, poverty and social decimation of a neighbourhood such as Bedford-Stuyvesant provide precisely the climate in which such radical, dangerous, seductive preachers of hate find their captive audience. At the back is what appears to be a great number of carpet samples, rolled and stuffed into black bin bags, and on the other side is a collection of photographs and paintings of genuine heroes – Martin Luther King and Rosa Parks. Along another wall, a series of card tables displays a selection of home-made cakes sliced into neat wedges, and a pile of plastic forks wrapped in red paper napkins. Three women sit beside them in silence, apparently holding an extremely under-attended bake sale.

Eventually I select *The Illegitimacy of a People Called Jews* and another irresistible title, *The White Women* [sic] *is a Bitch (A Female Dog)*. I dither in the dusty store for a long time, like a teenage boy buying condoms, embarrassed to be seen with the DVDs and worried I'll be challenged. I'm not an obvious candidate for Nation of Islam conversion and wonder briefly if I should buy a slice of carrot cake as a diversion.

At a garden table at the back, on which a cash box serves as a till, the elderly man peers sternly at my purchases and then, jabbing his finger at each of them in turn, looks up at me. I brace myself. He pauses, and then eventually offers, 'These are on three-for-two.'

I offer somewhat surprised thanks and return to admire the remaining titles, eventually choosing *The Truth Terrorists Black Power House of Konsciousness*. He nods sagely, and hands me my purchases with no further comment. Later that night, my friend Cassim looks sorrowfully at my new DVD collection. 'On behalf of my co-religionists,' he says eventually, 'please let me say that the Nation of Islam are *not* real Muslims. They're *crazy*.'

That summer I ostensibly went to Brooklyn to learn about my father's childhood. I had wanted to see his house; his synagogue; the Jewish centre where he had walked, with trepidation, to his first day at kindergarten. But what I thought I was looking for was not there. When the obliging principal of the Beis Rivka Girls' School led me into a classroom – perfectly preserved from the 1940s when it was my father's yeshiva – the experience had little impact on me. For, once I looked honestly at my motivations; what I had wanted to find was my father as he was in my own childhood, not his. I now understand that

I will never find him in architecture, in street maps or in explorations of urban sociology, or by following the footsteps he walked in a childhood he was happy to leave behind. He is in other places.

On my last night in New York, sitting in the newly refurbished Second Avenue Deli, I find him in the pastrami on rye bread; in the solidly refrigerated chocolate fudge cake; in the gefilte fish like pallid, porous cannonballs daubed with neon-bright horseradish; in the Jewish warmth and irreverence and humour that suffuse everything in this restaurant, and in my own certain knowledge that he would love it there. I find him where I've always found him – in Art Garfunkel, who once, when I was high on my father's shoulders, said I was a cute baby; in Paul Simon's lilting ballad 'Bleecker Street'; in the pages of Henry Roth but never Philip; in Chaim Potok; and oddly, yet more powerfully than all of those, in Kermit the Frog, a wry and charming figure who has always, since childhood, reminded me of my father.

And I returned to find him here, in London, ill and fighting – but still waiting to hear about where I'd been. Concerned that I'd been careful in my exploration of what used to be his home. Equally concerned that I'd remembered to order my pastrami lean at the Second Avenue Deli. I came back with the nascent understanding that I felt drawn to look elsewhere because I have not yet come to terms with what has been taken from my family by his illness – that my attempts at reconstruction are my way of grieving, but that I must acknowledge what I've lost in order to appreciate, while I have it, what I have.

I had admitted little of this before I went to Brooklyn, having convinced myself that I was merely fascinated by the complex social evolution of Bedford-Stuyvesant, proclaiming to anyone with whom I discussed it that my desire to go there had as much to do with an interest in urban planning as it did with an interest in my own family.

But now that I'm home I realize that it was a far more significant experience than I'd known it would be, a shift that I had never consciously expected but had no doubt unconsciously hoped for. I understand that I may well have set off searching for him in the secret hope that I would return to find him cured, or that a focus on his past might somehow turn back time for him, or that my discoveries might restore what his illness has taken from him over many years. I suspect I believed that by learning more about where he had come from, I might be able to keep him present. ∎

A few months after starting university in Bradford, I came back to Norfolk and went to the football with my dad. I don't remember who Norwich played, or if we won; only what happened afterwards, as we walked away from the ground.

We heard shouting behind us and saw a black teenager being followed by a group of white teenagers. We couldn't hear what they were saying, but it looked hostile, and it was clear that he was trying, and failing, to get away. It looked like something was about to kick off, and since I thought I was street-smart now I instinctively drifted away. Dad, however, turned back.

Let's be clear: he's not a big man. He's never, as far as I know, been in a fight, and he usually avoids confrontation or complaint. He was a great father – supportive, caring, involved in our childhoods in a way we all took for granted at the time – but he never seemed heroic. He wasn't good at sport, we couldn't boast about his job, and we certainly couldn't threaten to set him on anyone who gave us trouble at school. He was just Dad; short, round-shouldered and inclined to shout, 'You twerp!' at football matches.

But here he was, pushing through the crowd, putting his arm around this lad's shoulder, quietly leading him away. The white lads kept on with the verbals, and Dad turned to face them, staring them down before saying, memorably, 'Just…push off, will you?'

He spoke loudly and clearly, without flinching, and if his voice trembled then it was with a righteous fury. Because did I mention that my older brother, who wasn't there that day, is black? And that growing up in Norfolk he'd had to put up with this kind of thing all his life? That it had mostly gone unchallenged, unpunished, and that my father had been unable to protect him from it?

I don't know if he was thinking about all that at the time, but I was, afterwards, after the white lads backed off and he kept walking with his arm round the black lad's shoulder, nudging through the crowd until they reached some kind of safety, while I followed on behind and thought about how much I had to learn if I wanted to be like

From left to right: my older brother Joe, my father, me, my mother holding baby
Matthew and my sister Catherine, New Cross, London, 1979

him, the words of his intervention ringing in my head like a line from
a Marlon Brando film. *Just push off, will ya?*

He retired this year, after thirty-nine years as an Anglican vicar.
He must have taken thousands of services in that time, but this still
feels like the holiest thing he's ever done. ■

LESSONS

Justin Torres

1. WE WANTED MORE

We wanted more. We knocked the butt ends of our forks against the table, tapped our spoons against our empty bowls; we were hungry. We wanted more volume, more riots. We turned up the knob on the TV until our ears ached with the shouts of angry men. We wanted more music on the radio; we wanted beats, we wanted rock. We wanted muscles on our skinny arms. We had bird bones, hollow and light, and we wanted more density, more weight. We were six snatching hands, six stomping feet; we were brothers, boys, three little kings locked in a feud for more.

When it was cold, we fought over blankets until the cloth tore down the middle. When it was really cold, when our breath came out in frosty clouds, Manny crawled into bed with Joel and me.

'Body heat,' he said.

'Body heat,' we agreed.

We wanted more flesh, more blood, more warmth.

GRANTA

THE MAGAZINE OF NEW WRITING

If you enjoy good writing, you'll love Granta – fiction, reportage, memoir, biography and photography four times a year

Subscribe to *Granta* or buy a subscription for a friend and receive, with our compliments, a *Granta* special-edition **MOLESKINE®** notebook

Subscribe online at **www.granta.com** or call **toll-free 1-866-438-6150** or fill in the **back of this card** and send to us

The Rise of the British Jihad
An Investigation by Richard Watson

'*Provides enough to satisfy the most rabid appetite for good writing and hard thinking*'
WASHINGTON POST
BOOK WORLD

Yes, I would like to take out an annual subscription to *Granta* and receive a complimentary *Granta* special-edition **MOLESKINE**® notebook:

PERSONAL SUBSCRIPTION
Your address:
FIRST NAME: LAST NAME:

COMPANY: ADDRESS:

CITY: STATE: ZIP CODE:

COUNTRY: TELEPHONE: EMAIL:

GIFT SUBSCRIPTION
Gift address:
FIRST NAME: LAST NAME:

COMPANY: ADDRESS:

CITY: STATE: ZIP CODE:

COUNTRY: TELEPHONE: EMAIL:

Billing address:
FIRST NAME: LAST NAME:

COMPANY: ADDRESS:

CITY: STATE: ZIP CODE:

COUNTRY: TELEPHONE: EMAIL:

NUMBER OF SUBSCRIPTIONS	DELIVERY REGION	PRICE	SAVINGS	AUTO RENEWAL PRICE	SAVINGS
☐	USA	$45.99	32%	**$35.99**	**47%**
☐	Canada	$57.99	32%	**$47.99**	**44%**
☐	Rest of World	$65.99	32%	**$55.99**	**43%**

I would like my subscription to start from: All prices include delivery

☐ the current issue   ☐ the next issue   GRANTA IS PUBLISHED QUARTERLY

PAYMENT DETAILS

☐ I enclose a check payable to '*Granta*' for $ _____ for _____ subscriptions to *Granta*.

☐ Please charge my ☐ MASTERCARD ☐ VISA ☐ AMEX for $ _____ for _____ subscriptions.

NUMBER ☐☐☐☐ ☐☐☐☐ ☐☐☐☐ ☐☐☐☐   EXPIRATION ☐☐ / ☐☐

SIGNED _____ DATE _____

☐ Charge my card automatically annually for only $35.99, a savings of 47%. Canada: $47.99 (savings 44%); Rest of World: $55.99 (savings 43%)

Our Best Offer
By signing up for automatic renewal, you will get the absolute best price on your *Granta* subscriptions. No more forms to fill out, no more renewal notices in the mail – we will automatically charge your card each year for your subscription, and send you a confirmation notice. (Don't worry – if for any reason you want to stop your subscription, it's easy to cancel.) Choose Auto Renewal by checking the box above!

☐ Please check this box if you would like to receive special offers from *Granta*.
☐ Please check this box if you would like to receive offers from organizations selected by *Granta*.

Please return this form to: **Granta Subscriptions, PO Box 359, Congers, NY 10920-0359**
Call toll-free 1-866-438-6150 or go to **www.granta.com**

Please quote the following promotion code when ordering online: BUS104PM

When we fought, we fought with weapons – boots and garage tools, snapping pliers – we grabbed at whatever was nearest and we hurled it through the air; we wanted more broken dishes, more shattered glass. We wanted more crashes.

And when our Paps came home, we got spankings. Our little round butt cheeks were tore up: red, raw, leather-whipped. We knew there was something on the other side of pain, on the other side of the sting. Prickly heat radiated upward from our thighs and backsides, fire consumed our brains, but we knew that there was something more, some place our Paps was taking us with all this. We knew, because he was meticulous, because he was precise, because he took his time.

And when our father was gone, we wanted to be fathers. We hunted animals. We drudged through the muck of the creek, chasing down bullfrogs and water snakes. We plucked the baby robins from their nest. We liked to feel the beat of tiny hearts, the struggle of tiny wings. We brought their tiny animal faces close to ours.

'Who's your daddy?' we said, then we laughed and tossed them into a shoebox.

Always more, always hungrily scratching for more. But there were times, quiet moments, when our mother was sleeping, when she hadn't slept in two days, and any noise, any stair creak, any shut door, any stifled laugh, any voice at all, might wake her – those still, crystal mornings, when we wanted to protect her, this confused goose of a woman, this stumbler, this gusher, with her backaches and headaches and her tired, tired ways, this uprooted Brooklyn creature, this tough talker, always with tears when she tells us she loves us, her mixed-up love, her needy love, her warmth – on those mornings, when sunlight found the cracks in our blinds, and laid itself down in crisp strips on our carpet, those quiet mornings, when we'd fixed ourselves oatmeal, and sprawled on to our stomachs with crayons and paper, with glass marbles that we were careful not to rattle, when our mother was sleeping, when the air did not smell like sweat or breath or mould, when the air was still and light, those mornings, when silence was our secret game and our gift and our sole accomplishment – we wanted less: less weight, less work, less noise, less father, less muscles and skin and hair. We wanted nothing, just this, just this.

2. HERITAGE

When we got home from school Paps was in the kitchen, cooking and listening to music and feeling fine. He whiffed the steam coming off a pot, then clapped his hands together and rubbed them briskly. His eyes were wet and sparkled with giddy life. He turned up the volume on the stereo and it was mambo, it was Tito Puente.

'Watch out,' he said, and spun, with grace, on one slippered foot, his bathrobe twirling out around him. In his fist was a glistening, greasy metal spatula, which he pumped in the air to the beat of the bongo drums.

My brothers and I, the three of us, stood in the entrance to the kitchen, laughing, eager to join in, but waiting for our cue. He staked staccato steps across the linoleum to where we stood and whipped Joel and Manny on to the dance floor, grabbing their wimpy arms and jerking them behind him. Me he took by the hands and slid between his legs and I popped up on the other side of him. Then we wiggled around the kitchen, following behind him in a line, like baby geese. We rolled our tiny clenched fists in front of us and snapped our hips to the trumpet blasts.

There were hot things on the stove, pork chops frying in their own fat, and Spanish rice foaming up and rattling its lid. The air was thick with steam and spice and noise, and the one little window above the sink was fogged over.

Paps turned the stereo even louder, so loud that if I screamed no one would have heard me, so loud that my brothers felt very far away and hard to get to, even though they were right there in front of me. Then Paps grabbed a can of beer from the fridge and our eyes followed the path of the can to his lips. We took in the empties stacked up on the counter behind him, then we looked at each other. Manny rolled his eyes and kept dancing, and so we got in line and kept dancing too, except now Manny was the Papa Goose, it was him we were following.

'Now shake it like you're rich,' Paps shouted, his powerful voice booming out over the music. We danced on tiptoes, sticking up our noses and poking the air above us with our pinkies.

'You ain't rich,' Papi said, 'Now shake it like you're poor.'

We got low on our knees, clenched our fists and stretched our arms out on our sides; we shook our shoulders and threw our heads back, wild and loose and free.

'You ain't poor neither. Now shake it like you're white.'

We moved like robots, stiff and angled, not even smiling. Joel was the most convincing, I'd see him practising in his room sometimes.

'You ain't white,' Paps shouted. 'Now shake it like a Puerto Rican.'

There was a pause as we gathered ourselves. Then we mamboed as best we could, trying to be smooth and serious and to feel the beat in our feet and beyond the beat to feel the rhythm. Paps watched us for a while, leaning against the counter and taking long draws from his beer.

'Mutts,' he said. 'You ain't white and you ain't Puerto Rican. Watch how a purebred dances, watch how we dance in the ghetto.' Every word was shouted over the music, so it was hard to tell if he was mad or just making fun.

He danced and we tried to see what separated him from us. He pursed his lips and kept one hand on his stomach. His elbow was bent, his back was straight, but somehow there was looseness and freedom and confidence in every move. I tried to watch his feet but something about the way they twisted and stepped over each other, something about the line of his torso, kept pulling my eyes up to his face, to his broad nose and dark, half-shut eyes and his pursed lips, which snarled and smiled both.

'This is your heritage,' he said, as if from this dance we could know about his own childhood, about the flavour and grit of tenement buildings in Spanish Harlem, and projects in Red Hook, and dance halls, and city parks, and about his own Papi, how he beat him, how he taught him to dance, as if we could hear Spanish in his movements, as if Puerto Rico was a man in a bathrobe, grabbing another beer from the fridge and raising it to drink, his head back, still dancing, still stepping and snapping perfectly in time.

3. THE LAKE

One unbearable night, in the middle of a heatwave, Paps drove us all to the lake. Ma and I didn't know how to swim, so she grabbed on to Papi's back and I grabbed on to hers and he took us on a little tour, spreading his arms before him and kicking his legs underneath us, our own legs trailing through the water, relaxed and still, our toes curled backward.

Every once in a while Ma would point out some happening for me to look at, a duck touching down on to the water, his head pulled back on his neck, beating his wings before him, or a water bug with spindly legs that dimpled the lake's surface.

'Not so far,' she would say to Papi, but he'd push on, smooth and slow, and the shore behind would stretch and thin and curve, until it was a wooded crescent impossibly dark and remote.

In the middle of the lake the water was blacker and cooler, and Paps swam right into a clump of slimy tar-black leaves. Ma and I tried to splash the leaves away from us, but we had to keep one arm holding on, so they ended up curling around in our jetty and sticking to our ribs and thighs like leeches. Paps lifted a fistful into the air and the leaf clump melted through the cracks in his fingers and disintegrated into speckles in the water and cigarette-sized fish appeared and nibbled at the leaf bits.

'We've come too far,' Ma said. 'Take us back.'

'Soon,' Papi said.

Ma started talking about how unnatural it was that Paps knew how to swim. She said that no one swam in Brooklyn. The most water she ever saw in one place was when one of the men from the block would open up the johnny pump, and water would rush and pour forth. She said that she never jumped through the spray like the other kids – too hard and mean and shocking – but instead she liked to stand further down, where the sidewalk met the street, and let the water pool around her ankles.

'I had already been married and pushed out three boys before I ever stepped into anything deeper than a puddle,' she said.

Papi didn't say when or where he had learned to swim, but he generally made it his business to learn everything that had to do with survival. He had all the muscles and the will, and he was on his way to becoming indestructible.

'I guess it's opposite with you, isn't it?' Ma called back to me. 'You grew up with all these lakes and rivers, and you got two brothers that swim like a couple of goldfish in a bowl – how come you don't swim?'

She asked the question as if she was meeting me for the first time, as if the circumstances of my life, my fumbling, terrifying attempts at the deep end, the one time at the public pool, when I had been dragged out by the high-school lifeguard and had puked up pool water on to the grass, 700 eyes on me, the din of screams and splashes and whistles momentarily silenced as everyone stopped to ponder my bony weakness, to stare and stare, waiting for me to cry, which I did – as if it had only just now occurred to Ma how odd it was that I was here, clinging to her and Paps, and not with my brothers who had run into the water, dunked each other's heads down, tried to drown each other, then ran back out and disappeared into the trees.

Of course, it was impossible for me to answer her, to tell the truth, to say I was scared. The only one who ever got to say that in our family was Ma, and most of the time she wasn't even scared, just too lazy to go down into the crawlspace herself, or else she said it to make Paps smile, to get him to tickle and tease her or pull her close, to let him know she was only really scared of being without him. But me, I would have rather let go and slipped quietly down to the lake's black bottom than to admit fear to either one of them.

But I didn't have to say anything, because Paps answered for me. 'He's going to learn,' he said. 'You're both going to learn,' and no one spoke after that for a long time. I watched the moon break into shards of light across the lake, I watched dark birds circle and caw, the wind lifted the tree branches, the pine trees tipped; I felt the lake get colder, and I smelled the dead leaves.

Later, after the incident, Paps drove us home. He sat behind the wheel, still shirtless, his back and neck and even his face a cross-hatch of scratches, some only deep red lines and broken skin, some already scabbing, and some still glistening with fresh blood, and I too was all scratched up – for she had panicked, and when he slipped away she had clawed on top of me – later, Paps said, 'How else do you expect to learn?'

And Ma, who had nearly drowned me, who had screamed and cried and dug her nails down into me, who had been more frenzied and wild than I had ever known her to be – Ma, who was so boiling angry that she had made Manny sit up front with Paps and she had taken the middle back, wrapping her arms around us – Ma replied by reaching across me and opening the door as we sped along. I looked down and saw the pavement rushing and blurring beneath, the shoulder dropping away into a gravel pit. Ma held open that door and asked, 'What? You want me to teach him how to fly? Should I teach him how to fly?'

Then Paps had to pull over and calm her down. The three of us boys jumped out and walked to the edge and took out our dicks and pissed down into the ditch.

'She really clawed you up like that?' Manny asked.

'She tried to climb on to my head.'

'What kind of…' he started to say, but didn't finish. Instead, he picked up a rock and hurled it out away from him as far as he could.

From the car, we heard the noises of their arguing, we heard Ma saying over and over, 'You let me go. You let me go,' and we watched the big trailers haul past, rumbling the car and the ground underneath our feet.

Manny laughed. He said, 'Shit, I thought she was gonna throw you out of the car.'

And Joel laughed too. He said, 'Shit. I thought you were gonna fly.'

When we finally returned to the car, Ma was up front again, and Paps drove with one hand on the back of her neck. He waited until the perfect moment, until we'd settled into silence and peace and we were thinking ahead, to the beds waiting for us at home, and then he turned his head to the side, glancing at me over his shoulder, and asked, all curious and friendly, 'So, how'd you like your first flying lesson?' And the whole car erupted in laughter; all was okay again.

But the incident itself remained, and at night, in bed, I remembered how Paps had slipped away from us, how he looked on as we flailed and struggled, how I needed to escape Ma's clutch and grip, how I let myself slide down and down, and when I opened my eyes what I discovered there: black-green murkiness, an underwater world, terror. I sank down for a long time, disoriented and writhing, and then suddenly I was swimming – kicking my legs and spreading my arms just like Paps showed me, and rising up to the light and exploding into air, and then that first breath, sucking air all the way down into my lungs, and when I looked up the sky had never been so vaulted, so sparkling and magnificent. I remembered the urgency in my parents' voices, Ma wrapped around Papi once again, and both of them calling my name. I swam towards their bobbing mass and there under the stars, I was wanted. They had never been so happy to see me, they had never looked at me with such intensity and hope, they had never before spoken my name so softly.

I remembered how Ma burst into tears and Paps celebrated, shouting as if he was a mad scientist and I a marvel of his creation:

'He's alive!'

'He's alive!'

'He's alive!' ■

The picture floats. Someone took it in the Seventies, but the white backdrop gives no clue. My dad owned that wide-lapel trench coat for fifteen or twenty years, typical thrifty child of the Depression. (He probably tried to give it to me at some point.) The beard's trim narrows the time frame slightly, that rakish full-goatee. So often in later years he wouldn't have bothered to shave his jaw to shape it. Put this in the early Seventies. Somehow it floated into my collection of paper trinkets, ferried off to college, then to California for a decade. The only copy. By the time I showed it to my father, last week, he hadn't seen the photograph for thirty-odd years. He couldn't be sure of the photographer, guessing at three friends with comically overlapping names – Bobby Ramirez, Bob Brooks, Geoff Brooks. (I remember all three of them, beloved rascals from my parents' hippie posse.) He settled at last on Geoff Brooks. The picture was never framed, nor mounted in an album, just shifted from file cabinet to cardboard box to file cabinet all this time. A scrap of Scotch tape on the left corner reminds me I had it taped up over a desk in Berkeley. In a family that, after my mother's death, scattered itself and its memorabilia to far corners of the planet, and reassembles now sporadically and sloppily, the picture's a survivor. But I've lived with it for thirty years, gazed into its eyes as often, strange to say, as I have my father's living eyes.

And it shows Richard Lethem as I dream him, my idol. His Midwestern kindness, prairie-gazer's soul, but come to the city, donning the beatnik garb, become the painter and poet and political activist he made himself, a man of the city. When I first knew my parents they were, paradoxically, just the two most exciting adults on the scene, part of a pantheon of artists and activists and students staying up late around the dinner table and often crashing afterwards in the extra rooms of the house. My parents were both the two I had the best access to and the coolest to know, the hub of the wheel. I wasn't interested in childhood, I wanted to hang out with these guys. The picture shows my dad meeting the eyes of a member of his gang, both of them feeling their oats, knowing they were the leading edge of the world. I wanted him to look at me that way. He often did. ■

CONTRIBUTORS

Alison Bechdel's comic strip *Dykes to Watch Out For* has become a cultural institution for lesbians and discerning non-lesbians the world over since it first appeared in 1983. Her graphic memoir *Fun Home* was nominated for a 2006 National Book Critics Circle Award. She lives in the woods near Burlington, Vermont.

Michael Bywater is a writer, broadcaster and culture critic. His previous books include *The Chronicles of Bargepole*, *Lost Worlds* and *Big Babies*.

Kevin Cummins was born in Manchester in 1953 and has lived in London since 1987. Despite photographing artists as diverse as Albert Finney, Rudolph Nureyev and Courtney Love, he is best known for his photographs of British rock musicians, including Joy Division, The Smiths, Oasis and Manic Street Preachers. He has published three monographs to date and a fourth, *Manchester:*

Looking For The Light Through The Pouring Rain, will be published in September 2009.

Emma Donoghue was born in Dublin in 1969 and earned a PhD from Cambridge before moving to London, Ontario. She is the author of nine novels, including *Hood, Touchy Subjects, Landing* and *The Sealed Letter.* 'Man and Boy' is taken from a sequence of true travellers' tales from the last four centuries.

Paul Farley is the author of three collections of poetry including *The Ice Age*, which was awarded the Whitbread Poetry Award in 2002, and, most recently, *Tramp in Flames*. 'Return to Netherley', co-authored with Niall Griffiths, appeared in *Granta* 102.

David Goldblatt has tried and failed at medicine, politics and academia, and is now a writer, broadcaster and teacher. His most recent book is *The Ball is Round:*

A Global History of Football. He was born in London in 1965 and now lives in Bristol.

Olga Grushin was born in Moscow in 1971. In 1976 her father found himself at odds with the state, and her family moved to Prague. She returned to Moscow in 1981. Her first novel, *The Dream Life of Sukhanov*, won the 2007 New York Public Library Young Lions Fiction Award and was shortlisted for the Orange Award for New Writers. In the same year she was chosen as one of *Granta*'s Best of Young American Novelists.

Kirsty Gunn's most recent book, *The Boy and the Sea*, won the Sundial Scottish Arts Council Book of the Year, 2007. She is professor of writing at the University of Dundee. She lives in London and Scotland.

David Heatley's work has appeared on the cover of *The New Yorker*, in the *New York Times* and *McSweeney's*. His graphic memoir,

My Brain is Hanging Upside Down, was published in October 2008.

Siri Hustvedt is the author of four novels: *The Blindfold*, *The Enchantment of Lily Dahl*, *What I Loved* and, most recently, *The Sorrows of an American*. She has also published two books of essays, *Mysteries of the Rectangle: Essays on Painting* and *A Plea for Eros*. She lives in Brooklyn, New York.

Reina James's first novel, *This Time of Dying*, was awarded the Society of Authors' McKitterick Prize for Best First Novel and shortlisted for a Commonwealth Writers' Prize. Her next novel, *The Old Joke*, will be published in April 2009. She lives in Sussex with her husband.

Ruchir Joshi is a writer and film-maker. He is the author of a novel, *The Last Jet-Engine Laugh*, and is currently working on another, set in Calcutta during the Second World War. 'Tracing Puppa' is the most recent addition to an ongoing series of irregular essays about memory and growing up. He has two sons, aged sixteen and twelve.

James Lasdun has published several books of fiction and poetry. He was the winner of the inaugural National Short Story Competition and his new collection of short stories, *It's Beginning to Hurt*, will be published in 2009. He last appeared in *Granta* 95 with a report from an American cemetery: 'Where is Thy Sting-a-Ling-a-Ling?'.

Jonathan Lethem is the author of a collection of essays, *The Disappointment Artist*, and seven novels, the most recent being *You Don't Love Me Yet*. His eighth novel will be published in 2009. He first appeared in *Granta* in issue 86 with 'Two or Three Things I Dunno About Cassavetes'.

Benjamin Markovits teaches at Royal Holloway, University of London. His most recent novel, *A Quiet Adjustment*, comes out in

paperback in January 2009. *Playing Days*, a novel about professional basketball, will be published next year.

Adam Mars-Jones is a writer and critic living in London. His recent novel *Pilcrow* restored a shy typographical symbol (¶) to its proper place in the breakfast conversation of millions. He was named one of *Granta*'s Best of Young British Novelists in both 1983 and 1993, and he last appeared in the magazine with 'Quiet, Please' in *Granta* 86.

Jon McGregor lives in Nottingham. He is the author of two novels, *So Many Ways to Begin* and *If Nobody Speaks of Remarkable Things*. He is currently working on a third novel. His first published story, 'What the Sky Sees', appeared in *Granta* 78.

Daniyal Mueenuddin graduated from Dartmouth College and Yale Law School. After a Fulbright Scholarship in Norway, he practised law in New York before returning to Khànpur, Pakistan. 'Provide, Provide' is taken from his forthcoming collection of short stories, *In Other Rooms, Other Wonders*, which will be published in April 2009.

John Naughton is Writer at Large for *GQ* magazine and a regular contributor to *The Word*. He is currently working on a book about Michael Caine.

Joseph O'Neill is the author of, most recently, *Netherland*, a novel, and a memoir, *Blood-Dark Track: A Family History*. He lives in New York City.

Francesca Segal is a writer and freelance literary critic. She is the *Observer*'s Debut Fiction columnist, and is currently working on her first novel.

Will Self's latest book is *Liver*. He first appeared in *Granta* 43 in 1993 when he was named a Best of

Young British Novelist.

Ali Smith was born in Inverness in 1962 and lives in Cambridge, England. She is the author of *Free Love and Other Stories*, *Like*, *Hotel World*, *Other Stories and Other Stories*, *The Whole Story and Other Stories*, and *Girl Meets Boy*. Her novel *The Accidental* was named the 2005 Whitbread Novel of the Year and shortlisted for the 2005 Man Booker Prize and the 2006 Orange Prize.

Justin Torres is finishing a collection of short fiction, from which 'Lessons' is taken. His stories have appeared in *Tin House*, *Gulf Coast* and other publications. He is currently pursuing an MFA at the Iowa Writers' Workshop.

Contributing Editors
Diana Athill, Jonathan Derbyshire, Sophie Harrison, Isabel Hilton, Blake Morrison, Philip Oltermann, John Ryle, Sukhdev Sandhu, Lucretia Stewart.

The Lotus and the Lion
Buddhism and the British Empire
J. JEFFREY FRANKLIN

"*The Lotus and the Lion* will have a unique place in criticism, forever changing our view of Victorian religion by placing it in its global context."

—JAMES NAJARIAN,
BOSTON COLLEGE
[288 PAGES / $35.00 CLOTH]

Adam Mickiewicz
The Life of a Romantic
ROMAN KOROPECKYJ

"*Adam Mickiewicz* fully demonstrates Koropeckyj's excellent biographical craftsmanship and, as such, it will be the main reference point for every student of Mickiewicz in the English-speaking world."

—BOZENA SHALLCROSS,
UNIVERSITY OF CHICAGO
[568 PAGES / $45.00 CLOTH]

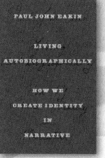

Living Autobiographically
How We Create Identity in Narrative
PAUL JOHN EAKIN

"In this fascinating, lucid, and deeply humanistic extension of his earlier work on autobiography, Eakin illuminates the acts by which we become players in a dynamic narrative identity system that is fundamental to our sense of self."

—JEFFREY WALLEN, HAMPSHIRE COLLEGE
[208 PAGES / $17.95 PAPER]

CORNELL UNIVERSITY PRESS www.cornellpress.cornell.edu

GRANTA | 105

LOST AND FOUND

The spring issue of *Granta* travels the globe to capture the people, places and things on the verge of disappearing, to celebrate moments of renewal and to mark the passing of time.

Elena Lappin journeys to Tel Aviv, Berlin and Prague on the trail of Kafka's missing papers; **Karen Wright** dissects the impact of the Russian oligarchy on the international art scene; and **Maurice Walsh** talks to Ireland's priests about how their role in the community is changing beyond recognition. Plus: **Tim Adams** on his great-grandfather, England's first ever goalkeeper; **Rick Gekoski** on a lost poem by James Joyce; and **Elizabeth Pisani** back in Tiananmen Square, twenty years on.

www.granta.com

In January 2009, *Granta* will introduce the second phase of its new Website, with even more fiction, interviews, reportage and content you won't find anywhere else, updated daily. Our new interactive features allow *Granta* readers to join in the debate about our latest pieces, while the magazine's entire archive of over one hundred issues will be freely available to subscribers. Visit granta.com to find out more and explore.

Granta is grateful for permission to quote four and a half lines from 'The Role of Idea in Poetry' from *Opus Posthumous* by Wallace Stevens, edited by Milton J. Bates, copyright © 1989 by Holly Stevens. Preface and Selection copyright © 1989 by Alfred A. Knopf, a division of Random House, Inc. Copyright © 1957 by Elsie Stevens and Holly Stevens. Copyright renewed 1985 by Holly Stevens. Used by permission of Vintage Books, a division of Random House, Inc., and Faber & Faber Ltd.; and five lines from 'Street' by George Oppen, from *New Collected Poems*, copyright © 1965 by George Oppen. Reprinted by permission of New Directions Publishing Corp.

Kevin Cummins wishes to thank Sally Williams for her help making contact with the Runcorn Wrestling Academy.